THE PROTO-NEOLITHIC CEMETERY
IN SHANIDAR CAVE

NUMBER SEVEN
Texas A&M University Anthropology Series
D. Gentry Steele, General Editor

THE PROTO-NEOLITHIC CEMETERY IN SHANIDAR CAVE

Ralph S. Solecki, Rose L. Solecki,
& Anagnostis P. Agelarakis

TEXAS A&M UNIVERSITY PRESS · COLLEGE STATION

Solecki, Ralph S.

The proto-neolithic cemetery in Shanidar Cave / Ralph S.
Solecki, Rose L. Solecki, and Anagonstis P. Agelarakis.—1st ed.

p. cm.—(Texas A&M University anthropology series ; no. 7)
Includes bibliographical references and index.
ISBN 1-58544-272-0 (alk. paper)

1. Shanidar Cave (Iran) 2. Neanderthals—Iran—Zagros
Mountains. 3. Excavations (Archaeology)—Iran—Zagros
Mountains. 4. Human remains (Archaeology)—Iran—
Zagros Mountains. 5. Burial—Iran—Zagros Mountains.
6. Zagros Mountains (Iran)—Antiquities. I. Solecki, Rose L.
II. Agelarakis, Anagnostis P., 1956– III. Title. IV. Series.
GN285.S65 2004

935—dc21   2003009958

CONTENTS

List of Figures   VI
List of Tables   IX
Preface, *Ralph S. Solecki and Rose L. Solecki*   XI
Acknowledgments   XV

CHAPTER

1. Introduction, *Ralph S. Solecki*   3
2. Catalog of the Burials in the Proto-Neolithic Cemetery,
    Ralph S. Solecki   11
3. The Stone Features, *Ralph S. Solecki and Rose L. Solecki*   32
4. Burial Offerings and Other Goods from the Proto-Neolithic
    Graves, *Rose L. Solecki and Ralph S. Solecki*   48
5. Cultural Materials Found in the Cemetery Fill, *Rose L.
    Solecki and Ralph S. Solecki*   64
6. Comparative Study of the Shanidar Cave Mortuary
    Practices and Those of the Levant during the Epipalaeo-
    lithic and Proto-Neolithic Eras, *Rose L. Solecki and
    Ralph S. Solecki*   82
7. Summary Discussion of the Proto-Neolithic Cemetery
    in Shanidar Cave, *Rose L. Solecki and Ralph S. Solecki*   105
8. The Zagros Proto-Neolithic and Cultural Developments in
    the Near East, *Rose L. Solecki and Ralph S. Solecki*   114
9. The Shanidar Cave Proto-Neolithic Human Condition as
    Reflected through Osteology and Palaeopathology,
    Anagnostis P. Agelarakis   159

Appendix A. Summary of the Proto-Neolithic Skeletons from
    Shanidar Cave, *Juan Munizaga*   185
Appendix B. Beads and Pendants from the Proto-Neolithic of
    Shanidar Cave and Zawi Chemi Shanidar Village,
    Peter Francis, Jr.   199

References   219
Index   229

FIGURES

1. Map showing the location of Shanidar Cave and the Zawi Chemi Shanidar village site, 121
2. Shanidar Cave: exterior view from the south, 122
3. Shanidar Cave: rear view—location of the Proto-Neolithic cemetery, 122
4. Shanidar Cave: overall view of the Proto-Neolithic cemetery looking to the northwest, 123
5. Plan of the excavations in Shanidar Cave and the location of the Proto-Neolithic cemetery, 124
6. Shanidar Cave: looking north over the cemetery area, showing the contact between Layers A and B, 124
7. Plan of the Proto-Neolithic cemetery in Shanidar Cave, 125
8. East Face—Squares B1 and B2, 126
9. North Face—Square C1, 126
10. North Face—Square B2, 127
11. East Face—Square C2, 127
12. North Face—Square C2, 128
13. North Face—Square D2, 128
14. East Face—Square D2, 129
15. Stages of excavation of Burial 1 (Cat. No. 279 IV)—Square C1, 129
16. Burial 1 (Cat. No. 279 IV)—Square C1, 130
17. Stone Features 6 (Cat. No. 353 IV) and 7 (Cat. Nos. 292 IV and 294 IV) and location of Burials 2 (Cat. No. 295 IV) and 18 (Cat. No. 377 IV)—Squares D1 and D2, 130
18. Burial 2 (Cat. No. 295 IV) and Stone Feature 6 (Cat. No. 353 IV)—Square D1, 131
19. Stone Feature 6 (Cat. No. 353 IV) and Burial 2 (Cat. No. 295 IV)—Square D1, 131
20. Stone Features 6 (Cat. No. 353 IV) and 7 (Cat. Nos. 292 IV and 294 IV)—Square D1, 132
21. Daub fragment, from wattle and daub construction, found between Stone Features 6 and 7 (Cat. No. 370 IV), 132
22. Burials 4 (Cat. No. 297 IV), 9 (Cat. No. 350 IV), and 20 (Cat. No. 379 IV)—Squares B1 and C1, 133
23. Burials 4 (Cat. No. 297 IV), 9 (Cat. No. 350 IV), and 20 (Cat. No. 379 IV)—Squares B1 and C1, 133

24. Fragments of carbonized matting found with Burial 4 (Cat. No. 297 IV), 134
25. Burials 5 (Cat. Nos. 298 IV and 371 IV), 21 (Cat. No. 380 IV), 22 (Cat. No. 381 IV), 23 (Cat. No. 382 IV), 24 (Cat. No. 383 IV), and 25 (Cat. No. 384 IV)—Squares B1 and C1, 135
26. Burials 5 (Cat. Nos. 298 IV and 371 IV) and 23 (Cat. No. 382 IV)—Squares B1 and C1, 135
27. Beads found with the burials and in the cemetery fill, 136
28. Slate tools and decorated objects found in the cemetery fill and beads found with the burials, 136
29. Plan of Stone Features 4 (Cat. No. 323 IV) and 5 (Cat. No. 337 IV a) and Burial 6 (Cat. No. 337 IV)—Squares B2 and C2, 137
30. Burial 6 (Cat. No. 337 IV)—Squares B2 and C2, 138
31. Burial 7 (Cat. No. 339 IV)—Squares C1 and C2, 138
32. Burial 7 (Cat. No. 339 IV)—Squares C1 and C2, 139
33. Burials 10 (Cat. No. 351 IV), 14 (Cat. No. 373 IV), and 17 (Cat. No. 376 IV)—Square C1, 139
34. Burials 10 (Cat. No. 351 IV), 14 (Cat. No. 373 IV), and 17 (Cat. No. 376 IV)—Square C1, 140
35. Burials 11 (Cat. No. 355 IV) and 26 (Cat. No. 385 IV)—Square C1, 140
36. Burial 11 (Cat. No. 355 IV)—Square C1, 141
37. Burials 13 (Cat. No. 372 IV), 11 (Cat. No. 355 IV), 10 (Cat. No. 351 IV), and 26 (Cat. No. 385 IV)—Square C1, 141
38. Burials 12 (Cat. No. 356 IV) and 25 (Cat. No. 384 IV)—Square C1, 142
39. Burial 13 (Cat. No. 372 IV)—Square C1, 143
40. Burial 15 (Cat. No. 374 IV)—Squares C1 and C2, 143
41. Burials 15 (Cat. No. 374 IV) and 20 (Cat. No. 379 IV)—Squares C1 and C2, 144
42. Burial 18 (Cat. No. 377 IV)—Squares D1 and D2, 145
43. Burial 19 (Cat. No. 378 IV)—Square C1, 145
44. Burial 19 (Cat. No. 378 IV)—Square C1, 146
45. Bone tools found with Burials 22 (Cat. No. 381 IV) and 24 (Cat. No. 383 IV), 147
46. Bone tools found with the burials and in the cemetery fill, 148
47. Burial 27 (Cat. No. 186 III)—Square D9, 149
48. Burial 27 (Cat. No. 186 III)—Square D9, 150
49. Stone Feature 1 (Cat. Nos. 283 IV and 293 IV)—Square B1, 150
50. Stone Feature 1 (Cat. Nos. 283 IV and 293 IV)—Square B1, 151
51. Stone Feature 2 (Cat. No. 331 IV a)—Square B2, 151

52. Stone Features 2 (Cat. No. 331 IV a), 3 (Cat. No. 331 IV b), 4 (Cat. No. 323 IV), and 5 (Cat. No. 337 IV a)—Squares B2 and C2, 152
53. Stone Feature 3 (Cat. No. 331 IV)—Square B2, 152
54. Stone Features 8 (Cat. Nos. 342 IV and 344 IV) and 9 (Cat. No. 324 IV)—Squares C3 and D3, 153
55. Stone Features 8 (Cat. Nos. 342 IV and 344 IV) and 9 (Cat. No. 324 IV)—Square C3, 154
56. Slate stone tools and decorated objects found in the cemetery fill, 154
57. Small stone pendants, shaped pebbles, chisels, and rubbers found in the cemetery fill, 155
58. Large pecked and ground stone tools found in the cemetery fill, 156
59. Flaked stone tools found in the cemetery fill, 157
60. Chipped stone tools from the area around Stone Feature 8 (Cat. No. 344 IV)—Squares C3 and D3, 158
61. Skeletal preservation and representation of Proto-Neolithic individuals by cranial, dental, and postcranial remains, 163
62. Aspects of demography: biological sex assessments, 165
63. Aspects of demography: age assessments, 166
64. Aspects of demography: lumped age subgroups, 167
65. Cranial view, 168
66. Dental mandibular arch, 168
67. Dental enamel hypoplastic defects, pitting, and linear enamel hypoplasias (LEH), 170
68. Dental enamel hypoplastic defects: individuals with deciduous dentitions, 171
69. Dental acquired enamel defects, cariogenic lesions, and periodontitis, 171
70. Dental mandibular surfaces and wear, 172
71. Inter-proximal carious lesions, 172
72. Maxillary Infectious-inflammatory dental conditions and periodontitis, 175
73. Prevalence of cranial periosteal reactions, 175
74. Auditory osteoma, 176
75. Prevalence of cranial trauma, 177
76. Prevalence of trauma affecting axial infra-cranial structures, 177
77. Prevalence of appendicular trauma, 178
78. Cranial vault trauma, 178
79. Schmörl's nodes, 181
80. Cleft vertebra, 182

TABLES

Table 1. Skeletal Counts for the Twenty-six Numbered Burials in the Shanidar Cave Cemetery, 28

Table 2. Cultural Materials Found in the Cemetery Fill, 65

Table 3. Population Distributions of the Shanidar Cave Proto-Neolithic and the Levantine Natufian Burials, 90

Table 4. Types of Grave Offerings Found with the Twenty-seven Shanidar Cave Proto-Neolithic Burials, 94

Table 5. Natufian and Shanidar Cave Burials with Personal Adornments, 96

Table 6. Shanidar Cave Proto-Neolithic Human Skeletal Collection: Demographic Table, 164

Table 7. Shanidar Cave Proto-Neolithic Human Skeletal Collection: Age Subgroups, 167

Table 8. Shanidar Cave Proto-Neolithic Human Skeletal Collection: Stable Isotope Ratio Analyses, 174

Table A1. Distribution of the Population According to Age, 192

Table A2. The Skeletons of the Proto-Neolithic Period of Shanidar Cave, 192

Table B1. Pink Calcite Disc Beads from Shanidar Cave (Cat. No. 373 IV), 200

Table B2. Pink Calcite Disc Beads from Shanidar Cave (Cat. No. 427 IV), 201

Table B3. Steps in the Manufacture of Thin Bone Beads (Subtype A), 205

Table B4. Steps in the Manufacture of Barrel Bone Beads (Subtype C), 208

Table B5. Perforation Characteristics at Zawi Chemi, 212

Table B6. Tapering Indices of Zawi Chemi Perforations, 213

Table B7. Flint Borers from Zawi Chemi, 215

PREFACE

RALPH S. SOLECKI AND ROSE L. SOLECKI

Shanidar Cave, a base camp, is the oldest prehistoric site with the longest history of occupation in Iraq, a country better known archaeologically for its later-period discoveries in Mesopotamia. Shanidar Cave is located about 400 kilometers north of Baghdad in northeastern Kurdistan, Iraq, at an elevation of 747 meters. It lies in the Baradost Mountains, one of the western folds of the Zagros Mountains, a chain composed of a series of rocks, of which hard dolomitic limestone is the main component. It is in this rock that are found weathered-out caves and shelters favored and used by humans up to the present time.

Shanidar Valley is located in a region with breathtaking mountain vistas. It is especially attractive in the spring, when the hill slopes are carpeted with multicolored wildflowers. The principal local trees are oak and, in the higher elevations, juniper. Wild animals, such as foxes, porcupines, and even wild boars and the occasional bear, are still to be seen in the valley and the mountains. Birds of prey and small game birds are frequently observed. Large fish (carp) are found in the Greater Zab River, which flows through the valley. This river is a major tributary of the Tigris River and in its course through the valley is joined head on with the Rowanduz River, draining the mountains to the east. This strengthened river makes an abrupt turn to the southwest to breach the last mountain range, emerging in the foothills leading to the Mesopotamian steppe plains.

Shanidar Cave today, as in the past, remains an attractive habitat for humans. It is easily accessible by foot and has a nearby permanent water source. The cave opening, a large triangle, is about 25 meters wide and 8 meters high at its mouth. It faces southwest with a view toward the Greater Zab River. Today, the cave floor covers an area of over a thousand square meters, most of which is unencumbered by rock falls. The vaulting interior is heavily blackened with the soot of countless fires.

Shanidar Cave was discovered in 1951 by Ralph S. Solecki during an archaeological survey for prehistoric cave sites in the greater Rowanduz area (R. S. Solecki 1998). The prehistory of Iraq was still virtually unknown at that time, the prime exception being the work of Dorothy Garrod (1930) in caves farther to the southeast in the Zagros. Solecki, accompanied by the district governor *(qaimakan)* and a representative of the Iraq Directorate General of Antiquities, recorded and examined about forty caves and shelters during the Shanidar-Rowanduz survey. From its situation and some telltale surface evidence, Shanidar Cave was selected as the one most likely to produce significant new data for the investigation of prehistoric development in the region. And it certainly has fulfilled its promise.

When first seen during the summer of 1951, the cave seemed to be unoccupied, although a number of temporary huts and animal corrals were present around the interior perimeter. Later it was learned that a small group of Sherwani Kurds along with their animals habitually wintered in the cave during the colder winter months. The central part of the cave floor, a communal area facing the opening, was clear and free of structures. At that time Solecki decided to test the cave deposits in this central open area. His later excavations in the cave expanded the original test trench in all directions. At the time of the original excavations in 1951, a stone wall and a habitation with an animal corral blocked access to the rear of the cave. Therefore, the rear portion of the cave, where the Proto-Neolithic cemetery was located, was not discovered during the early excavations at the cave. This area was untouched until 1960, when it was free for exploration.

Shanidar Cave was excavated by Solecki over four field seasons: 1951, 1953, 1956–57, and 1960. Field excavations were not possible after 1961, due to continuing political events in the region. Analyses of the cultural and physical remains recovered from the site, however, continue to the present. Four major cultural horizons were identified in the nearly 14-meter-deep (45 feet) major excavation. From top to bottom these cultural horizons are: Layer A (recent to Neolithic); Layer B, separated into two parts— Layer B1 (Proto-Neolithic) and Layer B2 (Zarzian or Epipalaeolithic); Layer C (Baradostian or Upper Palaeolithic); and Layer D, with the longest occupation down to bedrock (the Zagros Mousterian or Middle Palaeolithic). The skeletal remains of nine Neanderthals were recovered from Layer D, providing researchers with one of the most important samples of this extinct population (Trinkaus 1983).

The discovery of the cemetery in the upper levels of Shanidar Cave was made in the last days of the last season Solecki spent at Shanidar. The cemetery was identified as belonging to the Proto-Neolithic culture. It has greatly expanded our knowledge of this culture in the Zagros

Mountains. What makes the cemetery important is that a special assemblage of burial goods was associated with burials, as well as the remains of people, and such data is not found at the nearby contemporary open village site of Zawi Chemi Shanidar. The richness and types of burial goods found with infants and young children in the cemetery suggest that the parents lavished much affection upon their young, a very human condition.

From the human biological studies of the physical remains of the skeletons, it is inferred that the people were not living an isolated existence in peace and harmony in these remote mountain fastnesses. They evidently had close interrelations with other people over a fairly wide area in the mountains and steppe plains. Moreover, there is compelling evidence that the population experienced stressful environmental conditions during their lifetime (Agelarakis 1989).

The Proto-Neolithic period cemetery, dating to the eleventh millennium B.P.E., is the only known cemetery site dating to this period in the Zagros-Taurus Mountain area and the hilly flanks and northern steppe regions to the south of it. Proto-Neolithic peoples lived in Shanidar Cave for at least part of the year (Layer B1) and buried their dead in a special area to the rear of the site. It is also evident that they were culturally related to the inhabitants of the Zawi Chemi village, a contemporary site located some 4 kilometers downstream on the left bank of the Greater Zab River. We believe that the Zagros Proto-Neolithic culture was a local variant of the roughly contemporaneous Late Natufian/Proto-Neolithic cultural horizon of the Levant.

Although Shanidar Cave lies out of the main trade routes, its inhabitants maintained trade contacts with distant areas in order to obtain nonlocal materials such as obsidian, bitumen adhesive, exotic stones for beads, and so on. Such materials were recovered both in the cemetery and from the living areas in Shanidar Cave. In addition to these material items, cultural, social, economic, and religious customs were also being diffused throughout the area, for here we are on the threshold of the "Neolithic Revolution." This was a period of significant cultural change in the Near East. This examination of the Shanidar Valley Proto-Neolithic deals with such developments in the Zagros Region and thus adds a new geographic perspective to an investigation long dominated by the data and findings from the more extensively studied Levant area to the west. It also furnishes a new overview of the prehistory of Mesopotamia.

The Proto-Neolithic human skeletal sample recovered from the cemetery located to the rear of Shanidar Cave likewise represents a unique population data set. It provides a variety of new insights into the population of the Near East at a time of transition from an earlier hunting and gathering way of life to a full Neolithic one, dependent on domesticated plants and animals.

ACKNOWLEDGMENTS

We are deeply obliged to the members of the field-project teams who participated in the Proto-Neolithic period excavations at Shanidar and also to the scientists who cooperated in the laboratory on these findings. Their affiliations are given below. In the field were Jacques Bordaz, archaeologist; Dexter Perkins Jr., palaeozoologist, who also performed duties as archaeologist; and T. Dale Stewart, physical anthropologist. Contributors to the laboratory studies of the material remains were Juan Munizaga, of the University of Chile, and Denise Ferembach, both of whom made observations on the Proto-Neolithic skeletal remains. (Munizaga's report appears here as appendix A.) We are also obliged to Douglas Campana for his use-wear studies on certain bone artifacts; to Harald Rehder and David S. Reese for identification of the molluscs; to Gerald Brophy, R. N. Guillemette, and John Sanders for their study of certain lithic and mineral specimens; to Ms. Buthima Musslim for chemical analysis of one of the archaeological specimens; to Leonard Gorelick and A. John Gwinnet for their observations on the manufacture of the stone beads; and to A. Jaffe for interest in and comments on the Proto-Neolithic society of Shanidar Cave. Peter Francis, Jr., of the Center for Bead Research, Lake Placid, New York, is owed thanks for his detailed studies of the adornments recovered from both the Shanidar Cave and the Zawi Chemi Shanidar excavations. (His report is provided here in full as appendix B.) We owe deep thanks to Ibrahim el Zayri, who officially represented the Directorate General of Antiquities of Iraq in the field most conscientiously and efficiently. We are also heavily obliged for their support to the director of the Directorate General of Antiquities of Iraq and his staff, as well as to the staff of Columbia University, who piloted our affairs at home and abroad in connection with the 1960 project. We are much obliged to Argie Agelarakis, Mara Horowitz, and Helen de Wolf for making several of the drawings. Lastly, we are indebted to Gentry Steele, of the Department of Anthropology, Texas A&M University, for his support and guidance in seeing this study to press.

—Ralph S. Solecki and Rose L. Solecki

THE PROTO-NEOLITHIC CEMETERY
IN SHANIDAR CAVE

CHAPTER 1

Introduction

RALPH S. SOLECKI

A Proto-Neolithic period cemetery (R. S. Solecki 1963; R. L. Solecki 1981) dating from circa 10,600 years ago (R. S. Solecki and M. Rubin 1958, 1446) was found in the right rear portion of Shanidar Cave (figs. 2–7). The cemetery was found during the fourth Shanidar research project, at the end of the 1960 season.[1] The skeletal remains of thirty-five individuals were identified during the excavation of the cemetery. This is the only prehistoric cemetery site of its kind east of the Mediterranean area, comparable in age to the Late Natufian. Another Proto-Neolithic burial, dated on the basis of associated grave goods, was found toward the front of Shanidar Cave during the third Shanidar research season (1956–57) (R. S. Solecki 1957).

This report deals with the burial practices followed by the Shanidar Cave inhabitants who used the site during the Proto-Neolithic period: the preparation of the graves and the bodies; the cultural materials placed in the graves; the stone alignments and other stone features constructed in the cemetery area; and the materials found in the cemetery fill. There also is a comparative section, in which the Shanidar burials are compared to those from the Natufian of the Levant. This monograph also includes a summary of the palaeopathology of the Shanidar Proto-Neolithic skeletal remains and two appendices, one concerning the initial findings on the skeletal remains and one concerning the beads and pendants found with the burials.

The Shanidar Proto-Neolithic cemetery was found toward the end of the 1960 season, in the course of making an exploratory trench toward the rear of the cave, back from the main excavation. This work had not progressed very far when the cemetery was encountered. Unfortunately, the closeness of the end of the season did not permit completion of exploration in this area of the cave. The excavated part of the cemetery lay in Squares B1, B2, B3, C1, C2, C3, D1, D2, and D3, a large square measuring 6 by 6 meters (figs. 5, 6, 7). The burials and stone features described in this report were found within this area.

The skeletal finds from the cemetery were unpacked and studied in Baghdad in 1962 by Stewart, with the assistance of his colleague Juan Munizaga, of the University of Chile. Stewart concentrated his attention on the Neanderthal skeletons, while Munizaga spent some of his time unpacking, preliminarily sorting out, and examining the Proto-Neolithic burials. Munizaga wrote a short report based on his examination of the Proto-Neolithic skeletal remains. As this report has not been published to date, it is included here as appendix A for the purpose of historical documentation. Denise Ferembach, a French physical anthropologist with the Centre Nationale Recherche Scientifique (CNRS), examined the Proto-Neolithic burial collection in 1969 and published a report based on her study in the Iraq journal *Sumer* the following year (1970). Ferembach's use of the term "Zawi Chemi" to refer to the Shanidar Cave cemetery collection has caused some confusion (e.g., Mellaart 1975). All of the Proto-Neolithic human skeletal remains were found in Shanidar Cave. None to date have been recovered from the nearby village site of Zawi Chemi Shanidar (R. L. Solecki 1981). The express intention in the Ferembach report was to indicate that the Zawi Chemi culture was present in the cave. In 1981, Anagnostis Agelarakis, then a graduate student at Columbia University and now a professor at Adelphi University, restudied the Proto-Neolithic skeletons in the Iraq Museum in Baghdad. This study formed part of his Ph.D. dissertation at Columbia University (Agelarakis 1989). Agelarakis focused his attention on the pathology of the Shanidar Proto-Neolithic population and the environmental and dietary factors that may have produced the anomalous features found in the skeletons. Agelarakis then compared the Shanidar collection with a human-skeleton collection from the somewhat later village site of Ganj Dareh, in Iranian Kurdistan (Smith 1968, 1974). A summary of Agelarakis's study on the palaeopathology of the Shanidar collection is presented as a separate chapter (chapter 9) in this volume.

The Stratigraphy of the Proto-Neolithic Cemetery (Layers B1a and B1b)

Layer B was located below the uppermost cultural layer (Layer A) identified at Shanidar Cave. It was divided into two parts on the basis of its stratigraphy and cultural context (figs. 8–14). The top part, Layer B1, called the "Proto-Neolithic" layer, has been radiocarbon-14 dated (uncalibrated) as circa 10,600 +/- 300 B.P. (Rubin and Suess 1955). The Shanidar Cave Proto- Neolithic layer is coeval with the basal layer, Layer B, of the Zawi Chemi Shanidar village, which lies downstream on the Greater Zab River some 4 kilometers from Shanidar Cave. It has a radiocarbon-14 (uncalibrated) date of circa 10,870 +/- 300 B.P. (R. S. Solecki and M. Rubin 1958). This would fall into the brief cold episode called the Younger Dryas (Broecker 1987, 79–80; Broecker et al. 1989). The lower part of Layer B at Shanidar Cave (Layer B2) has been radiocarbon-14 dated (uncalibrated) as circa 12,000 +/- 400 B.P. (Rubin and Suess 1955). This latter cultural horizon contained a Zarzian industry first identified by Garrod (1930) from a cave site to the southeast of Shanidar in the lower folds of the Zagros Mountains. Layer A (Neolithic to recent), located above Layer B1, was a markedly dense occupational zone containing a totally different assemblage of much younger cultural materials. The Proto-Neolithic layer (Layer B1) was stratigraphically clearly delimited from the Layer A deposits (fig. 6). There was no evidence in any of the cave excavations to suggest that there was an immediate reoccupation of the cave after the Proto-Neolithic period. The time interval between the base of Layer A and the top of Layer B1 was probably about six thousand years, based on the associated cultural remains. The deposits of Layer B1 sloped gently downward to the west (the left side of the cave), as did almost all of the cave sediments.

Layer A was a very dense occupational zone and contained many bands of large and varicolored hearth lenses with inclusions of animal bones, potsherds, and a great quantity of goat and sheep dung in its upper parts (fig. 6). Probably some of the widespread burnings evidenced in Layer A were done for sanitary purposes in an effort to rid the habitat of vermin. It is also probable that some of the burnings were accidentally caused by the ignition of dried animal dung, which the modern Kurdish inhabitants of the cave used as an auxiliary fuel. Within the cemetery area, the top of the Layer B deposits was located at various depths in contact with Layer A, suggesting an uneven contact or disconformity between Layers A and B. There was some pitting from Layer A into Layer B. By the time the deposits of Layer A were laid down, the presence of the cemetery must have been long forgotten. Traces of a pit were found in Square D2, cutting into Layer B1 to a depth of about 80 centimeters. It measured about 50 by 90 centimeters, in a slightly constricted ovate plan. Its contents included stones, some pottery, stone tools, and animal bones in soft dark-brown sediment. Another pit, in Square C2, reached a depth of 107 centimeters into the top of the Proto-Neolithic layer. Finds included mullers, choppers, animal bones, and flints. A third pit was found in Square B1 and contained pottery and animal bones in soft sediment.

The Proto-Neolithic deposits in most of the excavated sections of the cave consisted of a rather uniform loose brown sediment, with traces of heavy occupations and numerous flints. The deposits of the cemetery area, however, had a noticeably different configuration. Two distinct stratified beds were evident in the cemetery area (fig. 8–14). There was an upper horizon of dense yellowish loam, relatively free of hearths and organic matter. This lay conformably over a lower horizon of gray-colored, less compact sediment. The latter had many traces of organic matter, ash, and charcoal and contained the burials. No burials were found in the yellowish loam. For purposes of identification the upper yellow loam is here called Layer B1a, and the underlying gray sediment is called Layer B1b. The contrast between the yellow loam of Layer B1a and the underlying gray sediment of Layer B1b in the cemetery area was clearly marked—so much so, in fact, that an initial impression might be that they belonged to two different cultural horizons. However, the detailed analysis of the stratigraphy of the cemetery area, in addition to the study of the cultural remains recovered from both B1a and B1b, resulted in the conclusion that both were specialized but related cemetery deposits.

Shortly before the Proto-Neolithic occupation, there had been a large rockfall from the ceiling of the cave. It had concentrated its force mainly in the area south of the cemetery. Hearths were made in the free areas among the stones north and south of these rocks before the cemetery was laid down. At the time of the establishment of the cemetery, boulders were still visible on the cave surface to the south of the cemetery, but the cemetery area itself was free of large stones. It is reasonable to assume that whatever portable stones lay in this zone were cleared away before burials were made there. In effect, this area appeared to have been situated in a kind of protected niche of the cave, screened off from the front by large boulders.

The excavation of the Proto-Neolithic cemetery was in the northern extension of the main Shanidar Cave cut, that is, in Squares B1 to B3, C1 to C3, and D1 to D3 (figs. 5 and 7). This made a large square measuring 6 by 6 meters. The burials and stone features described in this report were found within this area. The cemetery appeared to extend somewhat to the north and east, into the unexcavated portions of the cave.

The Yellow Loam Layer (B1a)

This distinctive yellow-colored layer covered the entire excavated area of the Proto-Neolithic cemetery. Only occasional patches of similarly colored sediment were found in other parts of the cave deposits. The most obvious of these were located around a large boulder near the lip or entrance of the cave (Squares B13 and C13), from the base of Layer A to the top of Layer B.

Layer B1a was circa 40 centimeters thick in the northern part of the cemetery (Squares B1, C1, and D1), from the depth of 57 to 97 centimeters below "o" datum. Toward the central part of the cemetery, the bed thickened to about 55 centimeters, from the depth of circa 60 to 115 centimeters below "o" datum, and then gradually thinned and finally disappeared beyond the cemetery limits to the south. Layer B1a extended to the north, east, and west beyond the limits of the cemetery excavations. In shape it seemed to be roughly an elongated ovate, oriented NE-SW, and probably measured at least 5.5 meters wide and 7.0 meters long (including the unexcavated portions (fig. 5). It covered the lower cemetery area conformably like a protective cap. In the middle of the cemetery, where the B1a deposits were thickest, a marked bulge could be observed at its upper limits.

Although the B1a deposits were composed primarily of the characteristic yellow loam sediments described above, interspersed through them were undulating bands of ashes and charcoal (figs. 10, 11). At least seven such discrete bands, some over two meters in width and up to four centimeters thick, cut through the yellow-loam deposits of B1a. Possibly they represented the debris of small hearths whose remains were dispersed following their use. This is the normal fate of a dead, open, or unbounded hearth in a trafficked area. If the Proto-Neolithic population had acquired the habit of keeping animals—for example, sheep, as at the nearby village site of Zawi Chemi Shanidar (R. L. Solecki 1981)—a few of these animals could have easily scattered the hearth remains. The burning of widespread patches of vegetation growing at the site was probably very unlikely because the configuration of the cave would have inhibited such growth.

The depositional processes that produced the distinctive sediments of Layer B1a in the cemetery area, we believe, were the result of human agents engaged in a series of recurring activities over an extended period of time. The occurrence of the yellow-loam bed directly over the burial area could not be due to coincidence. We also believe that Layer B1a cannot be interpreted as the result of a single, large-scale event. We do not believe, for example, that running water could have been responsible for the deposition of the yellow loam of B1a. There are no openings or swallow holes in the ceiling of Shanidar Cave above the cemetery area. We could not find any opening to the outside in the rear of the cave through which sediment could have filtered into the cave. Limestone blocks could have disintegrated to form sediment of this kind, but certainly not in the time span available here. Wind as a carrying agent might be a possibility. However, this is doubtful, because of the concentration of the yellow-loam deposit in a limited area of the cave, specifically in the cemetery locus. Another consideration makes wind and/or water transport of these sediments highly unlikely. The heavier artifacts found in the yellow loam, such as boulder querns and mullers, were certainly objects that had to be carried into the cave in individual lots by humans because of their weight. The associated smaller-sized chipped stone artifacts and other materials incorporated in the yellow loam could have been brought in with container loads of the sediment. However, we were not able to discern any traces of individual dump loads in the deposits. If present, this evidence could have been disturbed by human and/or animal agents. The traces of the in situ hearth bands, as discussed above, found in the yellow-loam stratum also militate against the possibility of wind and/or water transport of the sediment. The yellow loam of Layer B1a probably was most readily obtainable at the front and on the outside talus slope of the cave. Such sediments are found there today, deposited through natural agencies. Wind blowing about in the front area of the cave and runoff from the top and sides of the cave opening at the drip line are likely depositional agents.

We believe, therefore, that the yellow loamy sediment of Layer B1a was brought into the cemetery area by Proto-Neolithic people in some sort of communal effort. Perhaps the yellow sediments were brought in to cover the cemetery in order to lessen the unhealthy atmosphere of the shallow graves in this part of the cave. Perhaps the distinctive colored sediments were placed over the actual burial area as a marker in order to locate the exact position of the cemetery for additional interments or for the performance of ceremonies at the spot. The Proto-Neolithic cave inhabitants must have had the necessary manpower to bring in the sediments contained in Layer B1a, estimated to be circa 24 cubic meters in volume. The sediments were possibly carried in by means of woven baskets, which they probably had, or in skin bags made from animal hides.

Characteristic Zagros Proto-Neolithic cultural materials were present in Layer B1a, but not in the same numbers or varieties as in Layer B1b. These materials included large and small ground stone tools, chipped stone debris and tools, and bone tools (see chapter 5).

The Gray Sediment Layer (B1b)

The gray sediments of Layer B1b lay conformably below the yellow loam of Layer B1a (figs. 8, 12, 13, 14) and generally coincided in areal extent with it. Layer B1b contained much occupational debris, many charcoal flecks, ashes, and snail shells. This was also the horizon that contained the Proto-Neolithic burials and the stone arrangements and pavements associated with the cemetery. The cemetery proper was bounded in part by a curving low stone wall to the west and by irregular patterns of stone pavements or clusters to the east. Apart from these purposeful constructions, there were relatively few stray rocks in Layer B1b.

Layer B1b was roughly elongate ovate in shape (fig. 5), oriented NE-SW. It probably measured at least 5.5 meters wide and 7.0 meters long, including the unexcavated portions—that is, an area of circa 40.0 square meters in extent. It extended to the north, east, and west, beyond the limits of the cemetery excavations. Its full thickness could not be determined because the base of Layer B1b was not reached in all sections of the cemetery during the 1960 season. The B1b deposits appeared to be thickest in the center of the cemetery area, a little over half a meter thick, and tapered off toward the west side, from a depth of about 90 centimeters below datum in the east wall to about 103 centimeters below datum in the west wall. The greatest depth for Layer B1b, reached at the close of the 1960 season, was 155 centimeters below datum in Square D3 (at the west side) and 140 centimeters in Square B3 (at the east side). The gray sediment dipped noticeably to the west, as did most of the other deposits in Shanidar Cave.

The two sublayers (B1a and B1b) in the cemetery area, as noted above, were both in fact markedly different from the Proto-Neolithic deposits found elsewhere in the cave. The distinctiveness of the yellow loam of B1a has already been discussed. The dark-gray sediment and broad ash and charcoal lenses of Layer B1b were also clearly distinct from Proto-Neolithic deposits outside the cemetery. No widespread concentration of ashy, dark-gray sediments, similar to those of Layer B1b, have been found elsewhere in the Shanidar Cave Proto-Neolithic deposits. We believe, therefore, that

Layers B1a and B1b were laid down when that part of the cave was an operating cemetery and that their deposition was solely related to burial activities. Most of the burials within the cemetery were found concentrated in a roughly ovate-shaped area measuring circa 2.0 by 3.0 meters, with the long axis extending from southwest to northeast. Only four burials were found outside this area of concentration, but still within the cemetery proper. A number of earlier graves in the heavily used area had been disturbed when later interments were made. Most of the burials in the cemetery lay on a 5- to 10-centimeter-thick bed of ashes and charcoal. Characteristically, the graves were located at much the same depth, circa 1.0 meter below the "0" datum line, or about 0.5 meters below the contact between the Ceramic Neolithic (Layer A) and the Aceramic Proto-Neolithic (Layer B1). Except for Burial 25, there was no evidence to suggest that special burial pits were dug in the cemetery.

One burial (Burial 27), that of a young adult, was found during the 1956–57 season (R. S. Solecki 1957), some 12.5 meters to the south of the cemetery (fig. 5). The burial goods associated with this burial and its stratigraphic position suggested that it too belonged to the Proto-Neolithic cultural horizon.

Note

1. The fourth Shanidar research project was cosponsored by Columbia University and the Smithsonian Institution in 1960 under a research grant from the National Science Foundation. As in previous seasons, the expedition worked in cooperation with the Iraq Directorate General of Antiquities. The Iraq Petroleum Company, as in the third research season (1956–57), lent generous material assistance to the expedition. The 1960 expedition staff included Ralph S. Solecki and Rose L. Solecki, Jacques Bordaz, and Dexter Perkins Jr., all at that time from Columbia University, and T. Dale Stewart of the Smithsonian Institution. Ibrahim el Zayri represented the Directorate General of Antiquities of Iraq . The expedition divided up its force into two working groups. One worked at the cave excavation under the direction of Ralph S. Solecki. The other worked at the nearby village of Zawi Chemi Shanidar (fig. 1) under the direction of Rose L. Solecki (1981). Bordaz and Perkins divided their time between the two sites. Stewart worked only at the cave. He left for Baghdad with the skeletal remains of the Neanderthals excavated earlier that season and from there went to the United States before the Proto-Neolithic cemetery was found. Therefore, practically all of the exhumation and recording of the burials was done by Ralph S. Solecki, Bordaz, and occasionally Perkins. We closed the excavation on August 31, 1960, expecting to return the next season. All of the human skeletal remains, as well as the cultural materials from the excavation, were sent to the Iraq Museum in Baghdad.

CHAPTER 2

Catalog of the Burials
in the Proto-Neolithic Cemetery

RALPH S. SOLECKI

Descriptions of the Burials

The descriptions of the twenty-six graves (including the skeletal remains of at least thirty-five individuals) from the Proto-Neolithic cemetery given in this section are based primarily on observations recorded at the time of excavation.[1] Also included here are brief descriptions of the associated grave goods and other items of cultural interest. These are more fully discussed in chapter 4.

Burial 1 (Cat. No. 279 IV, Square C1, 0.96 meters below datum)[2]
This was a primary burial (figs. 15–16) of an adolescent in an extremely flexed position; it looked as though it had been forced into the grave in a tightly bound condition. There were no signs of a pit. It lay somewhat above the general level of the burials, at the southwestern end of the main cemetery group. The burial occupied a space of circa 0.55 meters E-W and 0.45 meters N-S. The individual lay on its back and left side, legs drawn up and arms across the body. The head was pointed to the east and was lying on its side, twisted at a right angle to the neck. The back of the head was turned upward, and the face was downward. Imprints, possibly of plant stalks, were observed in the sediment beneath the burial. A fragment of a flint blade was found at the base of the burial. Also associated were four limestone pebbles, one use-retouched obsidian blade fragment, and one broken chert blade. These materials were probably part of the cemetery fill, not grave offerings. The burial lay partially over several other bodies, including Burial 10 to the north, Burial 14 to the northeast, and Burial 17 to the south. Evidently there was some disturbance in the area of earlier graves by later interments.

Burial 2 (Cat. No. 295 IV, Square D1, 1.18 meters below datum)[3]

This was a fragmentary secondary burial of an adolescent (figs. 17–19). Only a single bone, a partial calotte, was recovered from this burial. It was found resting on a small platform or pavement of stones (Stone Feature 6) (figs.17–20). The top of the skull was uppermost. The skull fragment lay in ashes and charcoal. There was no evidence of a burial pit. The stones of the platform were reddish colored, as though they had been burned. This feature extended eastward from an arc of stones (Stone Feature 7) laid end to end in this quarter (figs. 17 and 20). About 0.35 meters to the northwest of the calotte lay a fragment of burned daub from some sort of wattle and daub construction (fig. 21). It had stick or reed impressions on one face (Cat. No. 370 IV). A smaller fragment lay nearby. One quern lay circa 40 centimeters to the southwest of Stone Feature 6, and another quern fragment lay to the north of it. This burial was found to the west or outside of the main cemetery complex.

Burial 3 (Cat. No. 296 IV, Square B3, 1.17 meters below datum)[4]

The remains of this individual, believed to be a a secondary burial, were judged to be those of an adolescent. At the time of the excavation, several long bones, including the tibia, were recorded. These were encountered in the south wall of the excavation extension. The rest of the remains were not found. There was no evidence of a burial pit.

Burial 4 (Cat. No. 297 IV, Squares B1 and C1, 1.02 meters below datum)[5]

This burial comprised what appeared to be a very tightly flexed primary burial (figs. 22–23). It occupied an area of about 0.50 meters NE-SW and 0.22 meters NW-SE. The crushed head of this individual, thought to be a child, lay facing the northeast. The skeleton lay on its left side, arms and legs doubled up in front. The skeleton lay in burned orange-colored sediment above a bed of ashes and charcoal. No indications of a burial pit were seen. A large slab of flat limestone measuring about 0.30 by 0.28 meters was found immediately behind, or northwest of the skeleton. A collection of angular limestone chunks (Stone Feature 4) lay to the south of these remains. Burial 4 had associated with it a number of items of interest, the most important of which were several pieces of carbonized matting (fig. 24). At the neck was a barrel-shaped stone bead, and two other stone beads were also associated. Other items recovered in the area of the skeleton included a heat-cracked denticulate flint, a second denticulate tool, and other flints. These items were probably from the cemetery fill.

Burial 5 (Cat. Nos. 298 IV and 371 IV, Squares B1 and C1, 1.02 meters below datum)[6]

This was the tightly flexed burial (figs. 25–26) of an adult female. It lay on its right side, face to the north with the mouth agape. The head was twisted to the left and vertically upright in an unnatural position. The bones were in a good state of preservation. No burial pit or associated cultural remains were noted for this individual, although a stone was found just behind its crushed skull. The body lay in dark-gray powdery sediment on a bed of ashes and charcoal measuring between 5 and 10 centimeters thick. The feet and leg bones of Burial 22 (described below) were lying directly on the chest of Burial 5, as though the former was interred soon after the latter in a common grave. Also, on the basis of their relative positions it appeared that Burials 5 and 22 were interred after Burial 23 (described below) in the crowded part of the cemetery. To the immediate northeast of this burial, and between it and Stone Feature 1, were found two loose items of interest that probably were associated with Burial 5. One (Cat. No. 293 b) was a flat lenticular-shaped green copper mineral bead/pendant (figs. 27 [k] and 28 [h]) (R. S. Solecki 1969); the second was a rectangular-shaped three-holed spacer bead (Cat. No. 293 IV a) (fig. 27 [a]).

Burial 6 (Cat. No. 337 IV, Squares B2 and C2, 0.86 meters below datum)[7]

This was a tightly flexed adult male primary burial, fairly well preserved (figs. 29–30). The burial lay directly on a bed of ashes and charcoal in soft dark sediment; there was no discernible burial pit. The skull of Burial 6 abutted Stone Feature 5. Found in the area of this grave were some stray human bones, apparently from an infant. Burial 6 occupied an area of circa 0.65 meters N-S and 0.70 meters E-W. The adult skeleton lay on its right side, the head to the north. The face was oriented to the west and turned somewhat downward to the right. The ribs were crushed, and the left ulna was broken in situ near the distal end. The left arm was resting at the side of the left leg. The foot bones were missing. Two large flat limestone blocks were found up against the upper back of Burial 6. The condition of the skull and limb bones suggested that the skeleton had been crushed after burial. The skull appeared to have suffered breakage by some small half-fist-sized stones that lay above it; three half-fist-sized stones lay directly on its left side. There was a small cluster of stones (Stone Feature 5) to the north of the skull. The associated grave goods included a small, elongate, end-faceted slate tool found lying directly over the neck, with the pointed end directed away from the head. An unworked elongate pebble of larger size (pestle) was found over the left knee. A snail shell was picked out of the space between the radius and the ulna of the left arm. A pecking stone was found above the skeletal remains.

Burial 7 (Cat. No. 339 IV, Squares C1 and C2, 1.23 meters below datum)[8]

This was an adult female primary burial (figs. 31–32) placed in a flexed and contorted position. It occupied an area measuring 0.67 meters E-W and 0.57 meters N-S, with a depth of 15 centimeters. It lay in a light-gray powdery sediment. No evidence of a pit could be seen. Burial 1 partially overlapped these remains to the east at a higher elevation. The individual appeared to have been lying on its stomach, with the legs flexed to the right side. The right arm had been bent back, the wrist and hand jammed against its chest at an unnatural angle. The head had been rotated around 180 degrees and was bent back at an extremely unnatural cant, carrying the shoulders and neck back with it toward the east. The mouth was slightly open. The skull was crushed. A small block of limestone, measuring about 15 by 10 centimeters, was lying just to the east and touching the head. The pelvic girdle and some of the ends of the long bones were smashed. Found with the remains were a double-ended bone awl, a spall chopper, some snail shells, and a fish vertebra. Other items recovered in the area of the skeletal remains included one quartzite spall chopper, one flint scraper, two unretouched flint flakes, one small lump of burned stone, four fragments of ordinary pebbles, one core trimming flake, and one fragment of a small mammal jawbone. These items were probably part of the grave fill.

Burial 8 (Cat. No. 347 IV, Square C1, 0.89 meters below datum)[9]

This was the burial of a child, located in the north wall of the cemetery excavation. It lay in a dark sediment surrounded by a light-colored loam. No pit outlines were observed. This burial was only partially exposed in 1960; in order to have excavated it properly it would have been necessary to cut well into the north wall section. The burial lay about 0.35 meters northwest of the arc of stones (Stone Feature 7) and about 0.25 meters above the stone feature.

Because this skeleton was incompletely exposed, we could not ascertain if it was a primary or secondary burial. The skeletal remains recovered included several rib and long bones. Associated with the burial was a snail shell and some mammal bone fragments.

Burial 9 (Cat. No. 350 IV, Square C1, 1.02 meters below datum)[10]

This grave lot, on the basis of observations, included a damaged skull, probably from an adolescent, along with a group of miscellaneous bones. All the skeletal remains were found in a mass about 13 centimeters thick (figs. 22–23). Munizaga identified the miscellaneous bones as the fragmentary skulls of two infants, about one year old. From all indications, these remains suggest the practice of secondary burial. No evidence of a pit was found. The adolescent skull was found in dark sediment above a 3-centimeter deposit of ashes and charcoal. Although it had been smashed in at the top, there was still evidence of occipital flattening. The head was face down, and the upper jaw or maxillae was perpendicular to the ground; the lower jawbone could not be seen during excavation. A partial long bone was found under the forehead. The associated grave goods included a three-holed green stone spacer bead (fig. 27 [c]) at the left side of the neck. A second single-holed lozenge-shaped bead (fig. 27 [b]), also of bright green stone, was found loose near the grave. Also found were an obsidian blade and a quartzite spall tool.

Burial 10 (Cat. No. 351 IV, Square C1, 1.03 meters below datum)[11]

This burial (figs. 33, 34, 37), cataloged as an infant, was apparently interred at the same time as Burials 14 and 17. The three of them were uncovered, lying in a rough "T"-shaped form, with the three skulls at the three ends of the "T" and the lower limbs pointed inward. Burial 10 was located at the western end of the bar of the "T." It occupied an area of about 17 centimeters NW-SE and 18 centimeters NE-SW and measured about 14 centimeters in thickness. It lay in a gray powdery sediment above a bed of ashes and charcoal. No evidence of a pit was recorded. The skeletal remains noted at the time of excavation included the calotte and some unidentified long bones. The rear of the skull had been crushed, and the face was pushed back over the lower jaw. The skull was in an upright position, facing the northwest. No associated grave goods were found. However, part of a mammal lower jaw (sheep or goat?) stuck out below the skull, and a snail shell was found at its left jaw. A large snail shell was found under the skull. Two loose flint flakes were found close by. These items probably were part of the cemetery fill. Burial 1 had been interred above and to the south of Burial 10.

Burial 11 (Cat. No. 355 IV, Square C1, 1.06 meters below datum)[12]

Burial 11 was recorded in the field as containing the skeleton of a child lying in a tightly flexed position (figs. 35–37). It appeared to be a primary burial, and there was no evidence of a pit. The burial occupied an area measuring 0.32 meters N-S and 0.45 meters E-W. Burial 11 was lying on its back, with the head tucked in toward the body. The legs were drawn up to the right and left sides of the body respectively. The left arm and right arm were each doubled up under the left leg and the right leg. The head was to the east, and the face to the southeast. The skull was broken in. A flint was found touching the lower jaw. Burial 11 was extraordinary because of the rich associated goods, especially items of adornment. Strands of beads had been draped around the neck and the wrists and over the head. One stray bead was noted at the mouth of the child, and a stone spacer bead was picked off one of the eye sockets. Inside the broken skull were found about three dozen beads and a rib-bone fragment. Beads were grouped at the right side of the neck. A string of beads was observed at the left wrist. Also associated were three triangular stone spacer beads, each with five holes drilled through the long axis. One was found under the right side of the lower jaw, one under the right ear, and one about 5 centimeters farther down around the neck. According to the count made by Jacques Bordaz, there were about fifteen hundred beads associated with this burial. The beads were made of variously colored calcites. They were mainly red, white, or blue in color, but a few green-colored beads were also present. The beads were arranged into strands, with as many as ten beads per strand. Using "r" for red, "w" for white, and "b" for blue, the sequence of beads in one row appeared to be "rrrwwwbbb." Beads of the same color were placed at least in pairs, and a single strand was always multicolored. These beads were circular or disk shaped, and flat in section. They measured about 4.0 millimeters in diameter and 2.5 millimeters thick, with holes about 1.0 millimeter in diameter. Larger, well-fashioned stone spacer beads were found in place with these bead strands. A total of nine bead spacers was found. The beads also included a large pink disk bead, a barrel-shaped white bead, and three small gastropod shell beads. Other finds included the flint mentioned above, several tip ends of crab claws, five snail shells (unworked), and a number of heat-cracked stones.

Burial 12 (Cat. No. 356 IV, Square C1, 1.13 meters below datum)[13]

This burial (fig. 38), on the basis of the field observations, contained a child's skeleton. Although the grave had been disturbed, it seemed probable that the individual had been laid out in a flexed position. No evidence of a burial pit was found. The remains included fragments of the skull, leg bones, ribs, and the pelvic girdle. The burial area measured circa 0.36 meters N-S by 0.30 meters E-W and was about 14 centimeters thick. It was composed of a compact gray-colored sediment. Several Proto-Neolithic–type flint tools were found within the burial area. Burial 12 was located in a highly disturbed part of the northern periphery of the cemetery.

Burial 13 (Cat. No. 372 IV, Square C1, 1.31 meters below datum)[14]

This was an infant burial (figs. 37, 39), lying in a flexed position on its right side, the limbs folded upon themselves. The burial was found in dark loose sediment and occupied an area of 22 centimeters NW-SE by 14 centimeters NE-SW and was circa 5 centimeters thick. The head, lying on its right side, was to the southeast, with the face to the north. The skull was crushed. No sign of a pit was recorded. Some stone beads were found on the north side of the body, while others were found loose among the limb bones and the feet. They were evidently originally part of a necklace. Six gastropod shell beads were also associated.

Burial 14 (Cat. No. 373 IV, Square C1, 1.07 meters below datum)[15]

This burial (figs. 33–34), on the basis of field observations, was identified as that of an infant. It was part of a triple group burial (Burials 10, 14, and 17) already discussed under Burial 10. They occupied a total area of about 0.70 meters N-S and 0.55 meters E-W. Burial 10, as noted above, was at the western end of the bar of the "T," and Burial 14 was located at its eastern end. Burial 14 occupied a space measuring 0.40 meters E-W by 0.20 meters N-S. No evidence of a pit was recorded. This individual was lying in a flexed position, with its head to the west and the body on its left side and facing south. The skull was crushed. All of the bones of this child seemed to be in an undisturbed anatomical position. There was a small limestone fragment on top of the head.

This burial, like that of the child in Burial 11, was accompanied by an extraordinary amount of personal adornments. These were principally strings of stone beads of several types. There were at least two hundred small red beads to the left side of the skeleton (fig. 34). Close to the chin were about thirteen small beads, originally on a string. At the south side of the chest area there were about two dozen beads. Each of these beads measured approximately 2 millimeters long; they were originally strung on two strands, each about 18.0 centimeters long. There was also a smaller string of beads, measuring about 7.5 centimeters in length, which included the small beads described above, eight large barrel-shaped beads 9 millimeters long, and two stone disc beads. There were a number of green stone beads in the group. Strings of perforated crab claw tip ends, each about 2.0 centimeters long, were also recovered from Burial 14. The large and small stone beads and the crab claw tips were evidently strung separately. One large flint was found lying above the skull, and a snail shell was recovered nearby. Other items found in the burial area included one denticulate flake, one elongate slate pebble, one naturally smoothed ovate stone, and a fragment of stalactite.

Burial 15 (Cat. No. 374 IV, Squares C1 and C2, 1.02 meters below datum)[16]
This was, on the basis of field observations, the primary burial of a child very tightly flexed into a ball (figs. 40–41). There was no evidence of a burial pit. The body covered an area of 0.34 meters NE-SW by 0.27 meters NW-SE, with a depth of circa 0.18 meters. The burial was on a 5-centimeter-thick bed of ashes and charcoal, lying on its left side, the head twisted to the southwest and turned face down. The skull had been crushed in. Associated finds included a single gastropod shell bead found at the neck and several thin, purple-colored, large-holed stone beads. There were three retouched flints found near the right side of the lower jaw. Other materials with Burial 15 included a large number of perforated gastropod shells, one muller fragment, one retouched flint, and some mammal vertebrae.

Burial 16 (Cat. No. 375 IV, Square C1, 1.07 meters below datum)[17]
This was a badly disturbed primary burial of an infant, located in about the center of the cemetery group. It must have been disturbed when later interments were made. It occupied an area about 0.25 meters E-W by 0.20 meters N-S and about 4 centimeters thick. It lay in a dark sediment mixture above a thin 5-centimeter-thick bed of ashes and charcoal. No evidence of a pit was recorded. The remains included some ribs, long bones, and a skull fragment. The associated objects included one flint chip, a number of snail shells, and an animal tooth. These items were probably accidental inclusions from the cemetery fill.

Burial 17 (Cat. No. 376 IV, Square C1, 1.10 meters below datum)[18]
This primary burial, on the basis of field observations that of an infant
(figs. 33–34), was part of the "T"-shaped group burial described for Burials 10 and 14. Burial 17 was found at the bottom end of the leg of the "T." It
occupied an area measuring 0.45 meters N–S and 0.22 meters E–W, with a
thickness of about 12 centimeters. It lay in brown sediment just above a
bed of ashes and charcoal. No evidence of a pit was evident. The body lay
flexed on its left side, with its head to the south. The head was face down,
and the skull was badly crushed. Some stray human bones were also found
in this burial group. Munizaga identified these as from an adult. Materials
recovered in the grave area included a lot of snail shells; one flint chip;
two perforated crab claw tips (burned); and one small, flat, triangular-
shaped piece of limestone with several scratches at one end.

Burial 18 (Cat. No. 377 IV, Squares D1 and D2, 1.07 meters below datum)[19]
A partial skeleton, probably that of an adult male, was recovered from
this disturbed grave (figs. 17, 42). The remains occupied an area of about
0.40 by 0.34 meters, 8 centimeters thick. No pit outline was discernible. It
lay in the same dark sediment characteristic of the cemetery group, on a
thin bed of ashes and charcoal. The bones included a fragmentary skull,
a broken jawbone, several long bones, and part of the upper torso. The
skeletal parts that were still in correct anatomical positions suggested that
the individual had been interred in a very flexed position (bundle burial?),
lying on its left side with the head to the east. Burial 18 was found at the
western side of the cemetery area, on the same stratigraphic level as Stone
Feature 7, the arc of stones.

Two snail shells were found to the east of the burial, and a cluster of
others was found nearby. An inverted trough quern was found circa 0.35
meters to the south in the fill.

Burial 19 (Cat. No. 378 IV, Square C1, 1.05 meters below datum)[20]
This appeared, on the basis of observations, to be the primary burial of a
young child (figs. 43–44), which had been jammed into a small space in
the cave deposits. The burial area measured 0.28 meters NW–SE by 0.24
meters NE–SW and was about 0.14 meters deep. The burial lay in brown
mixed occupational sediment, above the usual 5- to 10-centimeter thickness of charcoal and ashes. There was no evidence of a pit, but it was noted
that the burial lay in a lighter-colored mixed brown sediment, different
from its surroundings. The burial had been disturbed, but it was evident

that it originally had been very tightly flexed. The head was pressed down over the body, possibly contorted into this position at the time of interment. The face was to the north, and the top of the head was to the south. The skull was crushed in. The ribs were in primary association. The right coxa of the pelvic girdle was upside-down. A loose flint, some snail shells, and mammal bones were found in the area of the burial.

Burial 20 (Cat. No. 379 IV, Square C1, 1.02 meters below datum)[21]

On the basis of field observations, this was a poorly preserved burial (figs. 22, 23, and 41) of an infant. Parts of the skull, a rib bone, and several long bones were recovered. It could not be determined if it was a primary burial or not. It occupied an area of about 0.24 meters N-S and 0.26 meters E-W. No evidence of a pit was recorded. The burial lay in mixed occupational sediment above a bed of ashes and charcoal. The bones were highly disturbed, and the original burial position could not be determined. This skeleton was evidently badly disturbed when Burial 4, a child, was interred next to it. Burial 15, also a child, was buried in the same area. No grave goods were found directly associated with this burial. Snail shells were noted in quantity in the burial area.

Burial 21 (Cat. No. 380 IV, Square C1, 1.19 meters below datum)[22]

This burial (fig. 25) appeared to include the disturbed bones of several individuals. The remains lay in mixed soft black sediment, in a small area about 0.14 meters in diameter close to the center of the cemetery area. No burial pit was recorded. The remains included the bones of a young child, the heel bone of an adult, and some skull fragments. The skeletal remains of a small infant were found under the skull fragments. This burial, which was on level with Burial 5 and below Burial 9, was probably disturbed when one or both of these graves were dug. In fact, Munizaga, in his report (appendix A) suggests that some of the bones from Burial 21 and Burial 9 belong to the same individuals.

Burial 22 (Cat. No. 381 IV, Square C1, 1.11 meters below datum)[23]

This, on the basis of the field observations, was a flexed primary burial of an adult (fig. 25). It lay in an area about 1.00 meters N-S by 0.65 meters E-W in soft dark sediment, above a bed of charcoal and ashes. No burial pit outline could be seen. This individual was laid out on its stomach, with its head upright, face slightly downward and turned to the left. The legs were drawn up to the left. Both arms were flexed, with the hands under the chest. The knees were fragmented. The feet of Burial 22 were close to the chest of Burial 5. Burials 23 and 24 lay close by as well. Associated grave goods found with Burial 22 included two large, well-fashioned bone implements (fig. 45 [a–b]). These were lying to the right side of the torso. One was a large, well-polished, pointed tool made from a mammal bone (fig. 45 [a]). The second (fig. 45 [b]) was also well polished and was made from the rib of a large mammal; it had been cut across at the end to form a straight edge rather than a pointed tip. These two objects were probably matting/basketry tools. About fifty small gastropod shell beads were found in the vicinity of the upper leg bones of the burial. Also found in the grave area were one obsidian blade and several chert blades.

Burial 23 (Cat. No. 382 IV, Square C1, 1.10 meters below datum)[24]

This burial (figs. 25–26), on the basis of observations, consisted of the partial remains of an adult male, an incomplete infant skeleton found near the adult, and miscellaneous human bones later identified by Munizaga as from an adolescent. No evidence of a burial pit was recorded. Burial 23 was found in a crowded part of the cemetery, in a cluster along with Burials 5, 21, and 22. Burial 23 lay just at the knees of Burials 22 and 5. It seemed likely that Burial 23 was disturbed when Burials 5 and 21 were interred in the cemetery. The crushed adult skull was found lying on the right side, facing east. No long bones were found that could be assigned to this individual. The skeletal parts assigned to Burial 23 occupied an area of about 0.25 meters NE-SW by 0.20 meters NW-SE. One flint was found near the adult skull.

Burial 24 (Cat. No. 383 IV, Square C1, 1.15 meters below datum)[25]

The partial remains of the main individual in this grave, located in the northern part of the cemetery, were those of an adult male (fig. 25), although skeletal parts from other individuals appeared to have been included with Burial 24. The adult male lay in dark brown sediment, but immediately below this the sediment changed, becoming more compact and lighter brown. There was no evidence of a burial pit. The skeletal remains were found in a disturbed and fragmented condition in an area of about 0.32 meters N-S by 0.48 meters E-W. The remains included several skull fragments and unarticulated distal extremity long bones. The individual was positioned with the head to the west and long bones lying to the east. One of the tibia bones had a green clayey substance coating one area, perhaps from direct contact with some cuprous material (not preserved). The most interesting find associated with Burial 24 was a bone knife (fig. 45 [c–d]) with the flint insert blade still in place, held fast with a dark, tarry-looking substance (R. L. Solecki and R. S. Solecki 1963). It was found between the fibula and the tibia of the right leg, which suggested that the artifact originally had rested on the knees of the interred individual. One flint blade and some snail shells were also found with Burial 24.

It is worth noting here that Burials 22 and 24 were located next to each other at the northern edge of the excavated portion of the cemetery. They contained the most elaborate bone tools recovered from either the cemetery or the contemporary occupational fill outside the cemetery.

Burial 25 (Cat. No. 384 IV, Square C1, 1.21 meters below datum)[26]

This burial (figs. 25 and 38) definitely was a pit burial. The pit outline, measuring 0.30 meters N-S by 0.30 meters E-W, was clearly visible in the very dry, powdery, gray cave sediment. Furthermore, the bones themselves were found to be limited to the area within the pit outline. The remains had a noticeably dry appearance and included parts of an adult skeleton, probably female (several skull fragments and long bones), and a number of bones of an infant. These were all mixed together. None of the bones were articulated or in correct anatomical positions. Burial 25 was located in about the center of the exposed cemetery area and was very likely disturbed when later interments were made. Burial 12 was located just to the west of Burial 25. One bone awl was found in association with Burial 25 (fig. 46 [b]).

Burial 26 (Cat. No. 385 IV, Square C1, 1.22 meters below datum)[27]

This was a primary burial of an infant or young child (figs. 35 and 37), occupying an area of about 0.20 by 0.16 meters and 4 centimeters in thickness. There was no evidence of a burial pit. The burial lay in soft or loose dark mixed occupational sediment. It appeared to be a disturbed burial. The remains consisted of a mass of skull fragments (the skull was crushed), several long bones, and at least two rib bones. Associated burial goods included five blue stone beads. They were found to the northwest of the skull, practically touching the lower left side of the skull of Burial 11, which lay just to the west. Also found with this burial were one fragment of a worked pebble and some additional scattered beads. An animal jawbone was collected between Burial 26 and the skull of Burial 10.

Loose Skeletal Remains

A number of loose human skeletal remains were found scattered in Square C1. These were recorded together as Cat. No. 388 IV. Because of the disturbed condition of this part of the cemetery, they could not, with certainty, be placed with any of the individually cataloged burials in the field.

Summary of the Burials

The contemporary Kurdish inhabitants of Shanidar village bury their dead in a small tree-shaded cemetery close to their homes by the Greater Zab River. We do not know why the Proto-Neolithic inhabitants of Shanidar Valley chose to bury their dead in the cave. Perhaps it was because the cave was recognized as an ancestral home from the distant past. Or perhaps it was felt that this was a safe place for the burials, protected from animals and the elements. No obvious burial markers were preserved to indicate that there was a cemetery in this part of the cave. However, it is possible that the stone querns, which were found lying flat in the cemetery, were originally set on end as grave markers. There was clear evidence that earlier graves were occasionally disturbed by later interments. We believe, however, that the cemetery was in use for only a short time and, therefore, that all the burials found in it belong to the Proto-Neolithic period.

The burial patterns found in the cemetery ranged from complete, articulated skeletons (the majority) to what appeared to have been partial burials. The average burial took up an area of about 0.50 meters in diameter. On the basis of the available sample, most of the interments seem to have been primary ones. Several of the individuals appeared to have been forced or jammed into their graves. In a number of cases, especially those of adults, heads were twisted over bodies and limbs were contorted into very unnatural positions. In several adult skeletons, the head was bent backward over the shoulders to such a degree that the neck must have been snapped.

Several adult skeletons (e.g., Burial 7) were found with crushed skulls. This damage could have been due to postdepositional traffic in the burial area. However, it should be noted that several of the burials with crushed skulls had small stones lying either directly on their heads or in close proximity to them.

Both individual and group graves were found in the cemetery. The identification of a group grave was made difficult because of the crowded nature of the main part of the cemetery (Square C1) and the fact that earlier graves were disturbed when later interments were made. On the basis of all the available data (notes, photographs, drawings, etc.) seven possible group graves have been identified, all from Square C1. These seven group graves accounted for twenty, or more than half, of the burials in the cemetery. The remaining fifteen graves were individual interments, as was the one burial found outside of the cemetery proper. Several of these group graves obviously represented a single burial event; that is, several individuals were buried together at the same time in a small space. One of the group graves was found in a purposely prepared pit, certainly representing a single burial event. On the other hand, a number of the group graves may represent accidental associations created by disturbances in the cemetery when new graves were dug.

The seven group graves were defined as follows.

Group I (fig. 25)

This group was called Burial 21. It included the bones of a young child, the heel bone of an adult, and the remains of a small infant. This group appeared to have been disturbed by Burial 5 or Burial 9.

Group II (figs. 22, 23, 40, and 41)

This group consisted of the skeletons of three infants/children. Burial 20 was an infant whose skeletal remains were disturbed at some time by the intrusion of Burial 4, a child. Burial 15, also a child, may or may not have been associated as part of this group. However, its remains lay close to the skeletal remains of the other two individuals.

Group III (figs. 33–34, and 37)

This group was represented by three infant burials, Burials 10, 14, and 17. These three individuals were buried in a rough "T" formation, with the feet close together and the heads at the distal ends of the "T." Burial 14 was buried with an extraordinary amount of bead ornaments.

Group IV (figs. 35–37, and 39)

This group included three burials, Burials 11, 13, and 26. Burials 11 and 26 lay close together, and Burial 13 also seemed to be part of the group because of its close proximity to the other two. Burial 11 was an elaborately decorated child, Burial 13 was a decorated infant, and Burial 26 was a decorated infant or small child.

Group V (fig. 25, 38)
This group included the remains of an adult, Burial 25, and some skeletal remains of an infant. These two individuals were found together in the only clearly defined burial pit in the cemetery. Neither the bones of the adult nor those of the infant were found resting in anatomical articulation.

Group VI (figs. 22–23)
This group was called Burial 9. It included a fragmentary skull, probably of an adolescent, and skull parts from two infants. This group was located near Burial 20 (which was part of Group II).

Group VII (figs. 25–26)
This group was called Burial 23. It included the remains of an adult male, an incomplete very young infant, and miscellaneous bones of an adolescent.

All the skeletons in the cemetery were found in flexed positions, ranging from loosely to tightly flexed. No extended skeletons were found. Some of the flexed skeletons were in very compressed positions, suggesting that the bodies had been bound or encased in some way. Preserved fragments of matting (fig. 24) were found with one burial (Burial 4). There seemed to have been no deliberate orientation or patterning of burial positions. The body and head were faced in no particular or consistent direction.

The average burial depth was about a meter below "0" datum elevation (ranging from 0.83 meters to 1.31 meters). The cave "0" elevation datum point was about the floor level of the cave in the cemetery area.

The concentration of most of the burials in a small part of the excavated cemetery (Square C1, an area measuring only 2 by 2 meters) indicated that the Shanidar Cave people had some method of locating this particular spot. Perhaps a marker, made of either permanent or perishable materials, was put in place to identify it. In any event, the people were able to return to this restricted space again and again. The fact that earlier burials were disturbed by later ones did not deter them from reusing this "special" place. Although we are unable to give the sequence of all of the burials, some observations can be made from the positions of several of the burials. Because the interment of Burial 5 appeared to have disturbed Burial 23, we infer that it was interred later than the latter. It is suggested that Burial 4 was interred later than Burial 20, because the former intruded into the Burial 20 space. Burial 22 may have been laid down after Burial 5, or contemporaneously. In turn, it appeared that Burial 9 had been interred later than Burials 5 and 21. In another area, Burial 1 appeared to have been interred later than Burials 7 and 10 by virtue of its position in the cemetery.

The Proto-Neolithic Burial Found Outside the Cemetery

Burial 27 (Cat. No. 186 III, Square D9, 2.35 meters below datum)[28]
One burial (figs. 47–48) of Proto-Neolithic age was found in the 1956–57 season outside the cemetery proper and toward the front of the cave (R. S. Solecki 1957, 170–71). On the basis of the associated cultural material, this burial was also Proto-Neolithic in age. It was a young adult, probably a female.

The remains were found at a depth of 2.35 meters below "0" datum. The surface of the cave sloped downward toward the cave front, accounting for the greater depth below datum of this burial than the burials in the cemetery. The burial lay in a rough, stone-lined grave especially prepared for the individual. There were nine limestone blocks, several measuring about 20 by 30 centimeters, in the enclosure. With the stones, the grave measured about 0.90 meters N-S by 1.20 meters E-W. Within the enclosure, the grave measured about 0.30 meters N-S by 0.90 meters E-W. The burial was lying in the east-west direction with the head to the east. The individual lay on its back, with its limbs in a loosely flexed position before it. The face was up, and the head was slightly turned to the left (south). The head was resting on a stone in a broad niche of the stone enclosure. The facial bones were badly crushed and in fragments. The spinal column was twisted slightly to the left, as though the body had been forced into the stone enclosure. The elbows of both arms were resting on stones on either side of the burial. The right forearm and hand were missing. It is probable that the right hand had rested on top of the right knee. The left hand was found in the area of the pelvis. Both legs were doubled up, with the left foot under the pelvis. The right knee, so far as could be determined, had been elevated. Under the right foot was a hand-grinding stone or muller. On top of the feet was a large, broken trough quern, placed upside-down. The quern and muller were both stained with red pigment, and it was clear that the pigment had been ground in the quern. Also associated with this burial was a gastropod shell bead necklace. The beads were small and neatly perforated. Most of the beads were at the right side of the neck. Traces of red pigment were also found at the right shoulder, staining the bones and the beads in that area, and at the left hip.

George Maranjian made the following observations concerning the skeletal remains. The best-preserved parts of the skull were the mandible (except for the rami), the occipital, the right parietal, and parts of the frontal area. The dentition was complete. The mandible had all of the teeth in place, with the exception of the third molar. The teeth seemed to be rather large. There were thirty-three teeth in all. The mastoid processes were fairly well developed. The bones of the skull vault were moderately thick. The brow ridges were very small, and the occiput showed very little thickening.

Most of the vertebrae were present, although badly preserved and either fragmentary or in broken condition. The clavicle and sternum were present and in fairly good condition. The scapulae were fairly well preserved. Most of the rib cage was preserved, but the ribs were broken. The pelvis was in a very poor state of preservation; little remained except for a portion of the left ilium.

Of the limb bones, the right humerus was in good condition, although the bones of the right forearm and hand were missing. The left humerus, radius, and ulna were present, but in broken condition. The leg bones were represented by a few fragments. Parts of the feet had survived, but were in poor condition.

It was estimated that this was the skeleton of a young adult, possibly about twenty-five years old. It was thought to be a female, but a robust one. The reason for the separate burial of this individual, outside the Proto-Neolithic cemetery area, could not be determined.

Summary of the Proto-Neolithic Mortuary Traits at Shanidar Cave

1. A separate cemetery, located toward the rear of the cave, was used by inhabitants of the cave over a period of time. A single isolated burial was also found toward the front of the cave.
2. Burial position was either flexed or semiflexed. No extended burials were found. No preferred body orientation was observed.

3. Both individual and multiple (family?) graves were present.
4. More child/infant burials than adult/adolescent burials were found.
5. Earlier burials were disturbed by later interments.
6. Both primary and secondary burials were present, although the former were more common.
7. Bundle burials may have been present. At least one burial seemed to have been wrapped in matting.
8. A definite burial pit was observed in only one grave in the cemetery. In addition, the single burial found outside the cemetery was placed in a special stone-lined grave pit.
9. The burials in the cemetery were laid out on a bed of ash and charcoal, and the entire cemetery was covered with a layer of yellow-colored loam.
10. No definite grave markers were identified in the cemetery, but perhaps the querns and quern fragments found there once served such a purpose.
11. Hearths and stone structures (clusters and pavements) were built in the cemetery. To date, similar stone constructions have not been found elsewhere in the Proto-Neolithic deposits of Shanidar Cave.
12. Stones were sometimes placed in the graves. These could be set against the back, above and under the head, or above the body. In the one grave found outside the cemetery, a muller was placed below the right foot and a quern above the feet.
13. Almost 50 percent of the graves contained grave goods. Most common were personal adornments, characteristically found in children's/infants' graves. Bone tools and pecked/ground stone tools were also occasionally placed in the graves, mainly with adults.
14. Snail shell concentrations were found in the cemetery, as were broken animal bones. Perhaps these represented the remains of funerary feasts.

TABLE 1. SKELETAL COUNTS FOR THE TWENTY-SIX NUMBERED BURIALS IN THE SHANIDAR CAVE CEMETERY

Burial and Cat. No.		Solecki	Munizaga	Ferembach	Agelarakis
1	279 IV	1 (adolescent)	1 (adolescent)	1 (adolescent)	1 (adolescent)
2	295 IV	1 (adolescent)	1 (adolescent)	1 (adolescent)	1 (adolescent)
3	296 IV	1 (adolescent)	Did not find	Did not find/study	Did not find
4	297 IV	1 (child)	3 (1 adult, 1 child, 1 infant)	Did not find/study	Did not find
5	298 IV	1 (adult)	1 (adult)	1 (adult)	5 (1 infant,
	371 IV				4 adults)

TABLE 1, CONT.

Burial and Cat. No.		Solecki	Munizaga	Ferembach	Agelarakis
6	337 IV	2 (1 adult, 1 infant)	1 (adult)	3 (1 adult, 2 infants)	2 (1 adult, 1 infant)
7	339 IV	1 (adult)	1 (adult)	Did not find/study	Did not find
8	347 IV	1 (child)	1 (child)	Did not find/study	Did not find
9	350 IV	3 (1 adolescent, 2 infants)	3 (1 adolescent, 2 infants)	Did not find/study	Did not find
10	351 IV	1 (infant)	1 (young child)	Did not find/study	Did not find
11	355 IV	1 (child)	2 (1 adult, 1 young child)	Did not find/study	Did not find
12	356 IV	1 (child)	2 (1 infant, 1 unidentifiable)	3 (1 adult, 2 infants)	3 (1 adult, 2 infants)[a]
13	372 IV	1 (infant)	1 (infant)	Did not find/study	Did not find
14	373 IV	1 (infant)	1 (young child)	Did not find/study	Did not find
15	374 IV	1 (child)	Did not find	Did not find/study	1 (infant/child)
16	375 IV	1 (infant)	1 (young child)	Did not find/study	Did not find
17	376 IV	2 (1 adult, 1 infant)	2 (1 adult, 1 young child)	Did not find/study	Did not find
18	377 IV	1 (adult)	1 (adult)	Did not find/study	Did not find
19	378 IV	1 (young child)	1 (young child)	Did not find/study	Did not find
20	379 IV	1 (infant)	1 (infant)	Did not find/study	Did not find
21	380 IV	3 (1 adult, 1 child, 1 infant)	1 (1 adult and odd bones probably belonging to Burial 9)	Did not find/study	Did not find
22	381 IV	1 (adult)	1 (adult)	4 (3 adults, 1 infant)	8 (2 adults, 4 adults/adolescents, 2 infants)
23	382 IV	3 (1 adult, 1 adolescent,	3 (1 adult, 1 adolescent, 1 infant)	2 (1 adult, 1 infant	2 (1 adult, 1 infant
24	383 IV	1 (1 adult)	3 (1 adult, 1 child, 1 infant)	5 (3 adults, 1 adolescent, 1 infant)	4 (2 adults, 2 infants)
25	384 IV	2 (1 adult, 1 infant)	2 (1 adult, 1 infant)	2 (1 adult, 1 infant)	2 (1 adult, 1 infant)
26	385 IV	1 (infant/child)	2 (1 adult, 1 infant, and fragments of Burial 14)	Did not find/study	Did not find
Totals		35	37	22	29

[a] Agelarakis found these remains in a bag marked No. 356–384 and described them with No. 384. Because he did not describe any skeletal material under No. 356 (Agelarakis 1989, table 1) in this report, we have listed them under No. 356.

Notes

1. It was evident that the observations provided the most accurate counts of the number of individuals placed in a single grave lot as cataloged at the time of excavation. These counts sometimes differed from those presented by the three physical anthropologists who studied the Shanidar Cave Proto-Neolithic remains stored in the Iraq Museum (table 1). Furthermore, there are differences in the counts given by Munizaga (appendix A) and his followers (Ferembach 1970; Agelarakis 1989; chapter 9) that can presumably be attributed to the fact that for various reasons the three investigators did not always analyze identical grave samples. The individual grave lots that were packed in boxes had been unpacked and repacked an indeterminate number of times in the Iraq Museum, probably even before Munizaga first cataloged them in 1962. Munizaga found twenty-four of the twenty-six grave lots identified in the field and described thirty-one individual skeletons from them. Ferembach, in 1969, selectively studied only the more complete skeletons, so it is not certain how many of the grave lots she looked at. She published on twenty-two individuals from nine graves as cataloged in the Iraq Museum (Ferembach 1970). Agelarakis, who studied the skeletal material in 1981, recorded twenty-nine individuals from eleven grave lots. With the later addition of more information, Agelarakis (this volume) raised his enumeration of individuals from the cemetery to thirty-one.
2. Munizaga, Ferembach, and Agelarakis all identified one adolescent from this grave lot.
3. Munizaga, Ferembach, and Agelarakis all identified one adolescent from this grave lot.
4. Munizaga and Agelarakis did not find this specimen, and Ferembach did not find/study it.
5. Munizaga recorded three individuals for this grave lot— one adult, one child(?), and one newborn infant. Agelarakis did not find it. Ferembach did not find/study it.
6. Munizaga and Ferembach both recorded a single adult female for this grave lot. Agelarakis recorded five individuals from it—four adults, including one female, and one infant.
7. All of the three physical anthropologists studied this grave lot. Munizaga recorded one adult male, Ferembach one adult male and two infants, and Agelarakis one adult male and one infant.
8. Munizaga recorded one adult female. Ferembach did not find/study this burial, and Agelarakis did not find it.
9. Munizaga recorded one child. Ferembach did not find/study this burial, and Agelarakis did not find it.
10. Munizaga recorded one adolescent and two infants. Ferembach did not find/study this burial, and Agelarakis did not find it.
11. Munizaga recorded one young child (with first milk molar). Ferembach did not find/study this burial, and Agelarakis did not find it.
12. Munizaga recorded one adult and one young child (with first milk molar). Ferembach did not find/study this burial, and Agelarakis did not find it.

13. Munizaga recorded one infant and one individual of indeterminable age, Ferembach recorded one adult and two infants, and Agelarakis recorded one adult and two infants. The latter were found in a bag marked with both Cat. No. 356 IV and Cat. No. 384 IV (Burial 25).

14. Munizaga recorded one newborn infant. Ferembach did not find/study this burial, and Agelarakis did not find it.

15. Munizaga recorded one young child (with first milk molar) for this burial. Ferembach did not find/study it, and Agelarakis did not find it.

16. Munizaga did not find this burial, Ferembach did not find/study it, and Agelarakis found only the head of a femur under this catalog number. He identified it as possibly belonging to an infant or a young juvenile.

17. Munizaga recorded one young child (with second milk molar). Ferembach did not find/study this burial, and Agelarakis did not find it.

18. Munizaga recorded one adult and one young child (with erupting second milk molar). Ferembach did not find/study this burial, and Agelarakis did not find it.

19. Munizaga recorded one adult male(?). Ferembach did not find/study this burial, and Agelarakis did not find it.

20. Munizaga recorded one young child (with second milk molar). Ferembach did not find/study this burial, and Agelarakis did not find it.

21. Munizaga recorded one newborn infant. Ferembach did not find/study this burial, and Agelarakis recorded one adult for this burial (Cat. No. 379 IV) and Burial 5 (Cat. No. 371 IV).

22. Munizaga recorded one adult for this burial, along with some odd bones that probably went with the adolescent and the infants of Burial 9. Ferembach did not find/study this burial, and Agelarakis did not find it.

23. Munizaga recorded one adult. Ferembach recorded three adults (two males and one female) and one infant, and Agelarakis recorded two adult males, four adolescents/adults, and two infants.

24. Munizaga recorded one adult, one adolescent, and one infant. Ferembach recorded one adult male and one infant, and Agelarakis recorded one adult male and one infant.

25. Munizaga recorded one adult, one child(?), and one infant. Ferembach recorded three adults (two males and one female), one adolescent, and one infant. Agelarakis recorded two adults (one male) and two infants.

26. Munizaga recorded one adult and one newborn infant, Ferembach recorded one adult female and one infant, and Agelarakis recorded one adult female and one infant.

27. Munizaga recorded one adult, one newborn infant, and cranial fragments belonging to Burial 14 (Cat. No. 373 IV). Ferembach did not find/study this burial, Agelarakis did not find it.

28. We are indebted to George Maranjian, then a physical anthropologist with the Arabian American Oil Company (ARAMCO) and also a member of the Shanidar research team in 1957, for the morphological observations on the skeletal remains.

CHAPTER 3

The Stone Features

RALPH S. SOLECKI AND ROSE L. SOLECKI

E ight stone clusters or pavements and one stone alignment or wall were associated with the Proto-Neolithic cemetery complex (fig. 7). The stone clusters were composed of fist-sized angular lumps of limestone, characteristically laid in a thin layer in a single course on the unprepared cave floor. These small rocks could have been picked up anywhere in the vicinity of the cave and therefore provided a readily available resource. We suggest that these clusters were probably functional hearths associated with mortuary rituals performed in the cemetery. After the burial ceremony was completed, the hearth debris was swept away off the hot stones. This could account for the accumulation of charcoal and ashes found in the cemetery area, reaching a thickness of between 5 and 10 centimeters under the burials. Since the interments were made over a period of time, it is assumed that the accumulation and spread of the charcoal and ashes from the hearths were the result not of one but of a number of burial rites. This would account for the overall appearance of the gray soil in the cemetery area, a localized phenomenon in the cave. A definite hearth was found directly upon Stone Feature 1, and traces of a hearth and burial were found upon Stone Feature 6. Conclusive evidence of burning was also associated with Stone Feature 8.

The stone alignment (figs. 4, 17, and 20) may have been constructed to serve as a kind of boundary between the living area proper of the cave and the burial area within. One of the stone clusters, Stone Feature 6, was found at the inner curved side of the alignment (figs. 17–20).

Catalog of the Stone Features

Stone Feature 1 (Cat. Nos. 283 IV and 293 IV, Square B1, 0.92 meters below datum)

This was a stone pavement or cluster with a small reddish hearth in the center (figs. 49–50). The hearth was located directly on the pavement. The pavement was composed of at least two hundred angular limestone fragments, each about 5 to 10 centimeters long. Each stone seemed to have been carefully and purposefully laid in place, covering the whole area without any bare spots. The stones were practically touching each other. The stone pavement was roughly rectangular in shape, with a slight protuberance at the southwest end. The feature measured 0.80 meters wide at the northern part, 1.10 meters wide at the southern part (measured E-W), and 2.10 meters long (N-S). It was 5 to 10 centimeters thick. One trough quern, trough face up, was found just to the east in the excavation wall; a second quern, trough face down, and a muller were recovered just to the south of this feature. At the west side of the pavement was found a large, three-holed, green stone spacer bead (fig. 27 [a]). This bead was probably originally from Burial 5, located just to the west. Other cultural materials, as well as unworked burned rocks, some animal bones, and snail shells, were found in the fill of Square B1 at the stratigraphic level of Stone Feature 1.

Stone Feature 2 (Cat. No. 331 IV a, Square B2, 0.80 meters below datum)

This was a cluster or pavement of fist-sized limestone fragments in the southeast corner of Square B2. It measured 0.70 meters by 0.35 meters and was shaped like a long oval (figs. 51 and 52). Two fragments of a trough quern were found near this feature.

Stone Feature 3 (Cat. No. 331 IV b, Square B2, 0.86 meters below datum)

This was a cluster or pavement of stones composed of about thirty-four fist-sized limestone fragments (figs. 52–53). It was one meter away from the larger stone cluster (Stone Feature 2) and near Stone Features 4 and 5 in the same square. Shaped in a roughly ovate form, it measured about 0.55 by 0.44 meters. A large, broken boulder quern, bottom side up, lay to the west of it. A trough quern fragment was located to the east of this feature. A pink calcite bead, ovate-round in shape, was also associated (fig. 27 [d]). Several centimeters to the southeast of Stone Feature 3 was a collection of mammal bones, identified as sheep, goat, Bos, and red deer, plus some bird bones.

Stone Features 2 and 3 were located close to each other in Square B2 and at approximately the same stratigraphic level. The cultural material found in the fill around them was collected under a single catalog number. Therefore, except for the items described above as definitely associated with either Stone Feature 2 or Stone Feature 3, the material from the fill was described as a single unit. Some fire-cracked stones were also associated with these features.

Stone Feature 4 (Cat. No. 323 IV, Squares B2 and C2, 1.00 meter below datum).

This feature was composed of a small number of stones, in a kind of pavement, close to Stone Features 3 and 5 (figs. 29 and 52). It measured about 0.45 by 0.30 meters. The feature was made of about twenty angular, fist-sized limestone fragments. Burial 4 lay to the north of it. An inverted, broken, large boulder quern lay just to the east of and above Stone Feature 4. Some charcoal flecks (Cat. No. 335 IV) were recovered from under the quern. The fill around Stone Feature 4 contained much cultural material. Among the faunal remains recovered near this feature were the bones of sheep, goats, Bos, bear, and turtle; snail shells; and large fish bones.

Stone Feature 5 (Cat. No. 337 IVa, Square B2, 0.83 meters below datum)

This small cluster of angular, fist-sized limestone fragments (circa 40 by 20 centimeters) was located at the head of Burial 6 (figs. 29 and 52). This structure was noteworthy because of its small size and close proximity to Burial 6. Two pieces of chipped stone and a flat muller were cataloged with Stone Feature 5.

Stone Feature 6 (Cat. No. 353 IV, Square D1, 1.15 to 1.23 meters below datum)

This was a cluster or rough pavement of stones (figs. 17–20). It measured 0.80 meters long (E–W) by 0.42 meters wide (N–S) and was built with about one hundred angular, fist-sized limestone chunks. It was two courses thick in part, but was generally only one course thick, loosely packed. Stone Feature 6 abutted the inner side of Stone Feature 7, the curved stone wall. Burial 2 was lying on top of Stone Feature 6, approximately in the center. A small, inverted boulder quern was located at the southwest end of Stone Feature 6. It was under a patch of charcoal and ashes, possibly detritus from the nearby hearth. A quern fragment lay to the north of Stone Feature 6. Two pieces of daub (fig. 21)—burned clay with finger-prints impressed on one face and sticks on the other (Cat. No. 370 IV)—were found to the east of Stone Feature 6 and Burial 2 and between them and the longer arm of Stone Feature 7 (see below). These fragments may have been a structural part of Stone Feature 7; an enclosing wall built with a stone foundation and a wattle and daub superstructure may have once stood in this location. These fragments are the only evidence for wattle and daub construction found, as yet, in Shanidar Cave. A variety of cultural items were recovered from the fill around Stone Feature 6.

Stone Feature 7 (Cat. Nos. 292 IV and 294 IV, Square D1, 0.98 to 1.08 meters below datum)

This feature consisted of a single course of eleven unworked, portable-sized rough limestone blocks laid down in a curving line or arc (figs. 4, 17, and 20). In plan view the feature is "L" shaped, the arms joined at a rounded corner. Stone Feature 6, as described above, abuts against the inner face of Stone Feature 7. The stone blocks of Stone Feature 7 had been carefully aligned, each one touching the next one in line. The complete length of Stone Feature 7 was 2.80 meters, terminating abruptly at both ends. The stones averaged about 28 by 18 centimeters and were 16 centimeters thick. Snail shell concentrations were found above and close to this feature at its southwest end, at a depth of from 1.00 to 1.08 meters. At about the same depth, in the northwest section of the feature, the presence of charcoal, dark-gray sediment, and bone fragments was recorded. A number of mullers (Cat. No. 292 IV) were located to the west of Stone Feature 7, and other cultural items were recovered from the fill around it.

Stone Feature 8 (Cat. Nos. 342 IV and 344 IV, Squares C3 and D3, 1.05 to 1.35 meters below datum)

Stone Feature 8, a roughly circular stone cluster about 0.65 meters in di-ameter, located in both Squares C3 and D3, was constructed of about twenty-five angular stone fragments, one course thick (figs. 54–55). From the appearance of Stone Feature 8, it seemed to have functioned as a hearth or roasting platform. Much cultural material was recovered from the area around Stone Feature 8, mainly in Square C3. A number of stone items were burned, and there were some small pieces of heavily burned animal bone. The large numbers and type of chipped stone flints recovered from this area indicated that the Zarzian layer (B2) had been partially cut into during excavation by the Proto-Neolithic people. A quern fragment and an animal shoulder blade were found in an ashy charcoal deposit close to Stone Feature 8. One complete inverted trough quern lay to the northeast of this feature.

Stone Feature 9 (Cat. No. 324 IV, Square C3, 0.85 meters below datum)
This was a cluster of fourteen stones in a rough pavement measuring 0.60 by 0.90 meters (fig. 54). No cultural materials were directly associated with it, but a large number of snail shells, some mammal bone fragments, an obsidian tool, several flint tools, and various small stones were noted in the area.

Summary of the Stone Features

All eight of the stone clusters or pavements in the cemetery area were built of fist-sized chunks of limestone, stones readily found in and around Shanidar Cave. The clusters had distinct bounded oval or oblong outlines in plan and were carefully laid out with each stone fitted into place. The smallest stone cluster measured 0.20 by 0.40 meters, and the largest was 1.10 by 2.10 meters. They were placed apart from the central, crowded burial section of the cemetery and somewhat peripherally to the graves themselves. An open area without stone clusters or burials bordered the cemetery proper to the southwest. Only three burials were located near a stone cluster (Burial 2 with Stone Feature 6, Burial 5 with Stone Feature 1, and Burial 6 with Stone Feature 5). All three of these burials were located on the inner side of the stone clusters or within the cemetery, not on the outer side (fig. 7). Most of the burials in the cemetery, therefore, were not placed near the stone clusters. The ritual activities that presumably took place at the stone clusters were for the most part in open areas away from the burials themselves.

The stone clusters were located in the ashy sediments of the lower cemetery layer (Layer B1b) and thus were stratigraphically level with the burials. It is here suggested that the creation of the distinctive dark-colored sediments of Layer B1b was related to the ritual burning/cooking activities that took place at the stone structures. It should also be noted here that, as yet, no similar stone clusters or extensive ashy/charcoal sediments have been found outside the cemetery area in the Layer B1 deposits of Shanidar Cave.

The stone clusters had miscellaneous cultural materials associated with them. They were for the most part similar to the materials recovered from the cemetery fill (see chapter 5). Querns and quern fragments, however, seemed to occur regularly with the stone clusters and were rare in the rest of the cemetery. Ten out of the eleven querns/quern fragments found within the cemetery came from excavation units (squares) that also contained stone clusters. Only one quern was recovered from a square (D2) that did not contain a stone cluster. This quern, however, was located near Burial 18, the only burial in the square. Only four complete or broken mullers were recovered from around the stone clusters. However, the field notes indicate that "mullers were found in quantity" to the west of Stone Feature 7 (the curved wall of stones), between it and the west wall of D3. Three mullers were also recovered from the squares without stone clusters. The placement of a quern and a muller with Burial 27 further suggests some special relationship between these large food-processing tools and burial ritual.

It is possible, but unlikely, that the mullers and querns found near the stone clusters in Shanidar Cave could have served as ordinary building stones. At the nearby village site of Zawi Chemi Shanidar, stone walls were composed of natural river cobbles and also fragments of querns, mullers, and other broken stone tools (R. L. Solecki 1981). However, a number of factors make this interpretation unlikely for the cave constructions: the cave clusters were neatly laid out and constructed of fist-sized limestone fragments found in the cave, while the querns and mullers were made of quartzite, a different raw material; the larger-sized and irregularly shaped querns and quern fragments also could not easily be fitted into the regular outline of the stone clusters. Parenthetically, it might also be noted that limestone retains heat better than quartzite, which the cave people may have realized.

The exact function of the stone alignment (Stone Feature 7) that bordered the western edge of the cemetery could not be established. It is possible that at one time this stone alignment was part of a larger construction that enclosed the entire cemetery. Several fairly large-sized stones were recovered during the excavation of the cemetery. These could have been part of a larger stone wall. The daub fragments with wattle impressions found close to Stone Feature 7 suggest the possibility that a wattle and daub wall once stood above a stone foundation wall (represented by Stone Feature 7). It is fortunate that the Shanidar Cave daub specimens were preserved by fire. At another site, according to Howe (1983, 45), two lumps of hardened clay with stick(?) impressions were found at the roughly coeval site of Karim Shahir.

In summary, the stone clusters may have served several functions in the cemetery area. Primarily, we believe that burial rituals were performed in association with them, rituals involving the use of fire/cooking. Secondarily, the stone clusters seem to have enclosed or bounded the cemetery, as did the stone alignment (Stone Feature 7). The clusters were found roughly around the known periphery of the cemetery, to the east, south, and west (here up against the stone alignment). The northern boundary of the cemetery is still unexcavated, so we do not know if the clusters were also present there.

Probable Functions of the Stone Features

Comparative ethnographic and archaeological data can provide useful insights into the function of the Shanidar Cave stone clusters as specialized hearths. Fire serves the needs of humans in a variety of ways: it provides warmth, light, and the means of cooking food (both animal and vegetable), and it serves as protection against animals, especially in cave locations. In addition, fire has long been associated with human myth and ritual and "not only appeals to man's rational mind but . . . has deep subconscious or sensual appeal" (Oakley 1961, 185). The construction of hearths and the use of fires in mortuary ritual have been well documented in the ethnographic literature. Evidence for human use of fire goes back to the Lower Palaeolithic, but it is not until the Middle Palaeolithic period that recognizable hearths are found, associated with the Neanderthals. Many broad hearths were found in the Middle Palaeolithic and Upper Palaeolithic occupational deposits at Shanidar Cave, but none of these were delimited or defined by stone constructions. The earliest evidence in the cave for the association of stone constructions with fire/burning comes from the Proto-Neolithic cemetery. It should be noted, furthermore, that no similar stone constructions—or, for that matter, human burials—have been found as yet at the nearby Proto-Neolithic village site of Zawi Chemi Shanidar.

Other Near Eastern sites dating from roughly the same period as the Zagros Proto-Neolithic (or slightly earlier or later) contained various types of hearths. Of prime interest for comparative purposes, of course, are those stone-hearth constructions found in mortuary contexts.

Many of the open and cave Natufian sites of the Levant contained human burials. In only two of them were the burials definitely arranged in separate cemeteries as at Shanidar Cave, namely at el-Wad and Nahal Oren (Fiedel 1979). At Shuqbah, Garrod (1942) did not indicate the exact loci of the Natufian burials, so it cannot be known if they were arranged in a cemetery or not. However, in all three of these sites, hearths were found near or under Natufian graves.

At Nahal Oren, Stekelis and Yizraely (1963, 11, pl. 3a) reported the presence of a large hearth in the Natufian cemetery. Its size and shape were defined by a ring of smooth flat stones, and it was filled with a layer of ash a half-meter thick. It has been suggested that this hearth functioned as an eternal flame in the cemetery (Stekelis and Yizraely 1963).

At el-Wad, two of the Natufian burials in the group burial in Chamber 1 were associated with hearths (Garrod 1937). Burial 4, that of a young adult, lay on a hard gray hearth that contrasted in color with the red soil that surrounded it. Burial 5, a young child, lay on a bed of limestone fragments surrounded by a very black hearth. The situation on the terrace of el-Wad, also Natufian in date, is more complicated because of the presence there of stone pavements, stone walls, and rock cut basins in addition to human burials. None of the burials on the terrace were associated with specific hearths, although Garrod (1942, 10) does note that in Layer B2 large areas were blackened by hearth materials. The rock cut basins on the terrace contained no traces of fire (Garrod 1942, 11). A hearth, filled with light gray soil and outlined by limestone fragments, was located next to a stone pavement on the terrace and near Burials 20 and 25.

At Shuqbah, in the Natufian layer, Garrod (1942, 5) reported finding a number of human remains. H1, a young child, was found immediately above a very black hearth. In fact, Garrod (1942, 7) noted that the Natufian layer was made up of soft black earth with traces of charcoal; these deposits apparently were formed in part by the detritus from the hearths found in the Natufian layer (Garrod 1942, 7).

At other Natufian sites, burials could be located within the living areas, thus making the separation of burial constructions difficult. The identification of special mortuary hearths at these Natufian villages was even more complex because stone-lined hearths were built on the floors of the domestic habitations. Hearths also were located away from or between the dwellings. Because of these characteristics of Natufian villages it is sometimes difficult to distinguish special mortuary hearths from those built for domestic purposes.

At the Natufian village site of Mallaha (Perrot 1957, 1966; Perrot and Ladiray 1988), the human burials were clearly placed within the areas of habitation. Perrot and Ladiray (1988, 81–82) believe that in most cases the burials found stratigraphically below the floors of the habitations were not placed there when the structures were in use; the only possible exception to this was for newborns. At Mallaha, therefore, there was no clear separation between living and burial areas. This situation creates the potential for confusion when researchers try to assess the relationships between stone habitations, the hearths, and the human burials—that is, to determine if any of the stone constructions were used for ritual (mortuary) purposes as well as domestic ones. The stone habitations of Mallaha characteristically have a central hearth, either square or ovate in shape, excavated in the floor and outlined by stones. On the basis of the original excavation report (Perrot 1957), it was suggested that Habitation 1, which contained a square hearth on its floor and also a severed human head, was built up over Burials 15 and 19 as part of a single major tomb complex. Anati (1963), on the basis of Perrot's report, suggested that when Burials 15 and 19 were interred, a ritual fire was lit and a human sacrifice, represented by the skull, was made. Perrot reviewed this situation twice (1966, 1988) and in the latest statement made it clear that Habitation 1 was not built as part of the mortuary ceremony (Perrot and Ladiray 1988, 15–19). In any event, there now seems to be no persuasive evidence to support the idea that a ritual fire and human sacrifice occurred in Habitation 1 at Mallaha as part of a mortuary ceremony.

At Hayonim, Natufian remains have been found both inside the cave and on the terrace. Stone structures as well as burials were present at both locations. The relationship between the Natufian occupations of the cave and the terrace is not yet clearly understood (Bar-Yosef 1991, 89). Within the cave, stone-outlined hearths were found in a number of the structures (Loci 4, 5, and 7), but the hearths were built up against the inner wall, not in the center as at Mallaha (Bar-Yosef 1991, 186–87, fig. 1). Bar-Yosef (1991, 87) has suggested that these structures may have served some special activity at one time because of the presence in them of incised slabs. A burned zone, larger than the average hearth, was located outside one of the stone structures (Locus 3) and close to some of the burials recovered from an open area (Bar-Yosef 1991, 186–87, fig. 1). It seems likely that the hearths located inside the structures were related to domestic activities; the function of the larger hearth, outside the built-up area and close to the burials, is not clear-cut.

The Hayonim terrace, as noted above, also had a Natufian occupation associated with a variety of stone constructions and human burials. Valla,

Le Mort, and Plisson (1991, 95) reported the presence of a hearth feature (Feature 8) located in a depression between Structure 9 and Burials 7, 8, and 10. It is described as follows (Valla, Le Mort, and Plisson 1991, 95, fig. 1):

> Il se présentait comme une couronne dense de très petits débris entourant une zone centrale de 50 cm de diamètre marquee par une terre noirâtre au sommet, puis grise et cendreuse dans laquelle des pierres s'organisaient autour d'un bloc plat d'une quinzaine de centimètres carrés, épais de 8 cm.
>
> [It looked like a garland of very dense small debris encircling a central zone 50 cm in diameter, marked by blackish earth at the top, then grey and cinders, among which the stones were arranged around a flat block 15 centimeters square and 8 centimeters thick.]

Although Valla, Le Mort, and Plisson (1991, 98) note that it was impossible to determine the precise function of this hearth, the suggestion was given that it was used for "cuisson a l'étouffé" (to cook by braising). Another concentration of small stones (Structure 7) at the site, circa 1 meter square, has been interpreted as a garbage pit, even though just above it was a large hearth from Level 1. Structure 7 was also located outside of one of the stone structures.

Stone hearths have been recorded at the Natufian encampment at the site of Beidha, perhaps better known for its later early Neolithic village (Byrd 1991). Although no stone habitations were found dating to the Natufian period, two different types of hearths or roasting areas were uncovered. The hearths were oval to round in plan (35 to 60 centimeters in diameter), shallow (up to 15 centimeters deep), and filled with dark gray ashy sand mixed with small pieces of charcoal and fire-cracked stones (less than 10 centimeters in diameter). Hearth cleanings were also observed in the areas around the hearths, mainly in the form of ashy concentrations. Also found in the Natufian encampment at Beidha were what were identified as large-sized roasting areas, outlined by large stones. Only two have been excavated so far. These measured 1.5 to 2.5 meters in diameter. Many animal bones were associated with these large, shallow roasting areas.

At the site of Mureybat, stone hearths similar to those just described for Beidha were found in the Natufian or lowest occupation layer. These continued to be built in Phases II and III at the site (into the eighth millennium B.C.) (Molist 1985, 41).

The well-described Natufian sites of the Levant dated from the thirteenth through the eleventh millennia B.P., a time range both earlier than and contemporary with the Shanidar Proto-Neolithic. Within the broad Zagros area, the closest parallel to the latter is to be found at Karim Shahir (Howe 1983). The site of Karim Shahir, roughly coeval in date and similar in culture to the Shanidar Proto-Neolithic, is located some 150 kilometers to the southeast of Shanidar, in the foothills of the Zagros, at an altitude of 850 meters. Although no definite stone structures could be identified at Karim Shahir, the single occupation layer at the site had survived as a relatively concentrated stone scatter or pavement, along with great quantities of cultural refuse (Howe 1983, 42). Fire pits or hearths were identified at the site. The most common hearths (nine examples) were pits filled with pebbles, cracked rocks discolored by heat, traces of discolored and partly baked earth, specks of charcoal, some ashy deposits, snail shells, burned bones, and occasional cultural debris. In addition to the hearths described above, Howe (1983, 42) describes two other pits that extended over a somewhat larger and flatter area, distinguished by vaguely defined patches of discolored earth. These contained a few rocks and some artifact litter. One of these pits, in addition, was smeared with red ochre across the bottom. The fill contained several artifacts, including two small, lightly baked clay figurines. Howe (1983, 42) suggests that "these features give ceremonial connotation to this pit."

Stone hearths are also known from a number of Near Eastern Aceramic Neolithic sites, for example, Aceramic Haçilar (Mellaart 1970) and Çayönü (Çambel and Braidwood 1980). Perhaps the best description of these hearths is from the site of Cafer Höyük (Molist 1985, 35–52). None of the hearths at Cafer Höyük were found within buildings. All of them were located either outside of a building or in an open area. Two types of hearths have been described for Cafer Höyük (Molist 1985, 35–52). The first and most common type is the simple basin hearth, and these occurred in two slightly different variants. The first was a small hearth (50–60 by 30–40 centimeters), built in a regular ovate shape. The second variety was larger (over a meter in size) and either roughly round or irregular in shape. All the basin hearths were quite shallow in depth, ranging from 6 to 12 centimeters deep. The basin hearths were filled with burned stones and pebbles mixed with some ashes and fragments of wood charcoal. Occasionally, burned bone or obsidian chips were found in the fill. The stones and other materials filled the basin hearths virtually up to their tops. Sometimes the walls and bottoms of the basins were reddened through use.

Located around the hearths were areas where hearth debris had been dumped—areas filled with burned animal bones or with heavy ash or charcoal concentrations. Interestingly enough, burned rocks were not found in these dumping zones. Molist (1985) suggests that the basin hearths were used as follows. First a layer of stones was placed on the floor of the prepared basin, and then a fire was made directly on the stones until they became heated. Molist notes the possibility that an earth cover or even a superstructure (which was not preserved) was built over the heated stones and the items to be cooked. Some sort of cover would have been necessary to create a true oven. Molist, however, feels that because no direct evidence of such a cover has survived at the site, he cannot say for certain how or if these hearths were covered.

The second general type of hearth, the pit hearth, is known from only one example at Cafer Höyük. This hearth was rectangular in shape (measuring 95 by 62 centimeters) and was deeper (38–40 centimeters) than the basin hearths. All the surfaces of the pit had been thoroughly reddened by fire use, and even the stones found in the pit were cracked and modified by the heat. The fill in the pit hearth was clearly arranged in layers. At the base was a distinct stratum of wood charcoal laid out in a regular fashion. Above this, a layer of rocks had been placed in the pit; these rocks showed evidence of intense heating. Above this was a layer of clayey soil, with traces of ash, some charcoal fragments, and some animal bones.

Stone-filled hearths, therefore, on the basis of archaeological data, have long been utilized by humans. But there also is a large literature on the use of these stone hearths from cultures in the historic past. It is not practicable to review the full geographic range of this ethnographic data. Suffice to say, however, that both in the archaeological past and in the ethnographic present or near-present, there are examples of various types of stone cooking hearths. We believe that a brief summary of this material will provide useful information on how stone hearths and the related earth ovens were built, how they were used, and the purposes for which they were used. As noted above, fire was used by humans for a number of different and important functions. These specially constructed stone-filled hearths, however, could not have been built to provide light or to generate heat in an open area. It should be noted that the hearths that we have already discussed from Early Neolithic sites were all built outside of the houses or in open areas. Some ethnographic evidence suggests that earth ovens with rock heating elements were used primarily for the cooking of plant foods that required long heating periods (up to forty-eight hours) to make them palatable, but could also be used to cook game animals, shellfish, and fish (Thoms 1997, 2000). Heated rocks were also used in steaming pits (pit hearths), for grills, and for stone boiling. The last named technique was not known, on the basis of the present information, in the Zagros Proto-Neolithic and was not commonly utilized until some sort of permanent containers had been developed, although stone boiling in skin-lined pits was practiced in the historic past in North America (Lowie 1954, 23–25). Hot rocks, of course, were also used for noncooking purposes, the most widespread of which was steam bathing.

The use of earth ovens in the ethnographic past has been the subject of a recent conference (Thoms 1997). One of the papers at this conference reviewed the process of cooking in an earth oven used by the American Indians of the Pacific Northwest (Thoms 1997). These people prepared vast amounts of camas bulbs, which had to be heated for a long period of time to make them edible. First, the hot rocks were heated to the required temperature, and then the camas bulbs were placed above the rocks between layers of green plants. Next, heaps of earth were placed over the oven, and the bulbs were allowed to cook for up to two days. Thoms also notes that earth ovens seemed to be more often used in those regions that were poor in wood fuel. In other words, "the rocks would capture and retain flame-generated heat from quick-burning brush and driftwood that otherwise yield only short-lived coals" (Thoms 1997). More recently, Thoms (2000) presented his findings at another conference.

There is also some ethnographic data on the use of stone hearths in the modern Near East. At Mureybat, the site with Natufian and early Neolithic remains described above, stone hearths are in use in the modern village (Molist 1985, 40–41). Although these are clearly related to the basin hearths, they are also different in that they have a clay flange or collar around them on the surface. They are used to bake bread. First, stones are placed in the base of the basin, and then brush is placed above the stones and lit. When the stones have been properly heated, the ashes and wood cinders are removed, and the uncooked flat bread is placed directly on the heated stones to be baked. Molist (1985) also describes a pit hearth used by the Bedouins to cook meat. First, a pit is dug in the earth; this is lined with flat rocks around the sides and across the bottom. Then a fire is made inside the pit until the stones are almost red-hot. The ashes are then removed, and a lamb (either complete or quartered) is placed in the pit, which is then sealed.

Watson (1979) has provided some interesting data on hearths in her ethno-archaeological study of village life in western Iran. In the village of Hasanabad, a Kurdish settlement of circa two hundred people, each living room within a house complex has a centrally placed, stone-lined, roughly rectangular hearth that is used for cooking, heating, and lighting (Watson 1979, 122, fig. 5.2). These hearths are reminiscent of the house hearths at the Natufian sites of Mallaha and Hayonim. According to Watson (1979, 157) outdoor hearths are sometimes built in the courtyards for cooking during the hot summer months. There is no mention in her report, however, of stone hearths, earth ovens, or pit hearths. Watson does discuss another question of interest to the present study, that is, the use of acorns as a food source. Oaks producing edible acorns grow in the Hasanabad area, as they do at Shanidar and other locations in the Near East (Watson 1979; Olszewski 1993b; R. S. Solecki and R. L. Solecki 1997). At Hasanabad, the villagers prepare the acorns by burying them in hearth ashes until they pop open and then shelling and eating them without further preparation. They do not grind them into a meal, as they are prepared at other locations in Kurdistan. The modern Kurdish inhabitants of Shanidar Cave and other local groups in the area use acorns today as emergency food in times of shortages (R. S. Solecki and R. L. Solecki 1997). However, unlike the villagers at Hasanabad, these people pound and grind the acorns into a flour. With the flour, they prepare acorn-meal cakes that are then baked. This discussion of the use of acorns by modern Zagros villagers is of interest because it suggests another possible use for the stone hearths in the Proto-Neolithic layer in Shanidar Cave.

In summary, both archaeological and ethnographic data indicates that hearths were built according to several design plans and that these constructions were used for different purposes and in different settings. Hearths were built within structures, just outside of structures, in open areas, or in special locations—for example, cemeteries or ceremonial buildings. The hearths associated with the Proto-Neolithic cemetery at Shanidar Cave were of a distinct type, the stone hearth. Until now, these stone hearths have been found only in the cemetery area in the cave. Furthermore, charcoal and ashes from many fires were found throughout the burial layer (B1b) of the cemetery, apparently sweepings from the hearths.

Two important issues in reference to the Shanidar Cave hearths need to be discussed further: (1) the ritual relationships, if any, between the hearths and the burials in the cemetery; and (2) the functions of these specialized stone hearths in general and in a cemetery context. As discussed above, the association of fire and hearths with burials has been recorded at a number of Natufian sites in the Levant. The Natufian both predated and was in part contemporary with the Zagros Proto-Neolithic. Therefore, on the basis of (1) the configuration of the Shanidar Cave cemetery and the associated stone structures and (2) the Natufian data, which also links fire and hearths with burials, we suggest here that the Shanidar Cave stone hearths should be considered as cemetery constructions, used during the performance of burial rites.

The ways in which the Shanidar Cave stone hearths were used and precisely what they were used for cannot be, as yet, completely understood. We would like to suggest the following as likely possibilities, based on both archaeological and ethnographic data. In our brief survey above, we have noted that different types of hearths were generally built in different locations. Small, stone-outlined, variously shaped hearths were found within habitations, usually in the center of the structure but sometimes at different loci. These hearths could have been used for heating, lighting, and cooking within the structures. Stone-filled hearths outside of habitations, built on the surface or in shallow or deep pits, could not have served exactly the same functions as those built within dwellings. The stone-filled hearths, due to the manner in which they were built and where they were built, could not have been very effective for lighting or for heating space in open areas. Therefore, it seems most likely that this type of hearth was used for the preparation of food. The stone-filled hearths found in the Shanidar Cave cemetery, therefore, were probably used for food preparation, for cooking mortuary meals. The Shanidar Cave hearths were constructed by laying down a closely packed, neatly arranged layer of stones. Then the stones were heated by means of a fire that was built directly upon them. When the stones were sufficiently hot, the ashes and charcoal were swept away, exposing the hot rocks. Then whatever was to be cooked was placed directly upon the hot rocks and allowed to cook. It could not be determined if some sort of temporary collar or earth cover was built around or above the heated stones to keep in the heat. There was also no evidence for the presence of grills above the hearths.

Probably the Shanidar Cave Proto-Neolithic people were cooking some kind of plant food or land snails on these stone hearths. There is also the possibility that meat was roasted on them, but the absence of concentrations of burned bones makes this less likely. Regarding plant foods, we know that the Proto-Neolithic people made numbers of large trough querns and mullers, apparently for the processing of plant foods. Shanidar

Valley is within the zone of the wild prototypes of barley and wheat (Helbaek 1959, 365, fig. 1). Therefore, it is quite possible that the Shanidar Cave and Zawi Chemi Shanidar inhabitants used these grains, which they pounded into a meal and then shaped into cakes to be cooked on the hot stones. Another likely plant food source is acorns, which are commonly found in the Zagros. Sweet acorns (those that do not have to be leached) grow in the Zagros Mountains today and are used by the local Kurdish populations. They could be roasted whole and eaten without any further processing. They were also ground into meal, made into small cakes, and then baked (R. S. Solecki and R. L. Solecki 1997). The roasting of land snails on the stone hearths is another very likely use for these stone constructions. Many large concentrations of snail shells were found in the Proto-Neolithic layer in Shanidar Cave, both within the cemetery area and outside of the cemetery. Similar snail shell concentrations were also found at Zawi Chemi Shanidar. These small animals obviously were an important protein resource for the Proto-Neolithic people of the Shanidar area.

CHAPTER 4

Burial Offerings and Other Goods
from the Proto-Neolithic Graves

ROSE L. SOLECKI AND RALPH S. SOLECKI

Burial goods were found in fourteen of twenty-six graves in the cemetery (Burials 4, 5, 6, 7, 9, 11, 13, 14, 15, 17, 22, 24, 25, and 26) and in one grave outside the cemetery (Burial 27). Items of adornment were the most common objects found in the graves, especially with children. Characteristically, the adult members of the group were buried without personal adornments. Stone food-processing tools and other large and small stone objects were sometimes placed in the adults' graves. Cobbles of stone also were recovered from some of the graves, placed on or near the skull and sometimes crushing the skull. Bone tools were also found in a small number of the graves.

Probably the Proto-Neolithic people wrapped their dead in some kind of woven plant covering. The tightly wrapped burial positions of a number of the bodies certainly suggest this. In addition, charred matting was found at the base of one of the graves (Burial 4).

Description of the Grave Goods
Bone Tools

Bone tools (figs. 45–46) were found in four of the graves in the Proto-Neolithic cemetery. Burial 7, identified as an adult female, contained a well-polished, double-pointed bone awl, 7.20 centimeters long, 0.80 centimeters wide, and 0.45 centimeters thick (fig. 46 [a]). A second awl (fig. 46 [b]) was associated with Burial 25. This specimen was a long, well-polished awl, with one pointed and one blunt end. It measured 13.20 centimeters long, 14.00 centimeters wide, and 0.80 centimeters thick. Burial

25 contained the remains of both an adult (probably a female, according to Ferembach and Agelarakis) and an infant.

Two large, well-made bone tools were found with Burial 22, an adult interment. One (Cat. No. 381 IV a) was a smoothed and polished, elongated, pointed tool, perforated circa 1.0 centimeters from the rounded basal end (fig. 45a). It was made from a large mammal bone. It measured 26.0 centimeters long and 3.2 centimeters wide at the basal end. The bone was slightly curved on the side or lateral section. The perforation at the basal end measured 5 millimeters in diameter and was bored from both faces. The piece was nicked at the basal end, and there were transverse scratch marks on the concave side of the tool, near the point. The other bone tool (Cat. No. 381 IV b) from Burial 22 was a flat bone spatula, made from the rib bone of a large mammal (fig. 45 [b]). It lay next to the specimen described above. This specimen was oblong in shape and measured 25.5 centimeters long, with a maximum width of 2.8 centimeters and a maximum thickness of 3 millimeters. It was smoothed and polished all over both surfaces. One surface had been smoothed so much that some of the inner spongy bone tissue was exposed as linear ovate depressions. Several cut marks were clearly distinguishable across the squared end of this tool, on both faces. These cut marks, presumably made with a sharp flint, were evidently the result of purposeful detachment of this bone section from a longer bone. The end opposite the squared end showed wear polish. The piece was chipped and broken when found, but it is complete. Both of the tools found with Burial 22 may have been used for matting or basketry.

Burial 24 (Cat. No. 383 IV), an adult interment, contained a compound cutting tool (fig. 45 [c–d]) composed of a bone handle and an insert chert blade (see R. L. Solecki and R. S. Solecki 1963 for a discussion of this type of tool). The handle of the tool was made from a large mammal rib bone. It measured 20.9 centimeters long, 2.4 centimeters wide, and 8.0 millimeters thick and was polished all over. In profile, viewed from the side, the bone handle was curvate. A hole, presumably for suspension, had been drilled through the tool 2.5 centimeters from the pointed end. In addition, a deep groove had been cut along one edge at the broad blunt end, a chert blade affixed in it with a mastic substance. The exposed blade measured 3.3 centimeters in length, 6.5 millimeters in width, and circa 3.0 millimeters in thickness. No detectable "sickle sheen" or wear polish could be discerned using a ten-power magnifying glass on the working edge of the blade. A black, tarry, lumpy-looking substance held the blade firmly in place in the bone handle. It looked very much like bitumen, but an analysis of the substance could not be made at the time of discovery. Bitumen can be found today about 165 kilometers to the south, in the plains near Kirkuk. Geologists surveying for the proposed construction of the Bekhme Dam, about 18 kilometers down the Greater Zab River from Shanidar, also reported finding tarry deposits in that area.

It is not known if this object was imported as a trade item with the blade already affixed in the bone haft or if the tarry material was itself imported and the implement made locally. It should be noted here that none of the many blades (both microlithic and standard-sized) from the cave deposits had any traces of similar adhesive on them, although a stone chopper found in the cemetery fill had traces of such a material (see chapter 3).

Howe (1983, 64–65) notes the recovery of stone artifacts "bearing black substance (Bitumen?)" at Karim Shahir, stating that tests on a dark crust adhering to a rough stone specimen revealed that it was bitumen. The identification of bitumen traces on other crusted specimens at Karim Shahir was not so clear-cut. Because of the age of these items (roughly coeval with the Zagros Proto-Neolithic), chemical changes had taken place that made analysis difficult. Howe, however, presumed that the dark material found on the edges of two flint blades from the site was originally bitumen.

Items made out of bone, mainly tools but also ornaments, were characteristic of the Zagros Proto-Neolithic culture. At the nearby village site of Zawi Chemi Shanidar, bone implements formed an important component of the tool kit (R. L. Solecki 1981). R. L. Solecki (1981, 52) observes that many of the bone tools from Zawi Chemi Shanidar were probably used for skin dressing and leather working or for matting, basketry, and netting. The heavier bone tools with broad spatulate ends also could have been used in skin working, possibly as fat scrapers. Campana (1979, 206), on the basis of his examination of the Zawi Chemi Shanidar and Shanidar Cave spatulate implements, believed that the fine scratches on them strongly suggest this use.

Campana (1979) examined microscopically the bone implements from the Proto-Neolithic occupations of Shanidar Cave and Zawi Chemi Shanidar. He examined 30 bone implements from Shanidar Cave and 171 from the Zawi Chemi Shanidar village site, for a total of 201 tools. For comparative purposes, he studied 321 bone tools from the Natufian sites of the Levant (Hayonim, Nahal Oren, el-Wad, Kebara, Mallaha, Rakefet, and Shuqbah). Campana discovered that many of the bone tools bore use traces that were clear enough "to permit confident inferences as to the manner in which a tool was used (moved back-and-forth, twisted, etc.)" (Campana 1979, 2–3). He notes that a majority of the implements were perforators or awls and also that a good number were used for working hides or leather. Some of the bone points were used in the fabrication of basketry. He also concludes that the Proto-Neolithic peoples of Shanidar did not use bone implements for hunting and fishing activities. Furthermore, Campana (1979, 74) comes to an important conclusion regarding the manufacture of Natufian versus Zagros Proto-Neolithic bone tools. He observes that nearly all of the Natufian implements that he analyzed were shaved into shape using flint implements. On the other hand, nearly all of the Proto-Neolithic specimens from the Zagros area were ground into shape using abrasive actions. He suggests that the introduction of abrasive techniques in the Proto-Neolithic bone industry represented an important technological achievement. From the point of view of manufacturing processes, the Natufian bone tools suggest continuity with the Upper Palaeolithic, whereas the Proto-Neolithic bone implements appear to represent a break with the Upper Palaeolithic and to be closer to Neolithic stone-working techniques (Campana 1979, 265–66).

Beads

The notes, drawings, and photographs all indicate that beads were found in association with ten of the twenty-six burials within the cemetery and with the one burial located toward the front of the cave (Burial 27). Seven burials (Burials 4, 11, 13, 14, 15, 17, and 26) were identified as young children or infants; one (Burial 9) as one adolescent and some odd bones (possibly from two infants); and three as adults (Burials 5, 22, and 27).

At the time of the excavation of the cemetery, it was not possible to make accurate bead counts for the individual graves. Each skeleton, with its associated cultural materials, was packed in a separate container, labeled with its field catalog number, sealed, and then shipped to the Iraq Museum in Baghdad. According to the field reports, there were close to two thousand beads found with the burials. J. Bordaz made a rough count of circa fifteen hundred beads with Burial 11 alone. Juan Munizaga reported that he had seen the beads with the skeletons in the museum in 1962. Unfortunately, in the intervening years, before detailed analyses of the small finds could be made, the grave goods evidently were disturbed in storage, with consequent losses of data. During our examination of the Proto-Neolithic collection in the Iraq Museum in 1978, only a small sample of the original number of beads could be found. Presumably, the missing beads had been stored separately from the skeletal remains; in any case, they could not be located in the museum collections. The bead descriptions given in this report are based on three kinds of evidence: original field descriptions, the sample studied in the Iraq Museum in 1978, and the small sample of beads that was the research team's share of the 1960 collections. This small sample was first stored at Columbia University but was sent about a decade ago to the U.S. National Museum, Smithsonian Institution, for permanent storage. Peter Francis Jr. of the Center for Bead Research in Lake Placid, New York, studied this small collection (including specimens from the Proto-Neolithic horizons of both Shanidar Cave and Zawi Chemi Shanidar) when it was at Columbia University. His report is included here as appendix B.

The beads are discussed first according to type of raw material and then by find locus (figs. 27 and 28 [h, i, m–q]). Those associated with the numbered graves are described first, followed by those recovered from the cemetery fill. The latter were probably also originally from individual graves, but disturbances in prehistoric times blurred their associations with individual bodies. The stone beads, the most common type, are described first, followed by those made out of gastropod shells *(Theodotus)* and crab claws *(Potamon potamios)*. It is interesting to note that no bone beads were recovered from the Shanidar Cave cemetery, although they were common at Zawi Chemi Shanidar. At the latter site, evidence for the local manufacture of bone beads was recorded (R. L. Solecki 1981). It could not be determined if the Shanidar Cave stone beads were manufactured at the site or not; certainly some of the stones used for them were of nonlocal origin. It is presumed that the stringing and arrangement of the necklaces were according to the local tastes of their owners.

STONE BEADS

The cataloged stone beads

Burial 4 (Cat. No. 297 IV)

Three large stone beads from this child's burial were present in the Iraq Museum collection in Baghdad. One was a brick red, irregular barrel-shaped bead, which measured 10.1 millimeters thick and 9.0 millimeters in diameter. The bead hole, circa 2.0 millimeters in diameter, had been drilled from both ends. The second was pink-red in color and an irregular cylinder in shape; it measured 8.0 millimeters thick and 7.0 millimeters in diameter. Again the perforation had been drilled from both ends; one end measured 2.0 millimeters in diameter and the other 3.0 millimeters. The third bead, also of brick red color, was an irregular barrel-shaped bead, 9.0 millimeters thick and 8.0 millimeters in diameter. There was an abortive hole on one end that measured 1.5 millimeters in diameter.

Burial 5 (Cat. Nos. 298 IV and 371 IV)

This was an adult female burial. Two stone beads were probably associated with this burial. One was a three-holed, green stone spacer bead (Cat. No. 293 IV a) (fig. 27 [a]). It measured 22.12 millimeters by 11.40 millimeters and was 7.89 millimeters thick. It was parallel-sided, lenticular shaped in cross-section, and rectangular in plan. The ends were flat. The holes were bored from opposite ends. The diameters of the three holes were 2.49 millimeters, 3.36 millimeters, and 2.81 millimeters. A copper mineral bead/pendant (Cat. No. 293 IV b) was also associated with this burial (figs. 27 [k] and 28 [h]). Because this was a unique specimen, it is described in a separate section below.

Burial 9 (Cat. No. 350 IV)

One large, lozenge-shaped bead and one three-holed spacer bead were found associated with this grave, which included one probable adolescent and two infants. Both beads were made out of green-colored stone. The lozenge-shaped bead was provisionally identified as a jadelike material by Professor John Sanders, then with the Department of Geology, Barnard College. It was 38.0 millimeters long, 24.0 millimeters wide, and 9.4 millimeters thick at the middle (fig. 27 [b]). The sides were edge rounded, and it was lenticular in cross-section. There was a single perforation running through the long axis of the specimen. The perforation measured about 4.8 millimeters and 3.8 millimeters in diameter at the ends. The edges of the perforation, flat at one end and angled at the other, showed considerable wear, as did both faces of the bead. Peter Francis Jr. (see appendix B) notes that the fine striae present on the surface of the bead indicate that it had been ground to shape against a flat surface in an oblique direction across the surface of the bead, the ends ground flat.

A three-holed spacer bead (figs. 27 [c] and 28 [i]) was found in the neck region of the adolescent in Burial 9. It measured 23.00 millimeters by 9.00 millimeters, almost the same size as the similar spacer bead found with Burial 5. The holes were imperfectly bored. Their diameters were 2.49 millimeters and 3.36 millimeters.

Burial 11 (Cat. No. 355 IV)

This child's burial, according to the notes, contained upward of 1,500 beads. However, only 135 beads were found of this number in the Iraq Museum storage collections, 132 made of stone and 3 of gastropod shells. On the basis of the study of this small sample and the notes, it is clear that a variety of ornaments were buried with this child. Some of these were placed in strings around the neck of the child. The most numerous stone beads were small circular ones, either white, red, blue-gray, or, rarely, black in color. A number of red beads were identified as pink calcite. Also associated with Burial 11 were a large, pink-colored bead (7.3 by 4.0 millimeters) and a large, white, barrel-shaped bead (5.3 by 3.7 millimeters). Spacer beads were also associated with these ornaments. There were a single triangular spacer bead with five suspension holes and eight rectangular spacer beads with either three or five suspension holes.

Burial 13 (Cat. No. 372 IV)

A total of eighteen beads, including twelve of stone and six of gastropod shell, were found with this infant burial. These included six gray disk stone beads averaging about 5 millimeters in diameter and 3 millimeters thick. There were also five rounded red stone beads and one red disk bead.

Burial 14 (Cat. No. 373 IV)

Strings of stone beads of several types were found with this infant burial. Necklaces of small red beads (some have been identified as red calcite) and red- or green-colored larger barrel-shaped beads were found on the chest of this burial. At least two hundred beads originally decorated this infant's body. Also found were some perforated crab claws, but these seem to have been strung separately from the stone beads.

Burial 15 (Cat. No. 374 IV)

Several thin, purple-colored stone beads and a large number of gastropod shell beads were found with this child's burial.

Burial 26 (Cat. No. 385 IV)

A number of blue-colored stone beads were found in the neck region of this infant's burial.

Summary of the Stone Beads

The most common stone beads were small in size and circular in top view, with almost straight sides. They averaged 5.0 millimeters in diameter and 3.0 millimeters in thickness and had suspension holes circa 1.8 millimeters in diameter. They were blue, red, white, or, rarely, black in color. All the blue beads from the cemetery belonged to this bead type. A collection of twenty-three red calcite beads of this type were found uncataloged in the research project's share of the collections; these were assigned Cat. No. 427 IV. They were similar in shape and size to the stone beads found with Burial 14 (Cat. No. 373 IV), and there is the possibility that they were part of the grave goods from that burial. The beads averaged 4.5 millimeters in diameter and 2.5 millimeters thick, with holes about 1.8 millimeters in diameter.

The next most common stone beads were small, flat ended, and barrel shaped, with rounded or excurvate sides. They averaged 5.0 millimeters in diameter and 4.0 millimeters in thickness, with drilled holes 1.5 millimeters in diameter. They ranged in color from white to pink to red. They were about the same diameter as the circular beads but had smaller drilled holes and thicker sides. They appeared to have been perforated by drilling exclusively from one end.

The next most common stone bead type included thin, disklike beads with circular outlines and central holes. They averaged 5.0 millimeters in diameter and 1.0 millimeter in thickness (or length), with drilled holes 0.8 millimeters in diameter. Only a few holes were not drilled from both faces. These beads were generally white in color.

The spacer beads formed a distinct category (figs. 27 [a] [c] and 28 [i]). These were large, well-made beads; characteristically, they were rectangular in shape, but there was one roughly triangular-shaped spacer bead. The latter had five suspension holes. The rectangular beads had either three or five suspension holes. The spacer beads were generally made from a distinctive green-colored stone. Three of the rectangular spacer beads measured 22.0 by 10.0 millimeters, 23.0 by 9.0 millimeters, and 35.0 by 10.0 millimeters in size. In one specimen the suspension holes ranged from 2.5 millimeters to 3.7 millimeters in diameter.

Finally there was a "catch-all" type for variously shaped large-sized beads. Here were placed the three red-colored asymmetric beads from Burial 4. They ranged from 7.0 to 9.0 millimeters in width and from 8.0 to 10.1 millimeters in length. Also in this group were the green-colored, lozenge-shaped bead (38.0 millimeters long, 24.0 millimeters wide) from

Burial 9 (fig. 27 [b]) and the pink, asymmetric disk bead from Burial 11 (7.3 millimeters in diameter, 4.0 millimeters thick). Also placed here was the barrel-shaped, reddish bead (fig. 27 [d]) found near Stone Feature 3 (10.2 millimeters long and 11.0 millimeters wide).

Stone beads were also found at the nearby village site of Zawi Chemi Shanidar (R .L. Solecki 1981), but in fewer numbers than in the Proto-Neolithic cemetery. Only eight stone beads were recovered from the occupation fill at Zawi Chemi Shanidar, although other bead types, for example, bone beads, were relatively common. The Zawi Chemi stone beads were shaped in various forms, including barrel, disk, and tubular shapes, and were larger in size than the common types at Shanidar Cave. Five of the beads from the village site were made of chlorite (none made of this material were found at the cave), one was made of calcite/marble, and the two disk beads were not identified as to material. The most common bead type at Zawi Chemi Shanidar was made from bone (mainly bird bone). Sixty-five whole or fragmentary bone beads were recovered from the site.

Stone beads obviously were much more time-consuming to make than bone beads or pierced gastropod shell beads. Some were also made out of exotic materials. Stone beads, therefore, were probably viewed by these Proto-Neolithic people as appropriate offerings for their departed loved ones, especially infants and children.

Dr. Leonard Gorelick of Great Neck, New York, and Prof. A. John Gwinnet of the State University of New York at Stony Brook also examined some of these beads. They analyzed six red calcite disk beads from the Shanidar Cave cemetery. The beads had a hardness of between three and four on the Moh's scale. The smallest diameter of the drilled holes was 1.5 millimeters. The largest was about 2.5 millimeters. In one specimen, Gwinnet detected an irregularity in the drilled hole, which to him indicated that the bead stock had been drilled from both ends. These investigators thought that multiple beads were probably made from a single tubular stock. This was drilled from both ends and then sawed into beads. The drilled holes were clean and showed no staining from ferrous or cuprous drills. Gorelick and Gwinnet suggested that on the basis of their experimental studies, the holes could have been drilled with a flint point, with the aid of sand and water (Gorelick and Gwinnet 1987).

There is ample evidence that the residents of both the Shanidar Cave and Zawi Chemi Shanidar received exotic goods from a widespread trade network located in the Zagros Mountains area. There was not enough evidence to determine if the stone beads were manufactured locally in the Shanidar Valley from imported material or were imported as finished beads into the area. No stone bead workshops have been recovered at either the village or the cave site. The fairly uniform size dimensions and the expert workmanship, particularly of the small pink calcite beads, suggest a specialized industry. It should be noted here that evidence for bone bead manufacture was found at Zawi Chemi Shanidar, but not evidence of stone beads.

At the roughly contemporary site of Karim Shahir, Howe (1983, 50, 105, fig. 11) reports the finding of nine marble, limestone, and serpentine (chlorite) ground stone beads. These were barrel shaped or discoidal or had a distinctive biconical/plano-convex form. No bead workshops were found at the site. The tradition of making stone beads continued into the early Neolithic period in the greater Zagros Mountains area. The processes involved in the manufacture of stone beads at Jarmo, an early Neolithic site dating from the ninth millennium B.P. and located some 150 kilometers to the southeast of Shanidar (near Karim Shahir), have been described by Moholy-Nagy (1983, 297–99). She notes that stone beads were found in quantity at Jarmo and that they exhibited much diversity in form, size, and material. Most of the beads were various shades of marble, but other raw materials were used as well. Green-colored beads, probably of chlorite, were present. Moholy-Nagy (1983, 298) has suggested that there was "home production of Jarmo beads."

Ground stone beads first appeared in the Zagros area during the Proto-Neolithic period, and their manufacture continued into the Neolithic and later periods.[1] The wealth of suitable raw materials available in the Taurus-Zagros region, as well as the development of new stone-working techniques, made this new industry possible.

GASTROPOD SHELL AND CRAB CLAW BEADS

Beads made of perforated gastropod shells (figs. 27 [i] and 28 [q]) and crab claw tips were recovered from seven graves in the cemetery proper and from the one grave located toward the front of the cave.[2] These beads may be called "poor man's beads" because they were easily made out of readily obtainable or even household materials. As with the stone beads, nearly all of these beads were deposited in the Iraq Museum with their associated skeletal remains. The crab claw beads were unavailable for study in the Iraq Museum.

Ornaments made with these beads were found in the following graves.

Burial 11 (Cat. No. 355 IV)

Three gastropod shell beads (diameter about 5.0 millimeters) and a number of crab claw tip ends, along with many stone beads, were found with this child's burial.

Burial 13 (Cat. No. 372 IV)

Six gastropod shell beads along with stone beads were recorded with this infant's burial.

Burial 14 (Cat. No. 373 IV)

Strings of crab claw beads, as well as strings of stone beads, were recorded with this infant's burial.

Burial 15 (Cat. No. 374 IV)

A large number of pierced gastropod shell beads and several stone beads were found with this child's burial.

Burial 17 (Cat. No. 376 IV)

Two perforated crab claw tip beads were found with this infant's burial. No stone beads were associated.

Burial 22 (Cat. No. 381 IV)

A string of some fifty gastropod shell beads was found associated with this adult's burial. No stone beads were recorded.

Burial 27 (Cat. No. 186 III)

This burial was found outside the cemetery area, as described above. A necklace of perforated gastropod shell beads was found around the neck of this burial, probably an adult female. No associated stone beads were recorded.

COPPER MINERAL BEAD/PENDANT

A double-perforated, flat, lenticular-shaped bead/pendant (Cat. No. 293 IV b) made of a copper mineral (figs. 27 [k] and 28 [h]) was recovered from an area near Stone Feature 1 (R. S. Solecki 1969). This specimen was later identified as probably belonging to Burial 5, an adult female. It was trapezoidal in cross-section and beveled around its perimeter. The suspension holes, as they were assumed to be, were situated at the opposite ends of the specimen, slightly off center along the long axis. The holes appeared to have been bored from the ventral or reverse face. They measured about 2.5 millimeters in diameter. Apparently, they were made before the edges of the specimen were beveled. The rim of one of the holes had been broken through in the beveling process. The other hole was complete and had an intact thin wall at the beveled edge. The basal or reverse-perimeter edge of the specimen was rather sharp compared to the top or obverse-face perimeter. The latter was dulled and rounded. The specimen was bright green in color, with a kind of scaly coating on its surface. It seemed to have been much worn. From a visual examination with a ten-power hand lens, the specimen appeared to have been ground and smoothed into shape.

A hand-lens examination by Gerald Brophy, then with the Department of Geology of Amherst College, identified the specimen as malachite, a "serpentine breccia containing native copper, which had weathered either to malachite or Chrysocolla. This type of mineral can be found widespread in a geological 'thrust zone' where intrusives have been exposed by erosion" (personal communication, April 6, 1968).

Chrysocolla has a specific gravity of 2.0 to 2.4, with a hardness of 2 to 4. It is massive and compact and associated with oxidized copper minerals. It gives a light blue streak on a stone plate. Its color is a light green to turquoise blue. Additional information on the chemical composition of this specimen was obtained in 1989 through the kindness of Miss Buthima Musslim, a chemist with the Iraq Directorate General of Antiquities in Baghdad. Using a laser microscope analyzer (LMA 10), Miss Musslim found that the chief elements in the bead/pendant were copper first and silicon second. She noted that copper was found in the specimen in a "good amount." The minor elements present in the specimen were selenium, antimony, manganese, cadmium, and iron.

The closest known possible sources for this copper mineral appear to be Ergani and Maden in Anatolia. Çambel and Braidwood (1980, 48) have found a number of copper artifacts dating from the tenth millennium B.P. at the site of Çayönü, near Ergani in southeastern Anatolia. This source area for the copper ore is about 400 kilometers west-northwest of Shanidar on the Tigris River. It is possible that the long river route downstream on the Tigris to the junction of the Greater Zab River, then up the latter river to Shanidar, was followed as a trade-route guide. A shorter route would have been along the mountain fronts to the headwaters of the Greater Zab River, then down this river valley to Shanidar. This would follow the obsidian route from the Lake Van area described by Renfrew, Dixon, and Cann (1966) and R. S. Solecki (1969).

Stone Tools

A small number of pecked, ground, or flaked stone tools were found in the graves. A large number of these tools were also recovered from the cemetery fill. The following stone tools were found with the burials.

Burial 6 (Cat. No. 337 IV)
A pestle was found over the left knee, a slate-faceted rubber over the neck area, and a pecking stone above the skeleton of this adult male.

Burial 7 (Cat. No. 339 IV)
A quartzite spall tool was found with this adult female burial.

Burial 9 (Cat. No. 350 IV)
A quartzite spall tool was found with this adolescent burial.

Burial 14 (Cat. No. 373 IV)
A slate pebble and a naturally smoothed ovate pebble were found with this infant's burial.

Burial 15 (Cat. No. 374 IV)
A muller fragment was associated with this child's burial.

Burial 17 (Cat. No. 376 IV)
A small, triangular piece of flat limestone with some scratches at one end was found with this infant's burial.

Burial 27 (Cat. No.186 III)
This adult female grave was located outside the cemetery proper, in Square D9 (figs. 47–48). A broken trough quern had been placed upside-down (i.e., with the trough face down) over the feet, and a muller had been placed below the right foot of this individual. The muller was almost circular in shape (9.2 by 9.5 centimeters) and had been pecked on only one face. It was a double-pitted type. Both the quern and the muller were stained with the same red pigment that covered much of the burial.

Chipped stone tools and debitage were also occasionally found within a grave context, but it seemed likely that these were accidental associations.

Miscellany

Noted here are the fragments of carbonized matting (fig. 24) found with Burial 4 and a piece of stalactite recovered from Burial 14. Of architectural significance are the daub pieces (Cat. No. 370 IV) with wattle impressions (fig. 21), found near Burial 2 and Stone Features 6 and 7. The larger piece measured about 13.2 by 7.3 centimeters and was about 3.3 centimeters thick. The daub was a burned clay, light brick red in color. It contained fine particles of limestone with a coarse aggregate of crushed limestone and fiber impressions. On one face there were very distinct impressions of two sticks; one was about 0.8 centimeters in diameter, and the other, a heavier stick, was about 4.0 centimeters in diameter. It appeared that the clay had been forced up against a stick framework, filling in the open gaps in the wattle. Very distinct impressions of hand and finger smoothing were present on what had been the outer surface of the daub, but no fingerprints could be discerned.

Burial 4 (Cat. No. 297 IV)

Three fragments of carbonized matting (fig. 24), all part of the same piece, were found in this child's grave. They were found under the body, adhering to gray, ashy sediment. They probably belonged to a woven mat used to wrap or cushion the body before it was placed in the grave. The fragments measured 6.7 by 6.7 centimeters, 4.0 by 2.8 centimeters, and 6.0 by 3.6 centimeters. They were circa 2.0 millimeters thick. The matting seemed to have been made of reeds or rushes, each measuring about 5.0 millimeters wide, woven in a simple twill pattern with triple-strand warps and wefts (Crowfoot 1954, fig. 260). Each square in the pattern measured about 2.0 by 2.0 centimeters.

Helbaek (1963, 44) reports the occurrence of a thin, carbonized rush carpeting associated with a burial at Çatal Hüyük in Anatolia. It was made of very fine rushes, woven in a pattern of quadruple warp and weft. The illustrated example from this ninth-millennium B.P. site looks similar to the Shanidar specimen.

Summary of the Cultural Materials
Associated with the Burials

Eleven (40.7 percent), of the twenty-seven Proto-Neolithic graves excavated at Shanidar Cave contained some sort of personal ornaments. Seven of these were infant/child graves, one was a disturbed multiple grave of an adolescent and two infants, and three were adult graves. The infant/child graves always contained the more elaborate ornaments. In addition, stone beads, presumably the most prized, were found mainly in these graves. Only two adolescent/adult graves contained stone bead ornaments. Burial 5, an adult female, was also associated with the most exotic item found in the cemetery—the copper mineral bead/pendant. The adolescent in Burial 9 also had stone bead decorations. The other two decorated adult burials contained only gastropod shell bead ornaments. These beads could have been quickly made out of locally available material.

More utilitarian objects were placed in the adults' graves—for example, the bone tools with Burials 22, 24, and 25 (this last named grave contained both an adult and an infant). Stone tools also were occasionally found in the graves. Probably some of these stone tools (especially the smaller-sized or broken ones) may have been introduced into the burial when the body was covered over with fill. In Burial 27, however, a quern and a muller were definitely in direct association with the body of a young adult. Any stones could have been chosen if the intention was to insure the immobility of the dead; it would not have been necessary to use a pair of milling stones.

The grave goods placed in with the Proto-Neolithic burials at Shanidar Cave do not seem to have been symbols of hereditary status, although personal status may have been indicated by the large bone tools found with Burials 22 and 24. Therefore, this study of the grave offerings does not provide any data to suggest that these people were divided into a class-structured society. Although infants and children were buried with elaborate ornaments, in a stratified society some of the adults should have had as elaborate or even more elaborate grave offerings—but they did not.

The study of the grave goods also has increased our knowledge of the material culture and the technology of these Proto-Neolithic people. The burial offerings included items not found to date in the domestic/living areas of either Shanidar Cave or Zawi Chemi Shanidar. So far, evidence of matting and adhesives for compound tools is known only from the cem-

etery context. The grave-goods study also increases the number of artifact types in the Proto-Neolithic bone tool inventory.

Another important result of this study is that it increases our knowledge of long-distance trade, probably in both raw materials and finished
products in the greater Zagros area. The variety of raw materials used for
the stone beads, the special green stone selected for and the evident standardization of the spacer beads, the distinctive copper mineral bead/pen-
dant, and the black adhesive material (bitumen?) all suggest the presence
of a trade network in the area. The Greater Zab River valley was a natural
route, with connections deep into Anatolia as well with the Mesopotamian
steppe to the south.

Finally, the fact that these Proto-Neolithic peoples buried their dead
with grave goods in a special cemetery with closely associated stone features provides us with new insights into their religious life. Also relevant
to this aspect of culture is the fact that they attached special religious/
magical significance to red pigment (ochre), a widespread custom found
in both earlier and later human societies.

Notes

1. No beads were found in the Baradostian (Layer C) or the Zarzian (Layer B2)
   deposits at Shanidar Cave.
2. The gastropod shell beads from the cemetery were identified by David S. Reese,
   then with the Department of Anthropology, The Field Museum of Natural
   History, Chicago (now at the Yale Peabody Museum, Yale University, New Haven,
   Connecticut), in a letter dated October 30, 1998, as having come from freshwater
   gastropods of the genus *Theodotus*.

CHAPTER 5

Cultural Materials Found
in the Cemetery Fill

ROSE L. SOLECKI AND RALPH S. SOLECKI

A variety of cultural materials were recovered from the cemetery fill.[1] These items were found in all the excavated portions of the cemetery, in squares both with and without stone features, but not equally distributed throughout the cemetery (table 2). Similar materials were also found in the Shanidar Cave Layer B1 occupational deposits outside the cemetery and at the village site of Zawi Chemi Shanidar. Recovered from the cemetery fill were bone tools; large and small pecked, ground, or flaked stone tools and objects; chipped stone tools and debitage; and miscellany.

Bone Tools (fig. 46)

Thirteen bone tools were recovered from the cemetery fill (fig. 46 [c–i]). At least three of these had been perforated for suspension. Five broken bone awls, variously shaped, were recorded (fig. 46 [c–g]). One of the almost complete bone tools (fig. 46 [i]) was large in size (17.3 by 2.1 centimeters), with a smooth, rounded working end and a perforated butt end. Like the bone tool found with Burial 22 (fig. 45 [a]), it may have been a matting tool. The other almost complete bone tool (11.2 by 2.4 centimeters) had a straight, blunt working end (fig. 46 [h]). The articulation head was still attached at the proximal end. Lastly, two fragments from unidentifiable bone tools were present.

The bone tools were not found equally distributed in the cemetery. None were found in Squares B1, B2, C3, or D1. Only three were recovered from the fill around the stone structures.

TABLE 2. CULTURAL MATERIALS FOUND IN THE CEMETERY FILL

Types	First Row of Squares						Second Row of Squares						Third Row of Squares						Total
	B1		C1[a]		D1		B2		C2[b]		D2		B3		C3		D3		
	No.	%	No.	%	No.	%	No.	%	No.	%	No.	%	No.	%	No.	%	No.	%	
Bone Tools	—	—	2	15.4	—	—	—	—	2	15.4	3	23.1	4	30.7	—	—	2	15.4	13
Small Ground Stone Pieces																			
Fancies[c]	3	42.8	—	—	1	14.3	1	14.3	1	14.3	—	—	—	—	1	14.3	—	—	7
Slate Pieces	1	5.0	1	5.0	2	10.0	—	—	1	5.0	2	10.0	1	5.0	1	5.0	11	55.0	20
Rubbers	—	—	5	41.7	4	33.3	—	—	—	—	3	25.0	—	—	—	—	—	—	12
Chlorite/Talc Objects	—	—	—	—	2	100.0	—	—	—	—	—	—	—	—	—	—	—	—	2
Large Ground Stone Pieces																			
Querns	2	18.2	—	—	2	18.2	4	36.4	—	—	1	9.1	—	—	1	9.1	1	9.1	11
Mullers	1	9.1	—	—	2	18.2	2	18.2	2	18.2	1	9.1	1	9.1	1	9.1	1	9.1	11
Pestles	—	—	—	—	—	—	—	—	—	—	1	100.0	—	—	—	—	—	—	1
Pebble Objects	4	80.0	—	—	—	—	—	—	1	20.0	—	—	—	—	—	—	—	—	5
Pecking Stones	2	40.0	—	—	1	20.0	—	—	—	—	2	40.0	—	—	—	—	—	—	5
Hammer stones	1	3.7	6	22.3	7	25.9	3	11.1	5	18.5	2	7.4	—	—	2	7.9	1	3.7	27

TABLE 2. CONT.

Types	First Row of Squares						Second Row of Squares						Third Row of Squares						Total
	B1		C1[a]		D1		B2		C2[b]		D2		B3		C3		D3		
	No.	%	No.	%	No.	%	No.	%	No.	%	No.	%	No.	%	No.	%	No.	%	
Flaked Stone Pieces																			
Small Chisels	1	25.0	1	25.0	—	—	—	—	1	25.0	—	—	—	—	—	—	1	25.0	4
Pebble Chisels	1	50.0	—	—	—	—	—	—	1	50.0	—	—	—	—	—	—	—	—	2
Pebble Choppers	1	16.6	—	—	—	—	—	—	3	50.0	—	—	2	33.4	—	—	—	—	6
Spall Tools	—	—	—	—	1	11.1	1	11.1	2	22.2	2	22.2	—	—	1	11.1	2	22.2	9
Unworked Miscellany																			
Smooth Pebbles	10	24.4	8	19.5	—	—	1	2.4	4	9.8	6	14.7	1	2.4	10	24.4	1	2.4	41
Taconite Pebbles	1	14.3	3	42.9	—	—	—	—	—	—	—	—	2	28.5	—	—	1	14.3	7
Red Pigment[d]	—	—	—	—	—	—	—	—	—	—	—	—	—	—	1	100.0	—	—	1
Totals	28		26		22		12		23		24		11		18		21		185
Chipped Stone																			
Tools and Debris	309	7.0	1	<0.01	119	2.7	369	8.3	148	3.3	106	2.4	1205	27.1	1122	25.3	1058	23.8	4437

[a] The majority of the burials were located in Square C1.

[b] Much of this material was found at the level of Stone Feature 4, located in Squares B2 and C2.

[c] This includes beads, pendants, and shaped stones.

[d] This specimen was found when cleaning the south walls of Squares B3, C3, and D3.

Pecked, Ground, and Flaked Stone Tools and Objects

With the exception of the stone beads, pecked, ground, or flaked stone objects, small or large, were not commonly placed in the graves. Stone tools and even decorated items, however, were recovered in numbers from the cemetery fill.[2] Some of these seem to have been associated with the stone features built in the cemetery, while others were probably dumped into the area as part of the earth fill. Probably some came from graves disturbed by prehistoric excavations in the cemetery.

Small Pecked and Ground Stone Tools and Objects (figs. 28, 56, 57)

BEADS

Only one stone bead (Cat. No. 331 IV) (fig. 27 [d]) was found loose in the cemetery fill, in Square B2 near Stone Feature 3. This was a barrel-shaped bead, made from pink calcite. It measured 12.5 millimeters long and had a diameter of 11.5 millimeters. The hole, about 2.4 millimeters in diameter, was bored from both ends.

PENDANTS

Two stone pendants were found in the cemetery fill. The one (Cat. No. 323 IV) recovered near Stone Feature 4 was burned, and only a fragment was preserved (fig. 57 [a]). It was narrow and elongate in shape (3.2 by 1.2 centimeters) and squared off at the remaining end. A large hole was drilled from both faces at this end. The second pendant (Cat. No. 353 IV) came from the area around Stone Feature 6 and Burial 2. It was a small (2.4 by 1.2 centimeters), highly polished white limestone/marble pendant, elongate-ovate in shape (figs. 57 [b] and 28 [l]).

SMALL SHAPED STONES

Four small shaped stones were recovered from the cemetery fill. These pieces were the right size and shape to have been used for pendants, but they were not perforated. All showed traces of purposeful smoothing or polishing. One rectilinear but unperforated limestone/marble piece (figs. 57 [c] and 28 [j]) was found while scraping the south wall of Square C3 at the cemetery level (Cat. No. 268 IV). It measured 3.1 by 3.0 centimeters. A small ovate limestone pebble with light scratches on both faces (fig. 57 [d]) was recovered from Square B1 (Cat. No. 289 IV). The third piece, also found in Square B1 (Cat. No. 283 IV), was a polished red-brown stone, elongate- rectangular in shape, with pointed rounded ends (fig. 57 [f]). It measured 4.1 by 1.1 centimeters. The fourth shaped stone was recovered from the area around Stone Feature 1 in Square B1 (Cat. No. 293 IV). It was a small, naturally polished gray stone, with evidence of abrasion along one face and at one end (fig. 57 [e]). These shaped stones resembled items found at Zawi Chemi Shanidar (R. L. Solecki 1981, pl. 8 [c–g]).

PLAIN AND DECORATED SLATE OBJECTS (FIGS. 28 (A–G) AND 56)
The items described under this heading were made of specially selected raw material, a metamorphic slatelike stone. At least two distinct types of objects were made from this raw material: (1) small decorated pieces and (2) elongated shaped tools. Twenty such items were recovered from the cemetery fill. For the most part, these were elongate, cigar-shaped tools with beveled ends. However, one perforated and two incised and/or carved pieces were also present. The distribution of these slate objects in the cemetery deposits seemed to suggest that they were part of the fill, and not grave offerings. Only one came from Square C1, the square with most of the burials. Twelve specimens came from Squares C3 and D3—squares with no burials, but with stone features. It should be noted here that slate objects of both types were found in the Layer B1 cave deposits outside the cemetery proper. Similar end-faceted pebbles were also found at Zawi Chemi Shanidar, but were characteristically made of different raw materials (R. L. Solecki 1981, 33–34, pl. 6, fig. 15 [h–j]).

Of particular interest were the two decorated slate pieces. One (Cat. No. 268 IV), from Square D3, was a flat stone object with decorations on both faces (figs. 28 [d] and 56 [a]). There were actually two fragments of this object, but they could not be fitted together. The illustrated fragment measured 4.1 by 2.1 centimeters. The design was created by an incised outline, filled in with crosshatching. The sinuous design appeared to represent a serpent (R. S. Solecki 1980, fig. 2 [k]). A small fragment with a similar design was found in the Layer B deposits during the second season of excavation at the cave (R. S. Solecki 1953). A similar serpentlike design was represented on a flat, decorated bone piece from Zawi Chemi Shanidar (R. S. Solecki 1980, fig. 2 [e]). Smoor (1978, 115), in his study of eastern Mediterranean iconography, finds the serpent motif especially interesting. It is recognized as a symbol of immortality and death. This motif is known also from the Natufian site of Nahal Oren (Smoor 1978, 43).

A second decorated slate object (Cat. No. 293 IV) was found in Square B1. Unfortunately, it also was not complete, so its overall shape and possible function could not be determined. The section of the object in hand (figs. 28 [e] and 56 [b]) was keel shaped in front profile, with a broad top and a thinned, narrow bottom section. A line was incised lengthwise along the top, and five incised lines were cut across this central incised line. This piece measured 4.2 by 1.6 centimeters.

Eighteen slate tools were found in the cemetery fill. Type I tools (figs. 28 [a–c] and 56 [c–f]) were naturally smoothed elongate pebbles, apparently selected for their size and shape. They were then worked in such a way that one or both ends became pointed, with beveled sides, or somewhat rounded. The second type (Type II) of slate tool (figs. 28 [f–g] and 56 [g–h]) was more extensively shaped to produce narrow elongated pieces, plano-convex or even concavo-convex in section. One example (figs. 28 [f] and 56 [g]) had been perforated from both faces, apparently for suspension.

The complete slate tools ranged in size from 3.4 by 0.7 centimeters to 8.0 by 1.0 centimeters, but one of the broken specimens measured 17.0 centimeters in length and 1.1 centimeters in width, larger sized than any of the complete ones.

FACETED RUBBERS

Two faceted rubbers were recovered in the cemetery fill (fig. 57 [i]). Both were from the same level in Square D1. Both were rather small in size (3.4 by 1.3 centimeters and 6.0 by 1.5 centimeters) and beveled on only one end, with use-wear on both faces.[3]

MISCELLANEOUS RUBBERS

Twelve such specimens were recovered from the cemetery fill (fig. 57 [j]). Characteristically smallish, naturally smoothed pebbles were used for these tools, ovate (3.2 by 1.8 centimeters to 5.1 by 2.4 centimeters) or elongate (5.3 by 1.5 centimeters to 8.2 by 3.5 centimeters) in shape. All had some traces of use-wear in the form of scratches or striae on one face, both faces, or, as in one example, along one side, almost beveling the piece.

CHLORITE OR TALC OBJECTS

Two fragmentary specimens were recovered from the cemetery fill. One was a tiny piece of chlorite broken from a larger object that had a rounded edge. The second specimen was the end fragment (3.3 by 3.3 by 1.0 centimeters) from a well-polished, flattish object with scratch marks on its surface.

Large Pecked and Ground Stone Tools

QUERNS

Eleven querns or quern fragments were found in the cemetery fill. Ten of these were found near the stone features built in the cemetery. Only one quern was found in a square (D2) that did not contain a stone feature. All of the querns were trough querns, with deep or shallow depressions on the working surface. They were made from quartzite boulders and were ovate in shape. The complete querns ranged in size from 20 centimeters long and 17 centimeters wide to 38 centimeters long and 26 centimeters wide, but two of the fragmentary ones were originally considerably larger.

The querns were found in the following squares, associated with six of the stone features.

Stone Feature 1 (Square B1)

One complete large trough quern was found in an inverted position to the south of Stone Feature 1 (fig. 49). A second quern was noted in the east wall of Square B1, to the east of Stone Feature 1. This quern was lying trough face up and seemed to be complete (fig. 49).

Stone Feature 2 (Square B2)

Two trough quern fragments were found near this feature (fig. 51).

Stone Feature 3 (Square B2)

One quern fragment, trough face up, lay to the east of Stone Feature 3 (fig. 52).

Stone Feature 4 (Squares B2 and C2)

The greater portion (circa three-quarters) of a large trough quern was found next to this stone feature. It measured 48.0 centimeters long and 26.5 centimeters wide. It was found in an inverted position, and charcoal flecks were found underneath it. The charcoal flecks seemed to have been localized under the quern (figs. 29 and 52).

Stone Feature 6 (Square D1)

One small inverted trough quern (fig. 17) was found located to the southwest of Stone Feature 6. A second quern fragment was found to the northeast of Stone Feature 6.

Stone Feature 8 (Squares C3 and D3)

One complete, inverted, shallow trough boulder quern (fig. 54) was found to the northeast of Stone Feature 8 in Square C3. Quern fragments from a second quern were noted among the stones of this feature, in Square D3.

Square D2

No stone features were found in this square. One inverted boulder trough quern was found in the northwest corner of this square. It measured 38 centimeters long by 26 centimeters wide.

It is clear from the distribution of the querns that most of them were located abutting or near one of the stone structures. The querns, when found, were lying either with the working (trough) face up or in an inverted (upside-down) position. The latter position was more common. Out of the seven querns for which this feature could be determined, five were lying inverted and only two had the trough face up.

MULLERS

Eleven fragmentary or complete mullers were found in the cemetery fill (fig. 58 [a]). Most of these mullers were fragmentary, having been broken or burned in antiquity. In addition, "a quantity" of mullers was observed in the west wall of Square D3, just west of Stone Feature 7 (the curved stone wall). Six of the mullers recovered from the cemetery fill were located near the stone features, which suggests some relationship between the stone features and the mullers, as well as the querns. The mullers were made from quartzite and were pecked into shape. The single-faced muller, either pitted or plain, seemed to be the preferred type. The sides and working face were pecked all over, while the back or reverse face was pecked only around the periphery, with a smooth, unretouched central portion. The measurements of the complete mullers ranged from 9.6 by 8.1 centimeters to 11.6 by 9.9 centimeters.

PESTLES

One pestle was found when cleaning the north wall of Square D2. It was made from a elongate pebble (13.3 by 5.7 by 3.7 centimeters). Both ends had been battered through use.

SUMMARY OF THE MILLING TOOLS

The milling tools (querns, mullers, and pestles) recovered from the cemetery fill apparently were associated with the stone features and the activities that took place around them. Rarely were they placed in graves. The most clear-cut example of a grave association was Burial 27 (Cat. No. 186 III), located outside of the cemetery. Burial 6 (Cat. No. 337 IV), also an adult, had a pestle over the left knee. A muller fragment was found near Burial 15 (Cat. No. 374 IV), a child, but it is not certain if this was a grave offering or not.

Milling tools, both compete and fragmentary, were also recovered in quantity at the village site of Zawi Chemi Shanidar. Many were found there incorporated in the rough stone wall constructions, as well as in the village refuse fill. The querns in the walls were characteristically placed there in an inverted position (trough side down), but they could occur in a variety of positions. It was presumed that the querns sat or fitted better in a stone wall if they were placed upside-down. It did not seem likely, however, that querns found in the cemetery were brought there to be used in the construction of the stone structures (see chapter 3).

The quern and muller found with Burial 27 (Cat. No.186 III) were stained with red pigment. Red pigment was also present on the bones of the individual in the grave. None of the other querns found in the cemetery showed any signs of pigment on their surfaces. None of the complete or fragmentary querns from Zawi Chemi Shanidar showed evidence that they had been used for pigment grinding (R. L. Solecki 1981). It seems unlikely, therefore, that these large querns were primarily made and used for pigment grinding. It is more likely that their original purpose was to process plant food (R. L. Solecki 1981).

Large-sized stone grinding/crushing tools have been recorded at other roughly coeval sites in the Levant (R. L. Solecki 1972). Limestone mortars were found in association with most of the Natufian burials at Nahal Oren, perhaps as grave markers, according to the investigators (Stekelis and Yizraely 1963, 11–12). Mortars were also associated with the Natufian horizon burials at Mugharet el-Wad (Garrod 1937, 15–19).

In summary, large-sized grinding/crushing stone tools were placed in or near Epi-Palaeolithic/Proto-Neolithic graves and cemeteries for a variety of reasons. They could have been used as grave markers, as part of a burial ritual, or just as mementos of personal possessions.

PEBBLE ABRADERS

Three complete and two fragmentary pebble abraders were recovered from the cemetery fill (fig. 58 [c–d]). These specimens were concentrated in the B row of squares: four from B1 and one from B2 and C2. The pebble abraders were made on elongated, flat, smooth pebbles. The ends of the specimens were neatly flattened through use. At least one of them had been reused as a chisel. The complete pebble abraders averaged 10.8 by 4.3 by 2.3 centimeters in size.

PECKING STONES

Five pecking stones were recovered from the cemetery fill (fig. 58 [b]). They were made on flat, ovate pebbles (sizes ranged from 8.0 by 6.9 by 2.5 centimeters to 11.2 by 4.5 by 2.2 centimeters). All of them showed signs of use-wear at the ends. In addition, one of them showed evidence of use along the sides. Also classified in this category are two tools that were used both for pecking and for rubbing or smoothing. The latter function was suggested by the scratch tracks present on the flat surfaces of these specimens. They averaged 7.1 centimeters long and 4.3 centimeters wide.

HAMMERSTONES

Hammerstones were found in all of the cemetery squares except Square B3.[4] Twenty-seven complete or fragmentary hammerstones were found in the cemetery fill. These tools were the most common large stone type found in the cemetery. Nine examples were associated with the stone features. Similar hammerstones were also found outside the cemetery proper in Shanidar Cave and at Zawi Chemi Shanidar. Particularly numerous were the distinctive "greenstone" hammerstones (eighteen examples) in both flattened-disk or rounded shapes (fig. 58 [e]). Squares C1 and C2, the two squares that contained the majority of the graves in the cemetery, also contained eight complete or fragmentary examples of these distinctive hammerstones. Also found in the cemetery fill were three ball hammerstones (fig. 58 [f]), one double-pitted one, and five variously shaped simple hammerstones.

Flaked Stone Tools

Several tool types are included here: small chisels, pebble chisels, pebble choppers, and spall tools.[5] Similar tools were recovered from the non–cemetery fill deposits at Shanidar Cave and from the village site of Zawi Chemi Shanidar.

SMALL CHISELS

Four such specimens were recovered from the cemetery fill. One was a highly polished, rectangular, flat slate stone (6.1 by 2.7 by 0.9 centimeters), red-brown in color. Both ends and one side were flaked to produce thinned chisel-like edges (fig. 57 [g]). Both faces also had obvious use-wear striae. The second chisel was made on a small (5.3 by 4.3 by 1.4 centimeters), flat, ovate limestone/marble pebble (fig. 57 [h]). It was whitish in color, with a natural polish. In shape, size, and raw material, it resembled the stones used for the two-holed pendants at Zawi Chemi Shanidar. At least one end of this specimen seemed to have been used as a chisel. Fine use-wear tracks were present on one face. The third small chisel was made on a spall broken from a pebble abrader. It had been used at one end as a chisel. It measured 4.6 by 4.1 by 1.3 centimeters. The fourth chisel was a very small (4.6 by 2.0 by 0.6 centimeters), flat, elongate pebble, with evidence of chisel usage at both ends.

PEBBLE CHISELS

There were two such specimens from the cemetery fill, both associated with the stone features. They resembled the pebble choppers. However, as they both showed evidence of pounding at the ends opposite the thinned flaked ends, it seems likely that they had been used as chisels. Both were made on flat pebbles, ovate or elongate in shape. They measured 9.5 by 6.9 by 2.7 centimeters and 11.8 by 5.9 by 2.1 centimeters. The former specimen (fig 59 [a]) was made of quartzite. The latter was a dark colored smoothed stone, with striated areas on both faces, and traces of red pigment. Both pebble chisels had shallow, pecked, pitted areas on both faces.

PEBBLE CHOPPERS

Six examples of pebble choppers were found in the cemetery fill, of which four were associated with the stone features. All of them were unifacial choppers. They also had shallow pitting on one or both surfaces near the working ends and striated areas that were evidently from usage. At least three of the choppers were made of a distinctive, dark green, naturally polished igneous stone. These choppers also had traces of red pigment on the pecked and striated surface areas (fig. 59 [b]).[6] One gray patinated chopper made of a fine limestone had traces of a black-colored material at the butt or nonworking end (fig. 59 [c]).[7] The choppers ranged in size from 5.4 by 9.4 by 3.0 centimeters to 9.7 by 11.7 by 3.5 centimeters.

SPALL TOOLS

Nine spall tools were found in the cemetery fill, four of which were located near the stone structures. These tools were naturally sharp spalls flaked from around the periphery or edges of quartzite boulders. Spall tools were very common at Zawi Chemi Shanidar and also occurred in the non–cemetery fill at Shanidar Cave. Only two complete specimens, both small, were available for measurement; one was 5.3 by 8.1 by 0.9 centimeters, and the other was 7.7 by 6.9 by 1.3 centimeters. The latter had traces of red pigment on its top surface (fig. 59 [d]). The cutting edge, which showed heavy use-wear or blunting, was 4.8 centimeters long. The proximal end showed battering traces.

Unworked Miscellany
Small, Naturally Smoothed/Polished Pebbles

Small, naturally smoothed or polished pebbles were recovered in numbers (over forty) from the cemetery fill. They were found in all squares except Square D1. More than half of the number were associated with stone structures. The pebbles were charactistically flat, elongate, or ovate in shape, but they could also be rounded, ball, or irregular in shape. They must have been purposely brought into the cave, probably for use as rubbers, pendants, disks, and so on. However, no traces of manmade use-wear could be observed on any of these specimens using a ten-power hand lens. Another possibility is that these pebbles served as "charm stones."

Taconite Pebbles

Seven lumps of lustrous taconite, unworked but obviously specially saved by the Proto-Neolithic people, were recovered from the cemetery fill. Four of these were located near the stone features. The other three came from Square C1, which had no stone features.

Red Pigment

A fragment of a red pigment stone was found in scraping the south wall of the cemetery excavation (Squares B3, C3, and D3). As already noted, traces of red pigment were found on three of the pebble choppers, one pebble chisel, one spall tool, and over the skeletal remains and grave goods of Burial 27.

Chipped Stone Industry

Many chipped stone specimens (almost forty-five hundred examples) were found in the cemetery fill (fig. 60). The majority of these (76.8 percent) were concentrated in the southern part of the cemetery (Squares B3, C3, and D3). According to data recorded in the notebooks, this area contained heavy occupation debris, including chipping debitage. Only one grave (Burial 6), in Square B3, was located in this southern section of the cemetery. Stone Features 8 and 9 (in Squares C3 and D3) and a small part of Stone Feature 2, in Square B3, were built there. Thus, it appeared that the cemetery was being expanded southward but that this section was never extensively used for burials. The presence of stone features in Squares C3 and D3 reinforces this interpretation, as the stone features seemed to have been constructed around the periphery of the cemetery. It should be noted in this discussion that Square C1, which contained the majority of the burials in the cemetery, had practically no chipped stone pieces (see table 2).

Typologically and technologically, the chipped stone assemblage recovered from the cemetery fill resembled that found in occupation fill from Layer B1, outside the cemetery in Shanidar Cave, and from the village site of Zawi Chemi Shanidar (R. L. Solecki 1981). One difference between the Proto-Neolithic industry of Shanidar Cave, found both within and outside the cemetery, and that of Zawi Chemi Shanidar is that the former contained a small amount of obsidian (thirty-three examples from the cemetery), while this raw material was apparently absent at Zawi Chemi (R. L. Solecki 1981). The majority (74.8 percent) of the chipped stone material from the cemetery fill at Shanidar Cave was lithic debitage. We may add the cores (2.5 percent) to the debitage figures, making a total of 77.3 percent. Standard-sized tools accounted for 13.1 percent of the tool assemblage. Microliths and microlithic-sized tools made up 6.8 percent of the collection (fig. 60).

Miscellany

Included here are one geode (unbroken), three fragments of calcite, and one invertebrate fossil.

Summary of the Cultural Materials
from the Cemetery Fill

The six 2-by-2-meter squares excavated in the Proto-Neolithic cemetery contained abundant cultural materials—for example, many pieces of chipped stone debitage and both standard and microlithic-sized retouched tools; 122 pecked, ground, or flaked stone tools or decorative items; and 13 bone tools.[8] A small number of exotic natural pieces were recovered, as well as over 40 small, naturally smoothed or polished pebbles. The function of the latter is unknown, but these items were evidently purposefully collected and brought into the cave. There were many burned rocks, some burned stone tools, and much ash and charcoal flecks in the cemetery fill, proof that fire was part of the mortuary tradition of these people. Also present were localized concentrations of snail shells (*Helix salomonica* and *Levantina mahanica)* and some scattered bones of food animals.

Only the chipped stone sample was large enough to furnish clear-cut spatial distribution patterns (see table 2). The other cultural items were found in such small numbers that such patterns were difficult to establish. For this reason, we have analyzed the cultural materials from the cemetery fill from five different perspectives, according to (1) associations with the stone features (Stone Features 1–9); (2) distribution within the squares with stone features (Squares B1, B2, C2, C3, D1, and D3); (3) distribution within the squares that lacked stone features (Squares B3, C1, and D2); (4) distribution within the three southern squares (B3, C3, and D3); and (5) distribution in Square C1, the square that contained more than 60 percent of the burials but no stone structures.

The most clear-cut conclusions derived from the analysis of the chipped stone sample from the cemetery fill are as follows (see table 2). The greater proportion (76.2 percent) of the chipped stone sample came from Squares B3, C3, and D3. This southerly area (one-third of the excavated cemetery area) contained only one grave (Burial 3 in Square B3), suggesting that this part of the cemetery was not the preferred burial locus and was not extensively used for this purpose. Furthermore, it seems probable, based on an analysis of the cultural materials recovered from the southern part of the cemetery, that its deposits were primarily composed of "in situ" Proto-Neolithic occupational fill that predated most of the cemetery. The northern row of squares (B1, C1, and D1) excavated in the cemetery area contained 76.9 percent of the graves, but only about 10 percent of the chipped stone specimens. Only two chipped stone items (a microlithic lunate and a core) were recovered from Square C1, the square that contained most of the graves (61.5 percent). There seems to be, therefore, no relationship between the graves and the chipped stone pieces from the cemetery fill—that is, the Proto-Neolithic people did not regularly use such items as grave offerings or part of burial ritual. Burial 24, however, did contain a bone-handled knife with an inset chert blade. This well-made object was definitely placed in with Burial 24 as a grave offering and probably represented a favored personal tool of the interred individual. In addition, there seems to be no relationship between the stone features and the chipped stone sample. All of the stone features except Stone Feature 8, which was located in Squares C3 and D3, had less than 5 percent of the chipped stone sample. The area around Stone Feature 8 had a high percentage of chipped stones (24.7 percent), undoubtedly due to its location in the southerly part of the cemetery, outside the main burial area.

The number of pecked, ground, or flaked stone tools or decorative items found in the cemetery fill was much smaller than the chipped stone sample. It is also not possible to lump all of the types together into a single broad category (as with the chipped stone). Such small, special, decorative items as beads, pendants, and shaped disks cannot be logically lumped with large stone items such as querns, mullers, and hammerstones. Therefore, it seems best to summarize most of these types individually, combining them together only when it seems appropriate. Thus the individual type samples are quite small.

There appears to be a definite correlation between the querns and the stone features, suggesting use association. Ten out of eleven querns recovered from the cemetery fill were located close to a stone feature. Only one quern was found in a square without a stone feature (Square D2). Square C1, which contained majority of the burials, had no querns. Although a quern was found with Burial 27, located outside the cemetery, no querns were found with any of the burials in the cemetery.

Six of the eleven muller/muller fragments were found associated with the stone features, and a total of nine were from squares that contained stone features. Also, just west of Stone Feature 7 (Square D1), in an unexcavated section, a quantity of mullers was observed in the west wall of Square D1. Therefore, we suggest the probability that there also was some special relationship between the stone features and the mullers.

Twenty slate pieces (tools or decorated objects) were found in the cemetery fill, the majority of which were fragments, broken in antiquity. Most of these pieces (65 percent) were found in the southern row (Squares B3, C3, and D3), an area that we believe contained mainly "in situ" occupation debris, an extension from the main living area toward the front of the cave. Even the slate fragment with the incised serpentine figures (figs. 28 [d] and 56 [a]) was found in Square D3. Four of the complete slate tools that were found in squares with graves could have come from disturbed interments, but there was no direct evidence for this.

The single stone bead, two stone pendants, and four small shaped stones all came from squares that contained at least one grave and possibly were grave offerings. All of the pebble rubbers (two faceted and ten plain) also were found in squares with graves. In fact, five of the plain rubbers were from Square C1, which contained the majority of the graves. None of the rubbers were recovered from the southern squares (B3, C3, and D3). Therefore, these tools and possibly also the three small chisels from Squares B1, C1, and C2 could originally have been associated with graves.

The other large stone tools found in the cemetery fill include a pestle, pecking stones, pebble abraders, hammerstones, pebble chisels, pebble choppers, and spall tools. In total, all of these add up to fifty-five specimens. Except for the hammerstones, with twenty-seven examples, these types were each represented by less than ten specimens. Grouped together, however, some useful distributional data may be obtained for them. Only five (9 percent) of these tools (two pebble choppers, two spall tools, and one hammerstone) were found in the southern row (Squares B3, C3, and D3), in contrast to the large numbers in the chipped stone sample (76.8 percent) from there. The greater portion (forty specimens, or 73 percent) of these large stone tools were found in the squares with stone structures. The distinctive greenstone hammerstones (eighteen examples) were found in all of the squares except B3 and C3. Square C1, which contained most of the graves, had six examples of complete or fragmentary greenstone hammerstones; in fact, these represented the only large stone tool type found in the fill of Square C1. We believe, furthermore, based on the evidence obtained from the graves and the fill found in Square C1, that the following large stone tool types were only rarely, if ever, used as grave offerings: pecking stones, pebble abraders, hammerstones (other than the special "greenstone" type), pebble chisels, and spall tools.

The thirteen bone tools found in the cemetery fill were mainly fragmentary specimens. Six (almost half) came from the third row of squares (B3 and D3) and, therefore, may be considered as part of the occupational debris characteristic of that part of the cemetery. The seven other bone tools came from the squares that contained graves and, therefore, may have been from disturbed graves.

In conclusion, it seems likely that the cultural items found in the cemetery fill came to rest there through several different processes. The material found in the southern part of the cemetery (Squares B3, C3, and D3) most likely was part of an "in situ" Proto-Neolithic occupational deposit that accumulated there before the cemetery was in full use. The small decorative items, small tools, and bone tools recovered from the squares with graves may well have come from disturbed graves. Some of the large stone tools (e.g., querns and mullers) clearly were related to the stone features built in the cemetery or the rituals that took place at them. The other large stone tools also may somehow have been associated with the stone features, because almost 75 percent of them were recovered from the squares with stone features. On the other hand, it seems unlikely that most of the large stone tools, numerous as they were, were regularly used as grave offerings.

Some further observations on the cultural materials recovered from the cemetery fill, based on negative evidence, should also be discussed. First, no celts with polished bits or chlorite grooved stones were recovered either from the graves or from the cemetery fill, although they were found elsewhere in Shanidar Cave and at Zawi Chemi Shanidar. At the latter site, celts were concentrated (fifty-seven out of sixty-two examples, or 91.9 percent) in the upper portion of the Proto-Neolithic deposits, suggesting that they were late additions to the Proto-Neolithic occupation at the site (R. L. Solecki 1981, 38). The thirteen examples of grooved stones from Zawi Chemi, on the other hand, were concentrated in the lower portion of the Proto-Neolithic deposits (all except two from the upper layer). We can conclude from this evidence that celts and grooved stones were not used as grave offerings at the Shanidar Cave cemetery. The absence of celts in the cemetery fill, especially in the southern part of the cemetery (Squares B3, C3, and D3) also suggests that these refuse deposits may have accumulated before the introduction of celts into the area. The absence of grooved stones in the cemetery fill, even fragmentary examples, cannot be explained on the basis of the present evidence. Two pieces of worked chlorite/talc (from nongrooved objects) were recovered from the fill of Square D1. This would indicate that the Proto-Neolithic people of Shanidar Cave who built the cemetery knew about the special natural characteristics of this raw material and used it for tool manufacture.

Notes

1. These items were not in direct association with a grave, although a few may have come from disturbed burials.
2. The tools and objects recovered from the cemetery fill and described here include all such specimens available to the authors for study.
3. R. S. Solecki (1994) suggests that the elongated pebble tools or rubbers with beveled ends were possibly used as flint-chipping implements either to blunt the backs of small chipped stone tools or to retouch them.
4. These hammerstone types have been fully described in R. L. Solecki 1981.
5. The flaked-tool types have been fully described in R. L. Solecki 1981.
6. R. N. Guillemette, of the Department of Geology and Geophysics, the Electron Microprobe Lab, Texas A&M University, analyzed three areas of red pigment on sample 323 IV, one of the dark green choppers. In his report dated July 30, 1998, he states that "the red pigment shows two major constituents, iron and silicon, along with oxygen, potassium, calcium, aluminum, and variable carbon. I believe that the pigment itself consists of hematite and quartz, with the other elements representing the substrate; the potassium, calcium and aluminum could also be present as a minor constituent of the pigment."
7. R. N. Guillemette also analyzed three areas of the black pigment on this chopper. His report notes that "the black pigment did not reveal any major elemental signature that could clearly explain the black color; one reason for this is that only a very minute quantity could be scraped from the surface, and most of the material scraped off probably consisted of substrate material. The color may be due to a small amount of carbon; this element does show in low to medium concentrations in all of the energy-dispersive X-ray spectra of the black pigment. Carbon is difficult to detect with energy-dispersive X-ray spectroscopy, and is also found as a common constitute of the mounting adhesive. The very small amount of sulfur present could also be ascribed to mounting adhesive or contamination, but if present in the form of iron sulfide it could also produce a dark color."
8. As noted above, the cultural material discussed in this section includes everything from the cemetery fill that the authors were able to study. Probably a small number of items, in storage in the Iraq Museum or sent to provincial museums, were not available for analysis.

CHAPTER 6

Comparative Study of the Shanidar Cave Mortuary Practices and Those of the Levant during the Epipalaeolithic and Proto-Neolithic Eras

ROSE L. SOLECKI AND RALPH S. SOLECKI

I n comparing the Shanidar Cave cemetery with Levantine mortuary
sites, we must point out at the beginning of the discussion that there
is a heavy numerical bias in favor of the latter area. The Shanidar
cemetery is the only one known so far from the entire Zagros area. Most
of the roughly contemporary comparative data on mortuary practices
comes from the Natufian culture of the Levant. The Natufian is well known
from many sites. It has been divided into three chronological phases—
Early, Middle, and Late Natufian, ranging from 12,500 to 10,200 years ago.
Therefore, it was in part earlier than the Zagros Proto-Neolithic and was
in part contemporaneous with it. We believe, in fact, that the Zagros Proto-
Neolithic and the Natufian of the Levant may be considered as regional
variants of the same broad Near Eastern tradition.[1] Both the Natufian
and the Shanidar Proto-Neolithic contain the earliest cemeteries known
in the Near East. Middle Palaeolithic Neanderthal skeletons have been
found in Shanidar Cave (R. S. Solecki 1963, 1971), but as yet no human
burials have been recovered from the Upper Palaeolithic (Baradostian)
or the Epipalaeolithic (Zarzian) deposits in the cave. In the Levant, there
are a handful of Late Upper Palaeolithic and also Early Epipalaeolithic
burials. Perhaps the most interesting of these is the H2 skeleton from the
site of Ohalo II (Nadel 1994). This individual was laid down in a shallow
pit, in a semiflexed position, with the head slightly elevated by three stones

placed under it. A large, round hammerstone was found between the legs, and an incised bone fragment was behind the head. Although the Ohalo II grave and those few others found at Late Upper Palaeolithic/Early Epipalaeolithic sites in the Levant do not appear to have been as standardized or elaborate as those of the subsequent Natufian, they do reflect what was to develop in the Natufian.

Before detailed comparisons can be made between the Natufian and the Zagros Proto-Neolithic mortuary practices, several terms need to be defined. In this chapter, the term *cemetery* is used as defined by Fiedel (1979, 110, 114). "By *cemetery* I refer to an area devoted exclusively to interment or other forms of disposal of the dead. A single isolated burial does not constitute a cemetery; there must be some indication, in the form of multiple interments, that the area was used repeatedly for the same purpose."

The meanings of the terms *primary burials* and *secondary burials,* as applied to the Natufian, vary with different researchers. Fiedel (1979, 134) defines primary burial as "an interment of the body shortly after death, when it is still intact," and secondary burial as "interment some time after death; in the interim the body has undergone transformation, usually resulting from the initial mortuary treatment (e.g., excarnation by exposure on scaffolds)." On the other hand, Belfer-Cohen (1990, 300), for the site of Hayonim Cave, defines primary burials as "burials of complete or nearly complete skeletons in anatomical articulations" and secondary burials as "disarrayed clusters of bones or isolated bones." The problems here do not so much involve primary burials as they do secondary ones. Because there was so much prehistoric disturbance in the Shanidar Cave cemetery as new burials were made, in this chapter, the term *secondary burial* is limited to those burials that seemed to have had more than a single mortuary treatment.

There is also some confusion in interpreting the use of the terms *semiflexed, flexed, contracted, twisted,* and so on, for a wide range of body positions. In this chapter, the terms *semiflexed* and *flexed* are used to cover the entire range of body positions found in the Shanidar Cave cemetery.

As noted above, this comparative section, to some degree, was affected by the differences in sample size and spatial range of sites available for the study of the Zagros Proto-Neolithic and the Levantine Natufian. Shanidar Cave contains the only cemetery site yet known for the Zagros Proto-Neolithic, and the sample from it is only twenty-six graves, with a minimum of thirty-five individuals. The total of Proto-Neolithic graves found in the cave is twenty-seven (thirty-six individuals), including the isolated one located toward the front of the cave. On the other hand, more than four hundred Natufian burials are known from Natufian sites (Belfer-Cohen 1995, 10).

Summary of Natufian Mortuary Practices

Natufian mortuary practices varied somewhat spatially from site to site and chronologically through time. Most of the four hundred–plus Natufian burials were found in the base camps in the central core area, including Mount Carmel, the Judean region, and to a lesser extent the Jordan Valley. Recent reviews of the main characteristics of Natufian mortuary practices (Fiedel 1979; Belfer-Cohen 1991a; Belfer-Cohen and Hovers 1992; Byrd and Monahan 1995; Bar-Yosef 1998) may be summarized as follows.

1. Burial Position

The positioning of the body and the placement of the body in the grave were not standardized in Natufian graves. Flexed, semiflexed, extended, and even seated positions were all used. The body could be placed on the left side, right side, the back, and even the front or stomach. There was no standard orientation of the body.

2. Single and Multiple Burials

Both single and multiple interments were found at Natufian sites. Multiple burials contained every possible combination of individuals and ages, including adult males, adult females, children, and infants. Multiple burials (80.1 percent) were more common overall in all periods than single burials (19.9 percent), although there were always some single graves (Byrd and Monahan 1995, 262).

3. Primary and Secondary Burials

Both primary and secondary burial practices were used. Sometimes this attribute was difficult to determine because of postdepositional prehistoric disturbances.

4. Population Demography

The proportions of adult and child burials at Natufian sites for all periods were: adults 62 to 78 percent, children 24 to 38 percent (Fiedel 1979, 170).[2] At the same sites, female burials ranged from 35 to 40 percent, while males made up 60 to 64 percent of the adult population (Fiedel 1979, 171).

5. Special Burial Areas or "Cemeteries"

The question of "graveyards" or "cemeteries" at Natufian sites is a complex one. Although the Natufians do not seem to have buried in or under occupied structures, they did bury their dead in abandoned structures. Such stone constructions as curving walls, pavements, lines of slabs, or curbs were found associated with the graves at most Natufian sites in the core area. At one time, most of these architectural features were believed to have been associated with the graves. However, it is now believed that these structures either predated or postdated the burials and were not constructed to receive burials or to delimit grave areas (Belfer-Cohen and Hovers 1992, 465). Many Natufian graves, therefore, were located in abandoned structures adjacent to but separate from contemporary living areas. Another question in reference to the Natufian grave sites is whether they should be considered as special burial areas, or "cemeteries." Fiedel (1979, 115–16) suggests that the term *cemetery* should be used only for two Natufian sites: Nahal Oren and the Chamber 1 burial area at el-Wad. Loci 1 and 2 at Hayonim Cave may be added as a third example.

6. Grave Construction

Most of the burials were placed into simple, unmodified pits in the earth. The pits could be shallow or deep and were only rarely outlined with stones or slabs or had stone slab covers. No evidence of associated perishable construction materials has been found.

7. Miscellaneous Stones within the Graves

Stones could be placed within the graves, either under, over, or to the side of the body or the head.

8. Grave Markers

Several types of weighty stone grave markers have been reported at Natufian sites. The most distinctive were the tall stone "pipe mortars" from Nahal Oren. At Mallaha (Eynan) the stone upright in Grave 23 may have served the same purpose. The cup-marked stones from Nahal Oren and Hayonim Cave may be included in this group. Rarely, stone circles were built around the graves to mark their location, for example, at Hayonim Cave.

9. Hearths

Such features were found near or under the graves at several Natufian sites (el-Wad, Nahal Oren, Mallaha, Hayonim, and Shuqbah). Of special interest is the large circular hearth located within the cemetery at Nahal Oren. It was made of flat, white stone slabs and was filled with a layer of ashes about half a meter thick.

10. Grave Goods

Grave goods were rarely placed in Natufian graves. Less than 10 percent of them contained burial offerings. Personal adornments—for example, head decorations, necklaces, bracelets, or belts—were by far the most common items. These ornaments were made primarily of dentalium shell beads and bone pendants, but bird bone beads and perforated animal canine teeth were sometimes used. To date, only twenty-four Natufian graves with offerings (see table 5) have been found from the sites of el-Wad, Mallaha, Hayonim Cave, and Erq el-Ahmar (Belfer-Cohen and Hovers 1992, table 1; Belfer-Cohen 1995, table 2.1). Bone tools may have been placed in Natufian graves, but to date there is only a single example (Hayonim Cave) with clear burial association (Belfer-Cohen 1990, 305, fig. 5.6).Other suggested grave goods from Natufian sites include a human-head carving in limestone and a turtle carapace from el-Wad; a bone figurine of a gazelle from Nahal Oren; gazelle-horn cores from Mallaha; and horse teeth from Erq-el Ahmar (Belfer-Cohen and Hovers 1992, 466; Bar-Yosef 1998, 104). Lumps of red ochre were occasionally found in Natufian graves, but only at Nahal Oren were the skeletons "covered with red ochre" (Stekelis and Yizraely 1963, 11). Other items have been recovered from the fill around Natufian burials. Some of these may have originally been placed in the graves (Fiedel 1979; Belfer-Cohen 1991a; Belfer-Cohen and Hovers 1992). These include bone tools, pestles, mortars, and chipped stone artifacts. At two Natufian sites, Mallaha and Hayonim Terrace, dogs were interred with human burials.

11. Skull Removal

The practice of separating the head from the rest of the body of the deceased was first recorded during the Late Natufian. This custom became more common during the succeeding early Pre-Pottery Neolithic period in the Levant.

Comparisons between the Natufian and the Shanidar Cave Proto-Neolithic Mortuary Practices
1. Burial Position

All of the Shanidar burials of complete or relatively complete skeletal remains within the cemetery were in a flexed position. Burial 27 (figs. 47 and 48), located outside the cemetery proper, was in a semiflexed position. Placement of the body was often on one of the sides (right or left), but some interments were on the back or the front. The two flexed bodies placed on their fronts were adults, but the other positions could be used for either adults or children. Natufian burials could be semiflexed, flexed, extended, or seated, but the semiflexed/flexed positions seemed to be the most common (Fiedel 1979, 159). However, according to Belfer-Cohen and Hovers (1992, 466), "No correlations were found between age or gender and time period or burial position other than a constant positive correlation between extended burial position and Early Natufian date (as in el-Wad and Hayonim Cave)." Perhaps there was spatial variation in Natufian burials as well. At Nahal Oren, the burial position seems to have been relatively uniform; most are semiflexed/flexed—or, as the excavators describe them, "in the contracted position" (Stekelis and Yizraely 1963, 11).

In summary, the burial position in the Zagros Proto-Neolithic culture seems to have been more standardized than in the Natufian. But this may well be a reflection of the temporally and spatially limited Zagros sample. However, both the Natufians and the Shanidar Cave inhabitants overall seem to have preferred semiflexed/flexed burials, for all ages and both sexes. The reason for this treatment is not hard to determine. Lacking advanced digging equipment such as shovels and using what equipment they had, it was most economical in terms of time and energy to make a shallow, round pit in the ground. Into this was fitted the body. This kind of grave accommodated semiflexed or flexed burials in the smallest possible space. At Shanidar, there is evidence that the bodies may have been wrapped in a matting made of rushes or reeds. There was no evident standardization in either the Levant or the Zagros for the placement of the body within the grave or for the orientation of the body according to the cardinal points.

2. Single and Multiple Burials

At Shanidar Cave, the identification of individual versus group graves was complicated by the fact that there had been much disturbance in the main section of the cemetery (especially in Square C1) when new interments were made. It was easier, therefore, to identify the individual burials at the site. There were fifteen individual graves, ten adults and five children. Seven group graves have been identified, but as all of them were found in Square C1, perhaps we are dealing in part with accidental associations caused by postdepositional disturbances. The multiple burials at the site contained only two or three individuals, always at least one child. The following variations were recorded: one adult and one child; one adult and two children; two adults and one child; and three children.

Both individual and group graves were present at Natufian sites. In general, however, group graves were more common than individual ones (Belfer-Cohen 1991a, 171). Natufian group graves contained every possible combination of adult males, adult females, and children. Three types of group graves have been outlined for the Natufian (Fiedel 1979, 151): (1) secondary burials of groups of three to seven individuals; (2) primary burials of more than three individuals, not necessarily buried at the same time; and (3) primary burials of two or three individuals clearly interred at the same time in one grave.

In summary, multiple as well as individual graves were present at both Shanidar Cave and the Levantine Natufian sites. However, at Shanidar Cave, the group graves always included at least one child. This was not true for the Natufian group graves containing only adults were found at several sites. Furthermore, the Natufian multiple graves contained up to seven skeletons in one group grave, while the Shanidar Cave group graves contained at the most only three individuals.

3. Primary and Secondary Burials

The difficulties involved in determining this attribute for the Shanidar Cave burials have been discussed above. Also, as noted in this chapter, the term *secondary* is limited to those burials that seemed to have had more than a single mortuary treatment. Only four graves from the site were recorded as containing secondary interments, and two more were identified as possible ones.

The four Shanidar Cave burials identified as secondary interments were:

Burial 2 (figs. 17–19)
This was represented solely by the calotte of an adolescent. It was found on top of Stone Feature 6 in Square D1 and had no associated grave goods.

Burial 3
This was represented only by the long bones of an adolescent. It was found in Square B3 and had no grave goods.

Burial 9 (figs. 22–23)
This was represented by the skull and long bone fragments from an adult (adolescent) and also two infant skulls. Burial 9 was found in Square C1. A small number of beads and a spall tool were associated with it.

Burial 25 (figs. 25 and 38)
This was the only definite pit burial recognized in the Shanidar Cave cemetery. It was represented by the bones of an adult and an infant, none of which were in correct anatomical position. Burial 25 was found in Square C1. One bone awl was associated with it.

Burials 21 (fig. 25) and 23 (figs. 25–26), both group graves in Square C1, also may have been secondary burials. Neither of these had associated grave goods.

All of the Natufian sites that have been adequately described also contained both primary and secondary burials (Fiedel 1979, 137). Even for the Natufian, with its much larger sample of burials, there has been no satisfactory and comprehensive explanation as to why both primary and secondary burials were in use at the same time. This was true for the Shanidar Cave cemetery as well, even with its much smaller sample. The Shanidar Cave secondary burials were not in any way special or elaborately decorated. In fact, most of them had no associated grave goods. Further-more, the individuals recovered from the secondary burials were not lim-ited to any particular age group. Perhaps the most likely explanation for the Shanidar Cave secondary burials is that they represent individuals who died away from the base camp and whose bodies were bundled up after death for eventual burial in the cave cemetery. Shanidar Cave, dur-ing the Proto-Neolithic as in recent times (R. S. Solecki 1979), was prob-ably occupied only during the colder winter months. During the warmer months the social group would move to an open village site in a favored location, for example, the nearby Zawi Chemi Shanidar village. One sec-ondary burial, however, Burial 2, does not seem to fit into this transhu-mance model. The burial was represented by only the skull cap or callote of an adolescent and was found centered on Stone Feature 6 in Square D1 (figs. 17–20). No other burials were uncovered in the immediate vicinity. It seems likely, therefore, that it had some special ritual significance.

4. Population Demography

The proportion of infant, child, adult, and adolescent burials (thirty-six burials) recorded at Shanidar Cave is given in row 1 of table 3.

The Shanidar Cave distribution table (table 3, row 1) agrees well with the typical population profile for prehistoric and medieval burial sites proposed by Angel (1971, 1) of a ratio of eight infants: five children: ten adults (table 3, row 3). The Natufian sites, on the other hand, had a notice-ably smaller proportion of infant and child burials and a greater pro portion of adult burials (table 3, row 2). The reasons for the under-representation of infant and child burials in the Natufian have yet to be

TABLE 3. POPULATION DISTRIBUTIONS OF THE SHANIDAR CAVE PROTO-NEOLITHIC AND THE LEVANTINE NATUFIAN BURIALS

	Infants	Children	Infants and Children	Adults and Adolescents
Shanidar Cave[a]	36.1 percent	19.4 percent	55.5 percent	44.5 percent
Natufian Sites	Not separated out	Not separated out	23.0 percent	77.0 percent
Angel Ratio[b]	34.8 percent	21.7 percent	56.5 percent	43.5 percent

Sources: Belfer-Cohen, Schepartz, Arensburg 1991, table 2; Angel 1971.

[a] *These percentages are based on the counts recorded during excavation.*

[b] *Ratio of eight infants: five children: ten adults*

satisfactorily explained (Fiedel 1979, 171–72). A number of factors may be suggested to explain the differences in death rates between the Natufian and the Zagros Proto-Neolithic. Specific cultural practices—for example, better nutrition or more extended periods of sedentism—could have increased the number of Natufian infants/children who survived to adolescence/adulthood. On the other hand, the Shanidar Cave people could have taken greater care with the burial of their infants and children. After all, these burials contained the most elaborate adornments in the Shanidar cemetery. Another possible factor could have involved preservation conditions at Shanidar Cave versus those at the Natufian sites: conditions that better preserved the fragile infant/child skeletons at the former site. Burial in a cave, as a protected site, might well have been the most important factor here. This view is supported by the high proportion of infants/children in the burials from Chamber 1 at el-Wad (Garrod and Bate 1937, 14–15).

5. Special Burial Areas or Cemeteries

The Shanidar Cave cemetery was placed to the rear of the cave, separated from the main occupation area located toward the front. So far as can be ascertained, the living area in Shanidar Cave was not abandoned during the time the cemetery was in use. The cemetery was used again and again, over a period of time, as a special place for the disposal of the dead. As such, it qualifies as a "cemetery." A small number of Natufian sites contained a separate "cemetery," close to but apart from the living areas (Fiedel 1979, 115–16). At other Natufian sites the dead were often found in the domestic living areas of the settlement. It is now generally believed that the stone structures (e.g., walls, pavements, curbs, etc.) found in these areas were not specialized mortuary constructions but structures that predated or postdated the burials found near them (Belfer-Cohen and Hovers 1992, 465). Boyd (1995), however, has suggested that at least for the site of Mallaha, there may be evidence for a relationship between a localized living area and a group of burials. In any case, unlike the Natufians, the Proto-Neolithic people of Shanidar Cave did not usually bury their dead in their main living space. We also believe that the stone constructions (the curved wall, the pavements, and the stone clusters) found in the Shanidar Cave cemetery were special mortuary structures. To date there is no good evidence for domestic stone structures in the main Proto-Neolithic living areas of the cave. Probably the Proto-Neolithic people did not require sturdy habitations within the shelter of the cave. Such stone structures, however, were found at the open village site of Zawi Chemi Shanidar (R. L. Solecki 1981), situated along the banks of the Greater Zab River. Today, the modern Kurdish seasonal inhabitants of Shanidar Cave build simple, single-room, temporary homes of woven wattle for their winter residences.

6. Grave Construction

Within the Shanidar Cave cemetery, only one definite and one possible burial pit were recorded, even though special care by the excavators was given to identify such features. No divisions or demarcations in the soil indicating the presence of individual burial-pit outlines could be discerned for most of the graves. It is possible that the crowding of the burials may have blurred such evidence. The dead, apparently, were placed above a thick lense of charcoal and ashes in a shallow pit and then covered over with cave fill. Over this was deposited a blanket of yellow loam.

The one Shanidar Cave grave (Burial 27) found outside the cemetery proper, however, was laid out in a specially prepared, stone-lined pit.

The Natufian burial pits seem to be similar to those described for Shanidar Cave: "The graves consisted of pits, either shallow or deep, only rarely revetted with stones or slabs. Occasionally the outline of a burial pit was preserved, but sometimes even that was obscured by on-going digging" (Belfer-Cohen and Hovers 1992, 465).

7. Miscellaneous Stones within the Graves

Five of the Shanidar Cave burials (Burials 4, 5, 6, 7, and 27) had stone blocks purposely placed within the graves. Four out of these five were adults, and one (Burial 4) was a child. The latter had a limestone slab placed up against its upper back. Burial 6, an adult male, had two flat blocks placed against his upper back, in the same position as in Burial 4. Burial 6 also had stones situated above its head and body, crushing the bones. Burials 5 and 7, both adult females, each had a block behind/above the head. The head of Burial 27, also an adult (female), was resting on a stone.

Stones under the body or head, or over the head, body, or limbs, have been recorded at most Natufian sites (Fiedel 1979, 129–33, table 1). "Pillowing," or the placement of the head on a stone/stones, was found at most Natufian sites in the core area (el-Wad, Hayonim, Nahal Oren, Mallaha). This placement was similar to that recorded for Burial 27. At Natufian sites, undressed stones could be placed above the various parts of adult skeletons, for example, the head, body, or legs. Again, the situation was comparable to that described for the Shanidar Cave burials.

8. Grave Markers

There was no definite evidence for grave markers in the Shanidar cemetery. Perhaps the querns and quern fragments found in the cemetery were brought there for that purpose. Several items that have been identified as probable grave markers have been reported from Natufian sites, the most distinctive of which were the "pipe mortars" from Nahal Oren.

9. Hearths

At Shanidar Cave some of the stone clusters/pavements in the cemetery were definitely used as hearths and identified as such from the associated physical traces. A hearth, with clear fire traces, was found directly on Stone Feature 1, and traces of others were still evident on Stone Features 6 and 8.The cleaning off of ashes and charcoal from the hot hearth stones, preparatory to use for cooking or other purposes, would account for the extensive accumulations of charcoal and ashes in the cemetery. Hearths in mortuary contexts were found near or under the graves at several Natufian sites (el-Wad, Nahal Oren, Mallaha, Hayonim, and Shuqbah). At Nahal Oren, ash concentrations were found "besides and/or over the graves" (Noy 1989, 55).

10. Grave Goods

Fifteen of the twenty-seven numbered burials (55.6 percent) from Shanidar Cave contained burial offerings. The most common were ornaments or personal adornment—for example, necklaces, bracelets, and probably belts made of strings of beads. These were fashioned primarily from different types of colorful stones of low or medium hardness. Strings of perforated gastropod shells or crab claws were also used for ornamentation. One grave (Burial 5, an adult) was associated with a unique copper mineral bead/pendant. Stone pendants were found in the Shanidar Cave cemetery fill, but not directly with any of the burials. Beads were found in eleven of the graves, the majority of which were infants/children (63.6 percent). Moreover, the more elaborately decorated burials were always of children. Only four adult/adolescent burials had decorations, and in two of these the ornaments were made exclusively of gastropod shell beads.

Bone tools were found in four of the graves, of which three definitely were adults. The fourth (Burial 25) included the skeleton of an adult and some stray infant bones, but the tool most probably belonged with the adult burial. One of the bone tools was definitely from a female burial, and another was with a probable female. A third bone tool was found associated with a male, and a fourth bone tool was found associated with the bones of an individual whose gender could not be determined.

Of the seven stone tools with grave associations, only two with certainty could be considered as grave offerings (i.e., not part of the grave fill). Both of these were from adult graves, one a male and the other a female.

In summary, offerings were placed in the graves of adults as well as in children's graves, but the types of offerings differed according to the age of the interred individual (see table 4). There were not enough sex-identified skeletons to determine correlations between the types of grave goods and gender. However, both adult males and females could be buried with offerings. Many of the children's bodies were buried with personal adornments, sometimes quite elaborate ones. The adults, on the other hand, were less often associated with ornaments, and these were not as elaborate as those found with the children. The adults were occasionally buried with bone or stone tools.

When compared to the Natufian data, a much greater proportion of the Shanidar Cave graves were found to contain grave goods—55.6 percent of the twenty-seven numbered Shanidar Cave burials, compared with less than 10 percent of the Natufian (Belfer-Cohen and Hovers 1992, 466).

TABLE 4. TYPES OF GRAVE OFFERINGS FOUND WITH THE TWENTY-SEVEN
SHANIDAR CAVE PROTO-NEOLITHIC BURIALS

Type of Grave Good	Total	Infants and Children		Adults and Adolescents	
		No.	%	No.	%
Beads	11	7	63.6	4	36.4
Bone Tools	4	—	—	4	100.0
Stone Tools	2[a]	—	—	2	100.0

[a] For this table only the two stone tools with definite skeletal associations were used.

Natufian mortuary offerings have been described as follows: "Grave goods are rather rare, the common ones being ornaments (head decorations, necklaces, bracelets, and belts), mostly composed of dentalium shells and bone pendants and occasionally of partridge tibio-tarsus beads and perforated wolf canines (Hayonim Cave, el-Wad, Erq el-Ahmar)" (Belfer-Cohen and Hovers 1992, 466).

At all Natufian sites, most of the ornaments associated with the burials were made of dentalium shells, although perforated animal teeth, bone beads, and bone pendants were also used. Pierced gastropod shells have been found at a number of Natufian sites. In addition, at the Negev Natufian site of Rosh Horesha, five stone beads were recovered during the excavations, four made of malachite and one of reddish limestone (Marks and Larson 1977, 200). Stone pendants were also found at Natufian sites. Decorated stone objects were characteristic of the Natufian sites in the core area (Noy 1991, 558–61; Belfer-Cohen 1991a, 574–76).

Bone tools, both decorated and plain, were regularly recovered from Natufian domestic sites in the core area. However, only one bone tool is reported to have a clear mortuary association. At Hayonim Cave, a large bone spatula, similar in size and shape to one of the bone objects from Burial 22 at Shanidar Cave, was found under the right arm of a female adult burial (Belfer-Cohen 1990, 305, fig. 5.6).

In summary, grave goods were placed more often in Shanidar Cave burials (55.6 percent) than in Natufian graves (less than 10.0 percent). At Shanidar Cave, moreover, the eleven burials decorated with ornaments were primarily of children (seven, or 63.6 percent), while only four (36.4 percent) were adults (table 5, row 5). The situation was reversed at all Natufian sites; in fact, only three (12.5 percent) of the twenty-four decorated Natufian burials were of children (table 5, rows 1–4). At the Natufian sites, more adult males than female adults had ornaments, but elaborate decorations could be found with both types of adults. At Shanidar Cave, none of the adults were elaborately bedecked with ornaments, and none of the four adults associated with burial ornaments could be positively identified as males.

At all of the Natufian sites, most of the ornaments were made from dentalium shells, although perforated animal teeth, bone beads, and bone pendants were also used. These were fashioned into necklaces, bracelets, belts, anklets, and head caps. At Shanidar Cave, the ornaments included necklaces, bracelets, and belts, but not the distinctive Natufian caps or beaded head coverings. Furthermore, dentalium shells, so characteristic

TABLE 5. NATUFIAN AND SHANIDAR CAVE BURIALS WITH
PERSONAL ADORNMENTS

Site	Total	Adults and Adolescents by Sex			Adults and Adolescents		Infants and Children	
		F	M	?	No.	%	No.	%
el-Wad	9[a]	1	7	—	8[a]	88.9	1[a]	11.1
Mallaha (Eynan)	10[a]	3	3	2	8[a]	80.0	2[a]	20.0
Hayonim Cave	4[a]	—	1	3	4[a]	100.0	—	—
Erq el-Ahmar	1[a]	1	—	—	1[a]	100.0	—	—
Shanidar Cave	11	2	—	2	4	36.4	7	63.6

[a] *Data from Belfer-Cohen 1995, table 2.1.*

of Natufian ornaments, were not found in the Zagros Proto-Neolithic
sites, either at the living site or associated with the burials. The reason for
this is obvious. There are substantial distances between the Mediterra-
nean/Red Sea sources for dentalium and Shanidar Valley. A single copper
mineral (malachite) bead/pendant was recovered from Burial 5 (an adult).
Although no copper mineral beads have been reported from Natufian
burials, four of them were found at Rosh Horesha (Marks and Larson
1977, 200). Stone pendants were found in the cemetery fill at both Shanidar
Cave and Natufian sites, but none were found with the burials.

Bone tools were recovered from four adult burials at Shanidar Cave,
but as yet, only one Natufian adult burial (at Hayonim) has been associated with a bone tool. At Shanidar, only two burials have firm associations with stone tools. For the Natufian, the situation is less clear, although
it is possible that stone pestles and mortars may have had direct associations with the burials.

Red pigment was found scattered on Burial 27 at Shanidar Cave, and
traces of the same material were found on stone tools in the cemetery fill.
At the Natufian site of Nahal Oren, red ochre was found scattered over
many of the skeletons, and ochre lumps were found in graves at Mallaha
and Wadi Hammeh 27. Finally, a most remarkable if rare Natufian mortuary feature is the joint burial of humans and dogs. Three such cases are
known, from Mallaha and Hayonim Terrace (Belfer-Cohen and Hovers
1992, 466). No such burials were found at Shanidar Cave.

11. Skull Removal

None of the Shanidar Cave burials had the skull separated and removed from the rest of the body. Burial 2 at Shanidar Cave was represented only by the callote, but the cultural explanation for this partial burial may be quite different from that behind the Natufian practice of the separation of the skull from the rest of the skeleton. This practice of skull (head) removal and separate interment became more common in the succeeding Pre-Pottery Neolithic cultures of the Levant.

Summary

Many similarities exist between the mortuary practices followed by the Epipalaeolithic Natufians of the Levant and the Zagros Proto-Neolithic peoples. Even so, there were differences, even when more or less similar practices were followed. There were also features of mortuary behavior absent in one area and practiced in the other. It should be noted here once again that the results of this comparative survey have been limited by the paucity of excavated Proto-Neolithic sites in the Zagros area.

Perhaps, however, the most important characteristic to be discussed here is the very practice of purposely burying the dead in a base camp, either in a special cemetery area or in abandoned living quarters. Boyd (1995, 21–22) has even suggested that for the Natufian site of Mallaha there may have been a long-term interrelationship between a special location, living quarters, and a burial ground. In broader perspective, however, both in the Natufian sites and at Shanidar Cave, the placement of the dead of the social group at the base camp certainly increased that group's ties to a traditional home site.

Further information on aspects of the social system can be derived from a study of mortuary practices. It has long been suggested (Wright 1978) on the basis of such evidence that the Natufians were socially stratified. This view has been challenged recently on the basis of an updated and enlarged Natufian data base: "Tempting as it is, evidence for social stratification in the Natufian, inferred from the decorated burials, is actually non-existent" (Belfer-Cohen 1995, 16). The authors of the present work have concluded, as well, that no evidence has been recovered from the Shanidar Cave cemetery to support the idea of a stratified society. At both the Natufian sites and at Shanidar Cave, grave goods were primarily personal adornments or the occasional personal tool.[3] There were no obvious symbols of rank, either in the grave goods themselves or in the way they were distributed in the graves. In fact, at Shanidar Cave, there were no elaborately decorated adult burials.

The types of grave goods found in both the Natufian and the Shanidar Cave graves were similar. For the most part they were limited to personal adornments made from strings of beads. Ornamented Natufian burials were rare; only 6 percent, or twenty-four out of four hundred–plus burials, were decorated (Belfer-Cohen 1995). Furthermore, in the Natufian, the ornaments were found primarily with the adults and only occasionally with the children (see table 5). At Shanidar Cave, on the other hand, a greater proportion of the children than the adults had ornaments, and the more elaborately decorated burials were always children. At Natufian sites and at Shanidar Cave, decorated burials were found in both single and group graves. When the group contained a decorated burial, that individual did not seem to have been given any special treatment.

The grave goods themselves, as noted above, were remarkably similar in the two areas. Natufian ornaments were made primarily from dentalium shells (either Mediterranean or Red Sea species), but shaped bone beads and pendants, pierced grastropod shell beads, and pierced animal teeth were also used. At Shanidar Cave, most of the beads were made from variously colored stones. Also present were beads made from pierced gastropod shells and crab claws. No dentalium beads were found at Shanidar, undoubtedly because the site lay too far from the sources of this material. Although the Natufian ornaments themselves appear to have been more elaborate in array than those of Shanidar Cave, it should be pointed out that the Shanidar stone beads were more difficult and time-consuming to make (and thus more valuable?) than the dentalium beads. With little preparation, the dentalium shells were ready for stringing.

In addition to the bead ornaments, bone tools were definitely associated with both Natufian (one example) and Shanidar Cave (four examples) graves. All of these were probably associated with adult burials. These bone tools were undecorated, although they could be well made and of large size. In fact, in both the Natufian and the Zagros Proto-Neolithic, the bone tools found in the graves were not representative of the richer bone industry recovered from the occupation fill.

At Shanidar Cave, ground stone tools were rarely placed in with the burials, and none as yet have been definitely reported from Natufian burials. However, a rich ground stone industry, including decorated pieces, has been found in the domestic fill at sites in both areas.

Both primary and secondary burials were found at Natufian sites and in the Shanidar Cave cemetery. As yet, there is no fully satisfactory explanation as to why both primary and secondary burials should have been practiced contemporaneously by the same social group. For the Natufian, Fiedel (1979, 140) notes, "There is no strong indication at any site that age, sex, or status differences were of critical importance in determining whether disposal would be primary or secondary." The same is true for the Shanidar Cave burials. Secondary burials were less common at Shanidar Cave than primary ones and were in no way special or elaborate. In fact, out of the six possible secondary burials, four were without grave goods of any kind. It seems likeliest, therefore, that the secondary burials represented for the most part individuals who died away from the base during the social group's annual rounds. They were prepared in some fashion immediately after death and either transported specially to the cave or carried along with the group until it returned to the cave. This interpretation again seems to strengthen the premise of the social group's close relationship with a particular location.

Red ochre was found sprinkled over the Natufian graves at Nahal Oren and also in Burial 27 at Shanidar Cave. In addition, lumps of red ochre were found associated with burials at Mallaha and Wadi Hammeh 27 and were found in the cemetery fill at Shanidar Cave. The association between red ochre or the color red and death is virtually worldwide and goes back far in antiquity. Many interpretations have been proposed for this special relationship between red ochre and burials (Fiedel 1979, 176–78). However, not all or even a majority of the Natufian or Shanidar Cave burials were so covered, once more reflecting the overall variability so characteristic of the mortuary practices in both areas.

It also seems probable that the hearths found in the cemetery area at Shanidar Cave and at some of the Natufian sites were used for religious/ceremonial purposes. There is no direct evidence, however, to determine exactly how or why these hearths were used during the burial rites.[4]

The Late Natufian practice of skull removal and separate burial of the skull is presumed to have had religious significance, probably related to an ancestor cult (Belfer-Cohen 1991a, 171). Nothing exactly like this practice is known from Shanidar Cave. Burial 2, however, represented by only the skull cap of an adolescent, was found by itself on top of Stone Feature 6. There were no other burials in the immediate vicinity. On the basis of

the present evidence, however, it cannot be determined if the same religious motivations that lay behind the Natufian custom of skull separation were responsible for Burial 2 at Shanidar Cave. However, the composition and positioning of Burial 2 do suggest religious connotations.

In rare cases, a dog was buried together with or alongside a human in
the Natufian culture. Such burials may have had religious significance,
but there is no evidence to support this. No joint human-dog burials have
been found in Shanidar Cave.

The identification of prehistoric special burial areas, or "cemeteries,"
as we know them today, could be complex. This was not a problem at
Shanidar Cave, where the burial area was clearly separated from the living area. This division between burial and living space has now been recognized at three Natufian sites: Nahal Oren, Chamber 1 at el-Wad, and
Loci 1 and 2 at Hayonim Cave. However, at other Natufian sites the dead
were buried in the living areas, actually within and between the structures. These buildings were made with stone foundations, with upper sections probably of brush and wood (Bar-Yosef 1998, 163). There was no
evidence for the use of mud bricks or wattle and daub in the Natufian
(Bar-Yosef 1998, 163). Bar-Yosef (1998) also suggests the possibility of special Natufian ritual architecture. As Fiedel (1979, 120) has noted, "Often
burials are associated with features which do not seem to have been used
in the daily activities of the living." These stone constructions included
curving walls, pavements, rock cut basins, rings of stones, stone hearths,
and several possible grave markers.

The Shanidar Cave burials, in terms of their spatial distribution, clearly
most resemble the burials at Nahal Oren, Chamber 1 at el-Wad, and Loci
1 and 2 at Hayonim Cave. Within the Shanidar Cave cemetery, there were
simple stone constructions, roughly equivalent to those recorded at some
of the Natufian sites. Nine stone features were excavated in the cemetery,
one curved wall and eight stone clusters or pavements. At least three of
the latter still had traces of hearths on them, while the remainder appeared for the most part to have been swept clean of charcoal and ashes.
It is believed that all of these structures were built to serve in mortuary
rituals and were not used for domestic purposes. There was no evidence
for the construction of stone-walled habitations in the living areas of the
cave. Two fragments of daub with stick impressions were found close to
the curved stone wall (Stone Feature 7) in the northwest corner of the
cemetery. Perhaps a wattle and daub enclosure once stood there. Such
simple constructions may have been used in the front and along the sides

of the cave for domestic shelters, but there is no direct evidence for this.

In addition to the special stone structures associated with the graves, undressed slabs or stones or even broken, large, stone grinding/pounding tools were placed in with some of the Natufian and Shanidar Cave burials. These stones could be placed above, below, or to the side of the head or the body of the burial. Sometimes the burials were so jammed into place with stones that the bones were considerably damaged. Occasionally the head was placed on a stone so that it was elevated or "pillowed," and sometimes the body was laid out on a bed of stones. These practices are reported to have been common in Natufian graves (Fiedel 1979, 129). Five such graves in direct association with stones were found in the Shanidar Cave cemetery. The cultural explanations for the placement of stones under the head and body are not necessarily the same as those for the placement of stones above or around the head or the body. In addition, there may have been regional variations in such practices among the Natufian sites, as well as between the Natufian and the Zagros regions. As Fiedel (1979, 129) points out, there are as yet no fully satisfactory explanations for the placement of the stones/slabs in the graves above the burials: "They may be grave markers in some cases, but in others they were clearly intended to weigh down the dead, presumably to keep them from haunting the living." Fiedel (1979, 130) also notes that all of the burials at el-Wad found with stones above the body or head were adults. The same is true for the Shanidar Cave cemetery. However, at Hayonim Cave, none of the burials were treated in this manner, although stones were found under the bodies or heads (Belfer-Cohen 1995, 16). The cultural motivations for this practice are not clear, as it is unlikely that a "bed" or "pillow" of stones was intended to increase the comfort of the deceased (Fiedel 1979, 133). Wright (1978) has suggested that the stones and slabs from the el-Wad burials should be considered as grave furniture. This interpretation, however, does not really help explain the presence of slabs/stones in mortuary settings. Even if the functions of these distinctive burial practices are not fully understood, it is important to point out in this comparative section that such customs were observed at both the Natufian sites and at Shanidar Cave.

Many of the same modes were employed for the disposition of the dead within the graves in the two areas. Burial positions and placement and orientation of the dead in the Natufian and Shanidar Cave graves were for the most part similar. The most obvious difference was the greater variation in burial position in the Natufian. This was probably due to the long time span and the geographic spread of the Natufian. Burial position was standardized at the Shanidar cemetery; all of the burials within its boundaries were in flexed positions. Only Burial 27, found outside the cemetery, was laid out in a semiflexed position. Natufian burials, on the other hand, could be flexed, semiflexed, extended, and, more rarely, even seated. Correlations between the extended-type burial and the Early Natufian phase have been suggested (Belfer-Cohen and Hovers 1992, 446). Overall, however, the semiflexed and flexed positions seem to have been most common for primary Natufian burials (Fiedel 1979, 159). In both the Natufian sites and Shanidar Cave, there was no regularly followed custom for placing the body of the dead within the grave. All of the following, plus variations, were known: on the right side, the left side, the back, and the front. There was also no standardized orientation of the body according to the cardinal directions.

Individual and group graves have been excavated at both Natufian sites and at Shanidar Cave. The determination of the depositional history of group graves can be a Sisyphean task. The prime problem is the unraveling of the sequence of burial events—that is, if all or some of the bodies were interred at the same time, if each was deposited at a separate time, or if there was some combination of the two methods. Another factor affecting the interpretation of group graves, at both the Natufian sites and Shanidar Cave, is the custom of using the same burial space over and over again, thus causing much disturbance to earlier interments.

Group graves in both areas could contain either primary or secondary burials. Overall, individual graves were more common than group graves at Shanidar Cave. In the Natufian, on the other hand, group graves were more common than individual ones, but this ratio varied through time and in space (Belfer-Cohen 1991a, 171; Belfer-Cohen and Hovers 1992, 466). In addition, the composition of group graves was different in the Natufian and Shanidar Cave. Shanidar Cave group graves always contained at least one child, while in the Natufian the group graves contained every possible variation of adult males, adult females, and children (Belfer-Cohen and Hovers 1992, 466). The Shanidar Cave group burials also included only two or three individuals, while the Natufian group graves could include up to seven individuals.

In conclusion, the general patterning of this mortuary trait (single or group graves) appears to have been similar in both the Levantine Natufian and the Zagros Proto-Neolithic cultures, although regional differences were also evident.

Yet to be discussed in this comparative section are mortuary customs practiced in one area but absent from the other. Joint human-dog burials (Bar-Yosef 1998, 164) have been recovered from two Natufian sites (Mallaha and Hayonim Terrace). Such distinctive interments have not been found at other Natufian burial sites, nor have they been found as yet at Shanidar Cave.

The practice of removing the skull from the dead was followed at three Natufian sites in the Late Natufian phase (Hayonim Cave, Mallaha, and Nahal Oren) (Bar-Yosef 1998, 164). There was no exact parallel to this custom at Shanidar Cave, but we have made the suggestion that Burial 2, consisting only of the calotte, may be comparable in some way. The practice of skull removal has not been reported from all of the Natufian burial sites.

At Shanidar Cave, there were no obvious grave markers similar to the tall stone "pipe mortars" at Nahal Oren. Perhaps the large stone querns or quern fragments served a similar purpose at Shanidar Cave.

In the actual preparation of the grave, the orientation of the body within the grave, and the placement of ornaments or tools with the burials, Shanidar Cave and Natufian mortuary practices were remarkably similar. The most apparent difference was in the absence of burials laid out in the extended position at Shanidar Cave and their presence at Natufian sites. However, extended burials apparently were not found at all Natufian sites: "Nahal Oren is unique among Natufian sites in that burials seem to be essentially uniform in position; most are flexed, with the knees at some distance from the chin, and the arms stretched out below the body" (Fiedel 1979, 162).

Notes

1. The chronological range for the Natufian is 12,500–10,200 B.P. The Natufian is known from a large number of sites and is well dated through a long series of radiocarbon-14 dates. The Zagros Proto-Neolithic is dated primarily on the basis of radiocarbon dates (uncorrected) from Shanidar Cave (10,600 +/-300 B.P.) and Zawi Chemi Shanidar (10,870 +/-300 B.P.) (R. S. Solecki and Rubin 1958, 1446). The site of Hallan Çemi Tepesi is located, as the crow flies, some 305 kilometers northwest of Shanidar Cave on another branch of the Tigris River (Rosenberg 1994). It lies in the mountainous area of eastern Turkey. Hallan Çemi Tepesi is culturally similar to the Zagros Proto-Neolithic. It has been radiocarbon dated to the second half of the tenth millennium B.P. (Rosenberg 1994, 123). When a broader

range of sites of the Zagros Proto-Neolithic is known, a wider time frame will no doubt be developed for it.

2. In this comparative section the term *adult* stands for adults and adolescents, and the term *children* stands for children and infants.

3. In both the Natufian burial sites and at Shanidar Cave, the identification of purposely placed grave offerings was made somewhat difficult by the practice of covering the dead with occupational debris full of cultural materials. Therefore, in this discussion, the term *grave goods* is used only for those ornaments found on the skeletons or other items found directly associated with the burials.

4. See chapter 2 for a full discussion of hearth usage.

CHAPTER 7

Summary Discussion of the
Proto-Neolithic Cemetery in Shanidar Cave

ROSE L. SOLECKI AND RALPH S. SOLECKI

The Proto-Neolithic occupants of Shanidar Cave not only lived in the cave but also used it to bury their dead. For the most part, the dead were interred in a "special area" or cemetery located toward the rear of the cave. Only one grave dating from this period has been found outside the cemetery, toward the front of the cave. A curved stone wall (Stone Feature 7) and a series of eight stone clusters or pavements (Stone Features 1–6, 8, 9) roughly enclosed and defined the cemetery. It is appropriate, therefore, to call the Shanidar Cave "special burial area" a cemetery—that is, an area devoted exclusively to the disposal of the dead and used over an extended period of time for that purpose. To date, the Shanidar Cave cemetery is the only mortuary site dating to the Proto-Neolithic (circa 10,600 B.P.) known from the Greater Zagros area. Many of the mortuary features that characterize the Shanidar Cave cemetery also were found in the better-known Epipalaeolithic Natufian sites of the Levant. The Zagros Proto-Neolithic was roughly coeval with the Late Natufian on the basis of radiocarbon-14 determinations. Zawi Chemi village, located some 4 kilometers downstream from Shanidar Cave, on the banks of the Greater Zab River, also dated from this same time period.

Like the modern Shirwani Kurds who live in Shanidar Cave during the winter season, the Proto-Neolithic inhabitants of the site also probably used the cave as a winter home. The latter summered outside the cave, possibly at the nearby Zawi Chemi Shanidar village, where they could gather a variety of plant foods and hunt animals along the river terraces.

The excavations in the area of the Shanidar Cave cemetery measured 6 meters by 6 meters (fig. 5). At the close of the excavations it was evident, however, that the entire cemetery had not been exposed.[1] The excavated portion of the cemetery contained twenty-six graves, from which the remains of at least thirty-five individual bodies were field identified. Because the cemetery was used over a period of time and earlier graves were disturbed when later interments were made, more individuals were probably originally laid to rest in the cemetery than the above count indicates, especially in the crowded, central part of the cemetery. Almost 70 percent of the graves were located in this favored burial locus. This area was crowded with bodies, but none of the stone constructions were located in this section of the cemetery.

The cemetery lay at a uniform depth of about 1 meter below the present cave ground surface, or about 50 centimeters from the contact between the Pottery Neolithic Layer A and the Aceramic Proto-Neolithic Layer B1. The burials were laid out on beds of gray, ashy sediment. A distinctive yellow-colored loam lay above the burials and sealed in the cemetery. This distinctive layer clearly defined the top of the cemetery as well as its limits.

The stone constructions built in the cemetery area have not yet been found in the domestic/living quarters of the cave. We believe, therefore, that these structures were used during mortuary rituals performed at the cemetery. These stone clusters and the wall unit were built roughly around the periphery of the main part of the cemetery, not in the section where most of the bodies were buried. Only three burials were found in close proximity to a stone structure. The most remarkable of these was Burial 2. This burial, represented only by the partial skull cap of an adolescent, was discovered sitting on Stone Feature 6. Direct evidence of hearths was found at three of the stone clusters (Stone Features 1, 6, and 8), but all of the stone clusters had traces of ashes and/or charcoal associated with them. It has been suggested here that mortuary rituals involving burning/cooking probably took place at these stone clusters and that such activities were responsible for the widespread dark-colored, ashy sediments characteristic of the cemetery. Despite this apparent association of fire with burial ritual, none of the skeletons was burned or charred, nor was there any evidence of cremation. The exact function of the stone alignment (Stone Feature 7) could not be determined. It seems to have been a boundary wall, built in the northeast corner of the cemetery. The daub fragments (fig. 21) from a wattle and daub construction found in the vicinity of this feature suggest that there may have been a superstructure wall built on a wicker work of twigs.

All but one of the large stone querns/quern fragments and a number of mullers (the hand stones) were found near the stone features, indicating some special relationship between these large plant-food-processing tools and the stone features or the rituals that took place at them.

As noted above, although stone constructions were built in the cemetery area of Shanidar Cave, no domestic structures built of stone or with stone foundations have, as yet, been associated with the Proto-Neolithic horizon in Shanidar Cave. Small, circular, stone-walled structures, however, were found at the nearby, roughly coeval village site of Zawi Chemi Shanidar (R. L. Solecki 1981). It seems probable that the Proto-Neolithic inhabitants of the cave site built only simple domiciles of wood and brush within the shelter of the cave. This is the same pattern followed by the modern Kurdish winter residents of the cave (R. S. Solecki 1979).

The Proto-Neolithic people of Shanidar Cave apparently followed culturally defined methods for burying their dead, although in practice variations did occur. The dead were placed, for the most part, in a special area at the base camp, clearly separated from the living quarters. Only a single isolated grave has been found outside the cemetery proper. Special stone constructions were built in the cemetery, apparently for the performance of mortuary rites. The cemetery was used over an extended period of time, and later interments definitely disturbed earlier ones. We do not know how long the cemetery remained in the memory of the cave inhabitants as a special burial area, but it was certainly for several generations. Definite grave markers have not been identified at the cemetery; perhaps they were present but were disturbed by later activities.

The Shanidar Cave burials were characteristically placed on a bed of dark ashy sediment. Only one definite burial pit could be identified in the cemetery proper, even though a careful search was made for such pits during excavation. The one burial outside of the cemetery, Burial 27, was in a specially prepared stone-lined pit.

In five of the graves (four were adults), stone blocks were placed above, below, or next to the body or head. The reasons for "pillowing" the head or holding down or enclosing the body are not fully understood. There was, however, clear-cut evidence in one of the graves (Burial 4) that the body had been laid on or wrapped in a woven mat. In addition, the extreme flexed position of some of the burials suggests that the body immediately after death had been tied up into a bundle. Perhaps the individuals who died away from the cave were tightly wrapped up for easier transport to the cave for burial.

Burial position was the most standardized mortuary practice followed at the Shanidar Cave cemetery. All the bodies were laid out in some variation of the flexed position. Some of the very flexed bodies were virtually crammed into the graves. No extended burials were found. Even though all the interments were flexed to some degree, there was much variation in placement of the body in the grave. Usually the dead were laid out either on the right or left side, but they could be placed on their front or back. There was also no standardization of body placement according to the cardinal directions.

Both individual and group graves were found, but some of the group graves may represent fortuitous accumulations due to prehistoric disturbances. Other group graves did not seem to have been disturbed. All the multiple graves included at least one child.

Both primary and secondary burials were present in the Shanidar Cave cemetery.[2] There is no completely satisfactory explanation as to why these Shanidar Cave people (and the Natufian of the Levant) practiced both primary and secondary burial at the same time. The Shanidar Cave secondary burials were not in any way special or elaborately decorated; in fact, most of them did not have grave goods. The likeliest explanation for secondary burial is that it was practiced when an individual died away from the cave and was bundled up and carried by the group until they returned to the cave. One secondary burial, however—Burial 2, represented only by a skull cap placed above Stone Feature 6—probably is the result of some special set of circumstances.

The thirty-six individuals from Shanidar Cave, including the one found toward the front of the cave, were separated into the following age groups: twenty infants and children (55.5 percent), five adolescents (13.9 percent), and eleven adults (30.6 percent). The adult skeletons that were complete enough to be sexed appeared to be equally divided between males and females. Infant/child mortality obviously was quite high at Shanidar Cave, much higher than at Natufian sites (see table 3). Several factors may be invoked to explain these differences: better nutrition and more extended periods of sedentism in the Natufian; more attention paid to children's burials in Shanidar Cave; or better preservation conditions in Shanidar Cave than at open village sites.

Grave offerings were found in fifteen (55.6 percent) of the Shanidar Cave graves. The most common offerings consisted of various kinds of bead decorations, usually composed of colored stone beads, but also of pierced gastropod shell or crab claw beads. The most elaborate decorations were always associated with infants'/children's graves. One of these graves contained over fifteen hundred stone beads. Such a great number of stone beads, we believe, represents a large investment, considering the number of human hours involved in making the beads. They also reflect the strong feelings these people must have had for their children. Bone and stone tools were occasionally also placed in the graves with adults. The bone tools were especially large, well-made tools and probably represented favored artifacts belonging to the deceased. Red ochre was found sprinkled over one of the graves (Burial 27), and red-ochre-stained tools and a piece of ochre were recovered from the cemetery fill.

The study of the Shanidar Cave offerings has provided new insights regarding the social and religious life of these people. The offerings placed in the Shanidar Cave graves were either bead ornaments or favored personal tools. There were no obvious symbols of rank, either in the grave goods themselves or in the way they were distributed in the graves. In fact, no elaborately decorated burials of adults were found. Therefore, this study of the grave goods found in the Shanidar Cave cemetery did not provide any evidence to suggest that these Proto-Neolithic people had a socially stratified society. There was good evidence, however, to suggest that they had a great fondness for their children and that they felt their losses very much. Perhaps, however, the most important conclusion in reference to social organization to be derived from this study concerns the very practice of purposefully burying the dead in a base camp, separated from the living areas of the site. In broader perspective, the placement of the dead of the social group at a base camp certainly increased that group's ties to a traditional home site.

Aspects of the religious life followed by the Shanidar Proto-Neolithic people also have been clarified by this study. These people obviously prepared a special place for the burial of their dead, followed certain traditional customs for the arrangement of the dead in the cemetery, and placed ornaments and tools with the departed. Red ochre was sprinkled over at least one of the burials. Also to be noted here are the special stone structures built in the cemetery, at which, we believe, mortuary rituals were performed. All of the above suggests that these people had developed traditional religious patterns involving burial rites and a belief in an afterlife.

This study has also enlarged our knowledge of the extent and importance of long-distance trade in the greater Zagros area and the types of materials exchanged there. The variety of raw materials used for the stone beads, including the copper mineral bead/pendant, illustrates the extent of this trade. Also pertinent to this discussion are the other imported raw materials found in the cemetery—for example, black adhesive (bitumen?), red ochre, obsidian, chlorite, and the distinctive green stone used for some of the hammerstones.

Shanidar Cave mortuary practices are comparable to those of other roughly contemporary cultures in the Near East. Most of the comparable data comes from the Natufian sites of the Levant. As discussed in the comparative section of this work (chapter 6), many similarities existed between the mortuary practices followed by the Shanidar people and those followed by the Natufians. Even taking into account the much larger size of the Natufian sample, along with the fact that it probably represents a time span of some two thousand years, there were significant similarities in mortuary practices between the Zagros and the Levant at that time. It should be noted here, however, that there also were some features found only in one of these areas and absent in the other. We believe that both the Zagros and the Levant should be considered as belonging to the same broad Near Eastern cultural horizon but that each also was part of a distinct regional/local tradition.

The skeletal collection recovered from the Shanidar Cave cemetery has been studied by three different physical anthropologists (see appendix A and chapter 9; Ferembach 1970; Agelarakis 1989). The three analysts—Munizaga, Ferembach, and Agelarakis—emphasized different sets of problems and worked with somewhat different samples (see table 1). All of the skeletal remains from the burials, along with all the associated cultural materials, were deposited in the Iraq Museum at the close of the 1960 season. It was not possible to immediately study the physical remains or the associated artifacts because the cemetery was found so close to the end of the 1960 season. Great care was taken to pack and number the materials from individual graves, both the skeletal remains and the associated cultural finds, and each individual burial was placed in a separate metal container. These containers were deposited in the Iraq Museum by R. S. Solecki in September 1960. T. Dale Stewart and his colleague Juan Munizaga went to Baghdad in 1962 to study the skeletal remains from the 1960 season. Stewart concentrated on the Neanderthals. Munizaga unpacked and studied the Proto-Neolithic skeletons. It appeared that the Proto-Neolithic burial remains and their associated materials were more or less intact in their containers up to the time Munizaga examined them. His count of the individual skeletal remains in the collection tallies in general with the records kept by R. S. Solecki in 1960, even though Munizaga apparently did not find Burials 3 and 15. Between the time of his departure from Baghdad and the arrival of Ferembach in 1969 and of Agelarakis in 1985, there was obviously some mixing of both the skeletal and the cultural contents of the containers, as well as some mislabeling of the bones.

The report by Agelarakis (1989) represents the most comprehensive of the three studies of the Shanidar skeletal remains, even though he did not have available to him the complete collection as it was deposited in the museum in 1960. In fairness to his predecessors, it must be stated that he spent more time in both painstaking laboratory study and subsequent research than they were able to devote to the project. Agelarakis was able to locate in the museum twenty-nine individuals out of the thirty-five recorded in the notes from the cemetery, or the thirty-seven described by Munizaga (see table 1). It was also obvious that at some time during or after Munizaga's study a number of the individual skeletons had been erroneously cataloged together. Even with these problems, Agelarakis's sample was large enough to provide important new data on the Shanidar Cave population. His contribution includes the palaeopathology of the Proto-Neolithic people; their physical condition, especially long- and short-term health problems; and their traumatic injuries.

The stratigraphic evidence from the cemetery, the standardization in mortuary practices, and the homogeneity of the grave goods all suggest that the Shanidar Cave cemetery was in use for only a relatively short period of time. There is no evidence to suggest that the individuals buried in the cemetery died during a single event, such as a plague, scourge, or similar catastrophe. We can also rule out death under rockfalls; such catastrophes would have produced massive injuries to the skeletal frame. Agelarakis (1989, 184), on the basis of his study of the skeletal remains, comes to the conclusion that the burials in the cemetery represent a small population: "[Because of] the similar morphological characteristic of the skeletal remains, [and] the frequent skeletal traits of non-metric variation, coupled with similarities among the disease patterns and other indications of stress evident on the skeletal bodies, it is suggested that these prehistoric individuals probably belong to the same group of people. There were no skeletal manifestations observed that could indicate 'distance' between the individuals involved."

Therefore, on the basis of both stratigraphic and skeletal evidence, it seems likely that the cemetery was in use for a relatively short period. Probably the Proto-Neolithic population of the cave was not greater than the modern Kurdish population of circa fifty persons; most likely it was around thirty-five or even fewer in number. To date, at least thirty-five individuals have been recovered from the excavated portion of the cemetery. Perhaps the unexcavated parts of the cemetery hold circa fifteen more bodies, making for a total of slightly over fifty interments. Using an estimated overall population death rate of 3 percent per year, we can estimate that the cemetery was in use for 33.3 years, given a population of fifty people; for 52.4 years, given a population of thirty-five; and for 66.7 years, given a population of twenty-five.[3]

Agelarakis (1989, 176–77) classifies the Shanidar Cave Proto-Neolithic population as follows: "The morphological characteristics of the skeletal remains revealed well built skeletal bodies which resembled the Proto-Mediterranean type of peoples called the Atlanto-Mediterranean or Eurafrican race (Ferembach 1970; Angel, personal communication; Persson, personal communication) with apparent sexual dimorphism; the males manifested significantly increased attributes of robusticity and emphasized muscular imprints."

Agelarakis's study (1989) has provided important new data on the general health of the Shanidar Proto-Neolithic people (see chapter 9 for a full discussion of this). Of particular interest is his evidence for stress periods during infancy and childhood. Agelarakis found physical indications of dental pathological conditions, some of which were due to periods of stress during early life. These pathologies were the result of malnutrition and/or trauma coupled with debilitating diseases. Other degenerative dental problems were also observed in the Shanidar Cave population.

Of special interest is Agelarakis's observation (also noted by Ferembach 1970) that the posterior teeth showed heavy wear patterns, even in young adults. This noticeably heavy tooth wear could be attributed to the presence of ground grains or nuts in the diet. We know that these people had milling equipment (querns and mullers made from quartzite), and grit from these tools could have easily gotten into their food. In fact, this heavy tooth-wear pattern is additional evidence for the use of plant food during the Proto-Neolithic.

The final subject to be discussed in this summary of the physical remains from the Shanidar Cave cemetery is the practice of artificial head deformation. At least two individuals—Burial 2 (Cat. No. 295 IV), an adolescent or young adult of sixteen to seventeen years, and Burial 6 (Cat. No. 337 IV), identified as an adult male—showed evidence of artificial cranial deformation (Agelarakis 1989, 46, 56–57; Meicklejohn et al. 1992,

89, 91). Meicklejohn et al. (1992, 93–94) so far have found evidence for such cranial deformation at four Near Eastern sites dating from circa nine thousand to eight thousand B.P., the earliest of which is Shanidar Cave.

Notes

1. Further excavations at Shanidar Cave, after the 1960 season, have not been possible, due to continuing political problems in the area.
2. In this work, the term *secondary* is limited to those burials that seemed to have had more than a single mortuary treatment.
3. From an unpublished manuscript (1983) by Abram Jaffe (deceased), statistician, formerly the director of Manpower and Population Program, Columbia University, New York.

CHAPTER 8

The Zagros Proto-Neolithic
and Cultural Developments in the Near East

ROSE L. SOLECKI AND RALPH S. SOLECKI

I n Shanidar Cave, the Proto-Neolithic horizon (Layer B1) lies above
the Epipalaeolithic Zarzian horizon (Layer B2). On the basis of the
radiocarbon-14 dates, there was a time gap of some two thousand
years between the two occupations at the site. To date, the Zarzian is the
only Epipalaeolithic industry identified for the Zagros region, and its development through time and its distribution in space are poorly understood. The Zarzian was named after the site excavated by Garrod in 1928 in
northeastern Iraq (Garrod 1930). The Zarzian may date to as early as 22,000
B.P., according to some researchers, and may have lasted until 12,000 B.P.
Zarzian sites have been located in northern Iraq, in northeastern Iraq,
and in adjacent areas over in Iran. They are generally situated at moderately high elevations and in much the same upland zones as the earlier
Upper Palaeolithic Baradostian. The Zarzian sites are, however, noticeably more common than those of the Baradostian, perhaps reflecting
somewhat ameliorative worldwide climatic conditions. The climate in the
Zagros during the Epipalaeolithic, however, overall continued to be cool
and dry and characterized by a steppe vegetation (Leroi-Gourhan 1981).

The Zarzian lithic industry has been viewed as "a direct development
out of the underlying late Baradostian industry at Warwasi" (Olszewski
1993b, 211). The Zarzian lithic assemblages were dominated by notched/
denticulate tools and a heavy microlithic-sized component. The latter, at
least in later phases, included geometrics such as triangles, lunates, and
trapezoids. In addition to the lithic industry, rare bone, shell, and stone
tools and decorative items have been associated with the Zarzian by some
investigators. At Palegawra these included simple, pointed bone tools; beads
and pendants of shell, teeth, bone, or stone; a polished celt; and a quern

fragment (Braidwood and Howe 1960, 58). Garrod (1930, 22) reports the following items from Zarzi: two fragments of worked bone, a grooved stone (called a schist polisher in the report), and a flat pendant made of schist. Both the Zarzi and the Palegawra reports were written before the Shanidar Layer B1 (the Zawi Chemi Shanidar horizon) was identified as a separate cultural entity from the Zarzian. Howe, in his brief report on the site of Palegawra, notes the following: "A sizable chipped and polished celt (mentioned above) from a depth of 80–100 cm., and scattered but definite traces of obsidian debris and distinctive implements suggest either disturbances or a very late phase of the Zarzian" (Braidwood and Howe 1960, 58).

We suspect, therefore, that at both Zarzi and Palegawra a Proto-Neolithic occupation may well have been present above the Zarzian.

The Proto-Neolithic peoples of Shanidar Valley lived in both open villages (Zawi Chemi Shanidar) and in caves (Shanidar Cave), probably on a seasonal basis. To date, the burials of these people have been found only at the cave site. Perhaps they chose the cave because it afforded better protection for their dead. Perhaps they also regarded the cave as their ancestral home (a tradition going back to the Zarzian) and had special socioreligious links with it.

The Proto-Neolithic in the Zagros area was a time of much cultural change and a period that can be viewed as transitional between the Epipalaeolithic and the later, fully developed Neolithic. In some features it exhibited ties to the earlier Epipalaeolithic culture, but at the same time it exhibited many innovative features in technology, settlement, subsistence pattern, etc. The Proto-Neolithic chipped stone industry, both typologically and technologically, resembles the earlier Zarzian, with an emphasis on notched and denticulated tools and a microlithic component that included geometrics. Much of the remainder of the Proto-Neolithic material culture, however, is reminiscent of the Aceramic Neolithic.

The Proto-Neolithic was, as noted above, a period of great innovation and variability in material goods. New technologies were developed and introduced to make new tools for a new way of life. For the first time, open villages, probably seasonally occupied, were established in favored locations. Permanent constructions in the form of stone-walled structures have been found at such an open-village site (Zawi Chemi Shanidar). The Proto-Neolithic people, who still lived in caves for at least part of the year, probably continued to construct shelters of perishable materials in such naturally protected areas. There was, however, also evidence for the use of wattle and daub construction in Shanidar Cave.

A variety of large pecked and ground stone tools—for example, querns, mullers, pestles, hammerstones, pounding and pecking stones, and so on— were all common for the first time. In addition, small ground stone tools and ornaments were also present. The full development of a worked-bone industry occurred during the Proto-Neolithic period, and a variety of bone tools and ornaments were common for the first time. Even simple, decorated worked-bone pieces were made. The bone and stone decorated items, plus the variety of personal ornaments used by these people, suggest a growing richness and elaboration of culture in Shanidar Valley at that time.

The Shanidar Valley Proto-Neolithic population also lived through a time that witnessed changes in the basic subsistence pattern. There was a new dependence on a broad spectrum of foodstuffs: a variety of wild plants and nuts, including grains (although there was no definite evidence for plant domestication); land snails (Helix salomonica and Levantina mahanica);[1] possibly crabs; red deer and wild sheep and goats; and, toward the end of the period, probably the keeping of sheep (Perkins 1964).

As noted above, at the present time there are no actual plant remains to suggest that the Zawi Chemi people practiced agriculture, although there are several lines of evidence to show that there was a lot of plant food in their diet. There is, however, physical evidence for domesticated plants at roughly coeval sites in the Levant and evidence from an even earlier time (circa 11,000 B.P.) at Abu Hurerya (Hillman 2000, 378). A brief review of the evidence for early food production in the greater Taurus/Zagros region would be relevant here, especially in light of the idea suggested by Bar-Yosef and Belfer-Cohen (1992, 38): "Thus it was in the 'Levantine Corridor,' from the Middle Euphrates through the Jordan Valley and into southern Jordan, that the first agricultural settlements were founded.... Within less than 1,000 radiocarbon years the settlements became four times larger than their ancestral villages and the new subsistence strategy was carried across the Taurus and Zagros Mountains into Anatolia and Iran."

The archaeological evidence from the Shanidar Cave cemetery and the contemporary living areas in the cave, as well as from the village site of Zawi Chemi Shanidar, refers to the time period from circa 10,900 to 10,500 B.P.—a time, on the basis of presently available evidence, before the establishment of sedentary agricultural villages in the Taurus/Zagros area. We believe that the Zawi Chemi people probably were semisedentary, changing their habitation site in the spring and then again in the late fall/winter. We do not believe, however, that they were nomadic hunters and collectors, making yearly rounds in small bands.

The Zawi Chemi people used a variety of local plant foods, for example, seeds, fruits, nuts, and so on. Shanidar Valley lies within the zone of "known and reasonably certain sites" of wild barley, einkorn, and emmer wheat (Harlan and Zohary 1966, figs. 1, 3, and 4). Leroi-Gourhan (1981) also notes an increase in Graminae pollen, Cerelia type, during the Zawi Chemi period, both at the village site and at the cave (R. L. Solecki, 1981, 58). The large numbers of querns and mullers, plant-processing tools, that were found at both the village site and the cave attest to the importance of plant food in the diet of the Zawi Chemi people. These heavy and large-sized grinding tools must have taken many human hours to produce. They could not have been easily carried about on yearly rounds by a small group. It should also be noted that these tools were not associated with the earlier Zarzian inhabitants of Shanidar Cave.

Another line of evidence supporting our suggestion that plant food played an important role in the diet of the Zawi Chemi people is supplied by bone isotope analyses made on a sample of the human skeletons from the Shanidar Cave cemetery (see chapter 9). These tests indicate that the Zawi Chemi people ate a typical herbivorous diet, with an animal-protein intake of less than 10 percent. It is notable that these results contrast with studies of the faunal remains from the Zawi Chemi village, where remains of sheep, goats, and red deer were found. Perkins (1964) even suggests that sheep may have been controlled by humans during the later phase of the Zawi Chemi occupation. Perhaps more hunting was possible in the summer (when the village site was occupied) than in the winter (when the cave was inhabited), especially during the colder Younger Dryas period.

The Zawi Chemi village, with its associated stone architecture, is the earliest known village site in the region. We are faced with the question of why the inhabitants of Shanidar Valley at this time established such a site, located on the banks of the Greater Zab River and out of the shelter of the cave. This was the period of the Younger Dryas, a cold and dry time that lasted several centuries sometime between 11,000 and 10,000 B.P. (Broeker 1987). To the west, in the Levant, this was a time when groups of people seemingly concentrated in the moister areas—for example, along rivers or lakes—while sites in the drier, more marginal regions were abandoned (Bar-Yosef and Meadow 1995, 70–71). We believe that this same process of severe environmental pressure was taking place in the Taurus/Zagros area. Along the banks of the Greater Zab River, the people could have taken advantage of the moister environment and the richer stands of wild plants that probably grew there. It is also possible that they used the small areas of rich river silt that accumulated along the riverbanks to sow some seeds of wild grains.

Agelarakis's study of the human skeletal remains from the cemetery has indeed shown that the Younger Dryas was a period of severe stress for the human populations living in the area at that time (see chapter 9). Agelarakis reports that there is a high frequency of stress markers, traumas, and diseases evident in the Shanidar cemetery population. These early-life stress conditions and subsequent manifestations of disease may reflect, according to Agelarakis, difficult environmental conditions leading to food scarcity or changes to a diet primarily dependent on plant foods. Agelarakis also observes a considerable amount of trauma indications in the Shanidar Cave population, primarily on the crania, but also on the vertebrae and the sacra. These findings suggest that some group fighting, perhaps over dwindling access to food supplies, may have taken place at that time. Some bone injuries may be attributable to habitual occupational stress.

After the Zawi Chemi occupations, both the cave and the village sites at Shanidar were unoccupied for some period of time. The next occupation of the cave came during some local ceramic Neolithic tradition. The village site was not reoccupied until about the sixth century A.D. This cultural horizon was dated by a Byzantine coin and the presence of "Christian ware" ceramics.

The aceramic Early Neolithic site of Hallan Çemi Tepesi (Rosenberg 1994; Rosenberg et al. 1998) is particularly pertinent to this discussion. It is located on the west bank of the Sason Çayi, a tributary of the Batman River (and in turn a branch of the Tigris River), in the foothills of the Taurus Mountains in eastern Turkey. It is about 320 kilometers northwest of Shanidar. A series of radiocarbon dates from the site places it in the chronological gap between the earlier Zawi Chemi on the one hand and such later sites as Nemrik, Qermez Dere, and basal Çayönü on the other hand (Rosenberg 1994, 131). Rosenberg et al. (1998, 38) suggest, furthermore, that the Hallan Çemi culture was derived from the regional Epipalaeolithic Zarzian tradition. We have suggested the same origins for the Zawi Chemi.

The village site of Hallan Çemi was abandoned toward the end of the Younger Dryas period, probably several centuries after the abandonment of the Shanidar Valley sites. Later, agricultural villages were established downriver from Hallan Çemi on the Tigris, as well as over a wide area in the Taurus/Zagros region. This movement of peoples most likely was related to the harsh environmental conditions of the Younger Dryas, as well as to the rapidly improving conditions that characterized the immediate post–Younger Dryas period.

On the basis of the excavations at Qermez Dere, Nemrik, and M'lefaat in northern Iraq, and the more recent work in eastern Anatolia at Halan

Çemi and Çayönü, Rosenberg et al. (1998) have suggested that the Taurus/Zagros arc was a second, largely autochthonous center of early Neolithic development in southwestern Asia. Small sedentary or semisedentary villages existed in the Taurus/Zagros region during the Younger Dryas. The culture practiced at these sites apparently had its primary roots in the Zarzian, a widespread Epipalaeolithic industry in this region and one that is distinct from the contemporary Epipalaeolithic industries of the Levant to the west. The subsistence strategies characteristic of the early Taurus/Zagros villages exhibited a good deal of variation, no doubt a reflection of local environments. They did not duplicate the subsistence patterns characteristic of coeval Levantine sites, especially in reference to the animals utilized. The diets of the Taurus/Zagros villagers included different mixes of the following: (1) wild plant foods, such as cereal grains, lupines, other seeds, nuts, fruits, and so on; (2) cereal grains sown by the villagers at choice spots, for example, in the rich soils along riverbanks (possible); (3) wild animals, especially sheep and goat, but also including red deer and pig; (4) a variety of minor foods including fish, shellfish, turtles, and land snails.

In conclusion, it seems evident to us that the Taurus/Zagros region should be viewed as a separate center of Neolithization and, furthermore, that it developed, initially at least, with little outside influence. We believe this, even though we acknowledge that more research is badly needed in Early Neolithic period sites in this area. The Taurus/Zagros Early Neolithic developed out of earlier cultural traditions, within a background that reflected both local environmental conditions and broader climatic events. We are therefore reluctant to accept the idea that has recently been put forward (Bar-Yosef and Belfer-Cohen 1992; Bar-Yosef and Meadow 1995) that food production occurred only once in southwestern Asia, in the so-called "Levantine Corridor," and spread from there throughout the region.

There is more evidence for the social and religious life of the Proto-Neolithic populations of Shanidar Valley than for earlier periods. A social group must have built and maintained the Zawi Chemi Shanidar village and the cemetery at Shanidar Cave. However, there was no evidence at either of these sites that a socially stratified society was present at that time. The Proto-Neolithic people buried their dead in a clearly defined cemetery area, further separated from the living areas by distinctive stone constructions. These stone constructions were probably used during mortuary rituals only. The maintenance of a cemetery over a period of time; the performance of burial rites; the interment of the dead according to traditional patterns; the decorating of the bodies, primarily those of infants and children, with ornaments; and the placement of tools in the graves of adults all suggest the presence of an organized religious life and a belief in life after death. Additional information on the religious practices of the Proto-Neolithic people of Shanidar Valley was recovered at Zawi Chemi Shanidar. Here a unique collection of wing bones from large birds and the skulls of wild sheep or goats was found deposited in a single mass, just outside the stone structure built at the site (R. L. Solecki and McGovern, 1980). This special collection included the skulls of at least fifteen wild sheep and/or goats and the bones (90 percent of them wing bones) from a minimum of seventeen birds, including four bearded vultures, one griffon vulture, seven white-tailed sea eagles, four small eagles, and one great bustard. This collection was certainly not the remains of an ordinary meal or even a feast and must represent the remains of some sort of ritual paraphernalia. The animal remains in this unique collection, especially those of the large predatory birds, suggest the hunting efforts of the group over a period of some time.

In many ways, the cultural developments we have just outlined for the Shanidar Valley were taking place in other regions of the Near East as well. There have been extensive investigations into Epipalaeolithic/Proto-Neolithic sites in the Levant, on the basis of which a long and detailed chronology has been established. The Proto-Neolithic way of life, on the basis of present data, seems to have begun earlier in the Levant than in the Zagros. The Early Natufian period, which dates from circa 12,500 years ago, some 1,500–2,000 years earlier than the Shanidar Valley Proto-Neolithic, already had what we consider to be a Proto-Neolithic way of life. A major problem in this study has been the incompleteness of the Zagros record for the Epipalaeolithic and Proto-Neolithic periods. When an adequate sample of Zagros sites in this time range has been investigated, a different reconstruction of the cultural developments in the two regions will probably emerge. More archaeological investigations in the Zagros region are badly needed.

Note

1. Harald Rehder, Department of Mollusks, U.S. National Museum, Smithsonian Institution. Unpublished report. It may be worth noting that most of the shells had been perforated or punctured, possibly to obtain the meat inside.

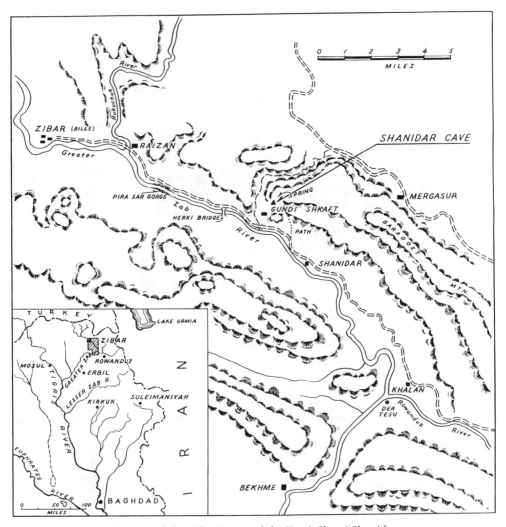

1. *Map showing the location of Shanidar Cave and the Zawi Chemi Shanidar village site*

122

2. Shanidar Cave: exterior view from the south

3. Shanidar Cave: rear view—location of the Proto-Neolithic cemetery

4. Shanidar Cave: overall view of the Proto-Neolithic cemetery looking to the northwest

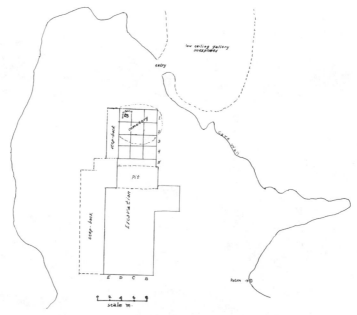

5. Plan of the excavations in Shanidar Cave and the location of the Proto-Neolithic cemetery

6. Shanidar Cave: looking north over the cemetery area, showing the contact between Layers A and B

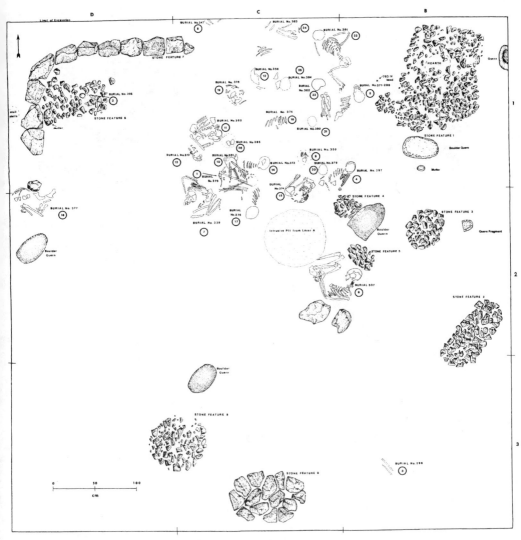

7. Plan of the Proto-Neolithic cemetery in Shanidar Cave

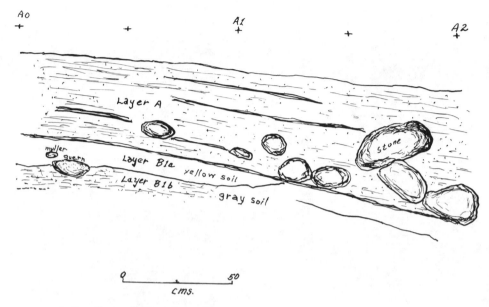

8. *East Face—Squares B1 and B2*

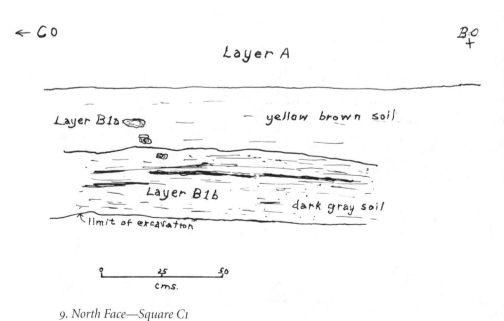

9. *North Face—Square C1*

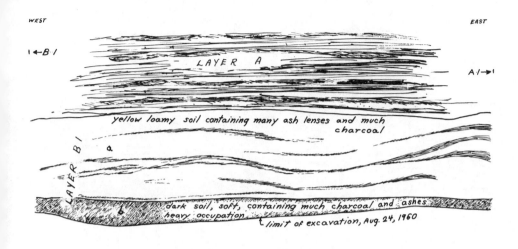

WEST   EAST

|←B·I

LAYER A

A I→|

yellow loamy soil containing many ash lenses and much charcoal

LAYER B I

a

dark soil, soft, containing much charcoal and ashes
heavy occupation

limit of excavation, Aug. 24, 1960

b

0   20   40
scale cms.

10. *North Face—Square B2*

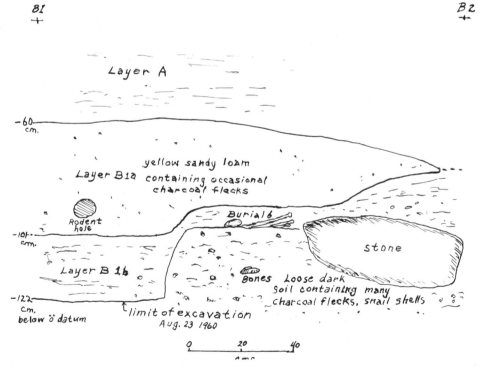

B1   B2
+   +

Layer A

-60 cm.

yellow sandy loam
Layer B1a containing occasional charcoal flecks

Rodent hole

Burial 6

-101 cm.

stone

Layer B 1b

Bones Loose dark soil containing many charcoal flecks, snail shells

-122 cm.
below ö datum

limit of excavation
Aug. 23 1960

0   20   40
cms.

11. *East Face—Square C2*

128

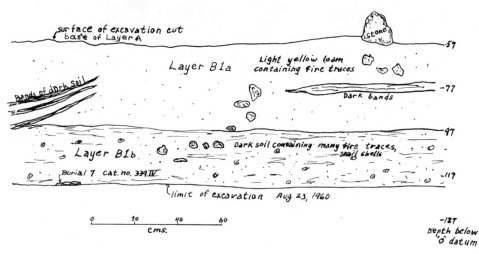

C1
+

B1
+

surface of excavation cut
base of Layer A

stone

-57

Layer B1a   Light yellow loam
containing fire traces

Bands of dark soil

Dark bands   -77

-97

Layer B1b   Dark soil containing many fire traces,
snail shells

Burial 7 Cat. no. 339 IV   -117

limit of excavation Aug. 23, 1960

0   20   40   60
cms.

-127
Depth below
"0" datum

12. North Face—Square C2

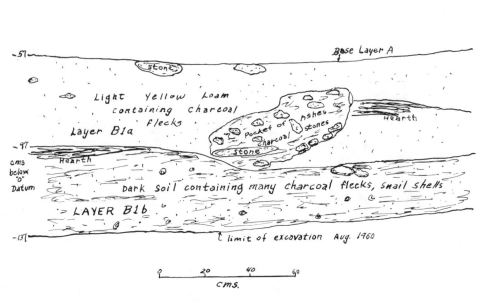

D1
+

C1
+

-57

Base Layer A

stone

Light   Yellow   Loam
containing   charcoal
flecks

Layer B1a

Hearth

Pocket of   ashes
charcoal   stones
stone

-97
cms
below
"0"
Datum

Hearth

Dark soil containing many charcoal flecks, snail shells

LAYER B1b

-137

limit of excavation Aug. 1960

0   20   40   60
cms.

13. North Face—Square D2

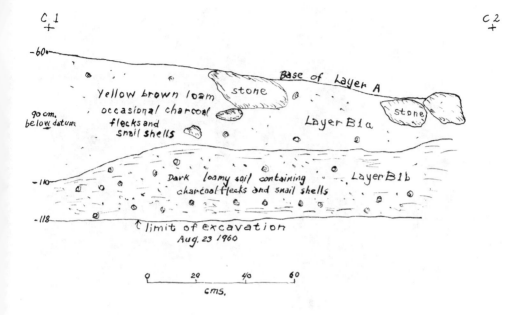

14. *East Face—Square D2*

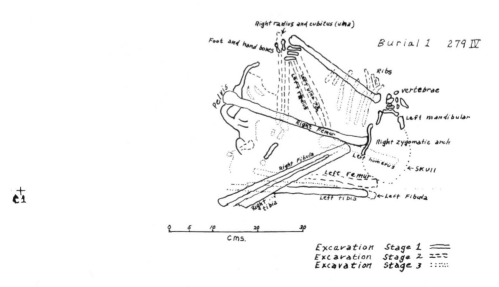

15. *Stages of excavation of Burial 1 (Cat. No. 279 IV)—Square C1*

16. Burial 1 (Cat. No. 279 IV)—Square C1

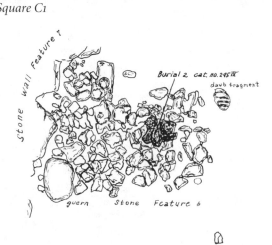

*17. Stone Features 6 (Cat. No. 353 IV)
and 7 (Cat. Nos. 292 IV and 294 IV)
and location of Burials 2 (Cat. No.
295 IV) and 18 (Cat. No. 377 IV)—
Squares D1 and D2*

18. Burial 2 (Cat. No. 295 IV) and Stone Feature 6 (Cat. No. 353 IV)— Square D1

19. Stone Feature 6 (Cat. No. 353 IV) and Burial 2 (Cat. No. 295 IV)—Square D1

132

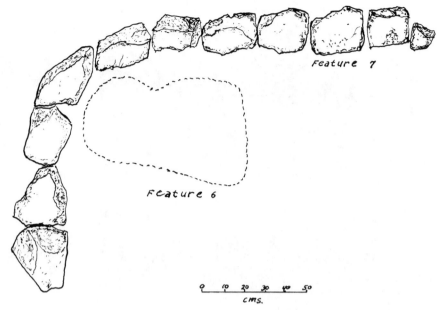

Feature 7

Feature 6

20. *Stone Features 6 (Cat. No. 353 IV) and 7 (Cat. Nos. 292 IV and 294 IV)—Square D1*

21. *Daub fragment, from wattle and daub construction, found between Stone Features 6 and 7 (Cat. No. 370 IV)*

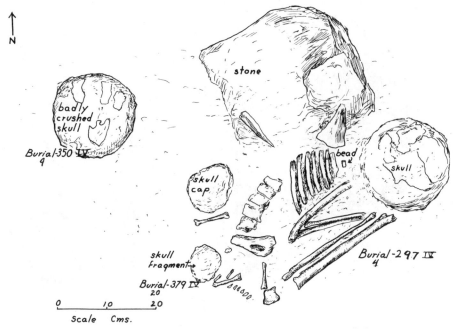

22. Burials 4 (Cat. No. 297 IV), 9 (Cat. No. 350 IV), and 20 (Cat. No. 379 IV)—
Squares B1 and C1

23. Burials 4 (Cat. No. 297 IV), 9 (Cat. No. 350 IV), and 20 (Cat. No. 379 IV)—
Squares B1 and C1

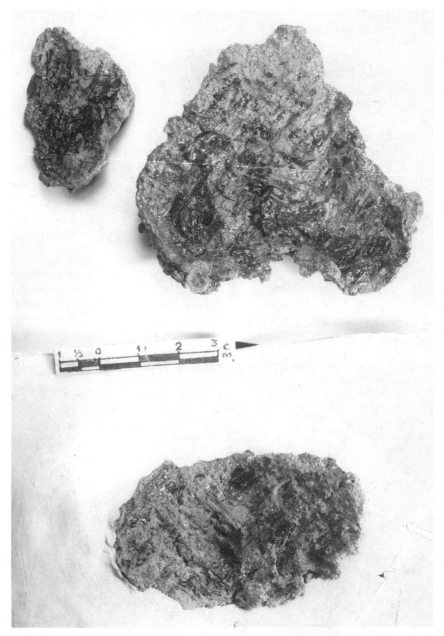

24. Fragments of carbonized matting found with Burial 4 (Cat. No. 297 IV)

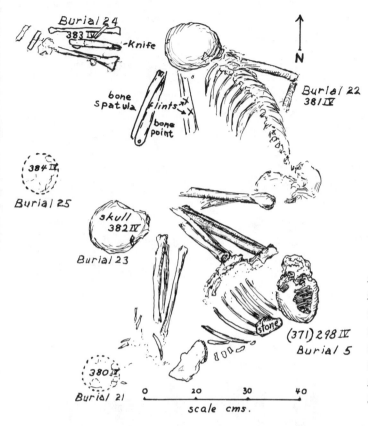

25. Burials 5 (Cat. Nos. 298 IV and 371 IV), 21 (Cat. No. 380 IV), 22 (Cat. No. 381 IV), 23 (Cat. No. 382 IV), 24 (Cat. No. 383 IV), and 25 (Cat. No. 384 IV)—Squares B1 and C1

26. Burials 5 (Cat. Nos. 298 IV and 371 IV) and 23 (Cat. No. 382 IV)—Squares B1 and C1

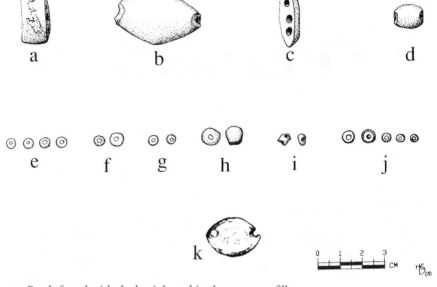

27. *Beads found with the burials and in the cemetery fill*

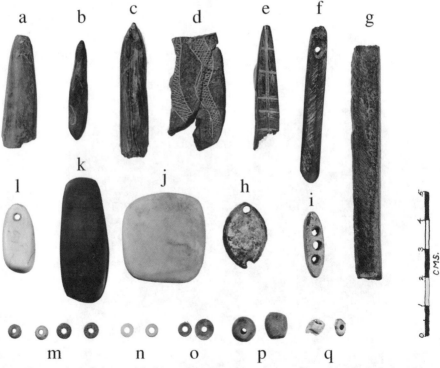

28. *Slate tools and decorated objects found in the cemetery fill and beads found with the burials*

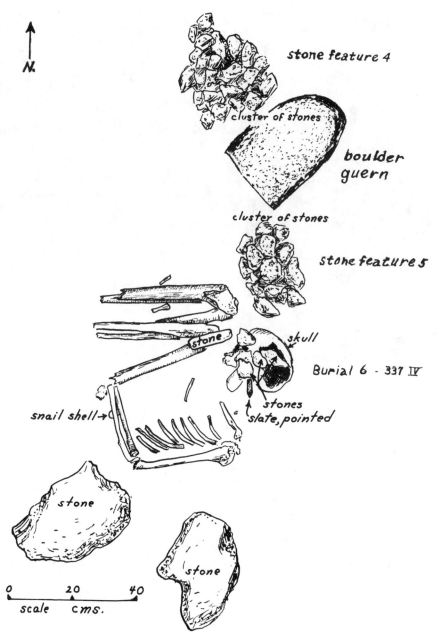

N.

stone feature 4

cluster of stones

boulder guern

cluster of stones

stone feature 5

stone

skull

Burial 6 - 337 IV

snail shell→

stones
slate, pointed

stone

stone

0   20   40
scale cms.

29. *Plan of Stone Features 4 (Cat. No. 323 IV) and 5 (Cat. No. 337 IV a) and Burial 6 (Cat. No. 337 IV)—Squares B2 and C2*

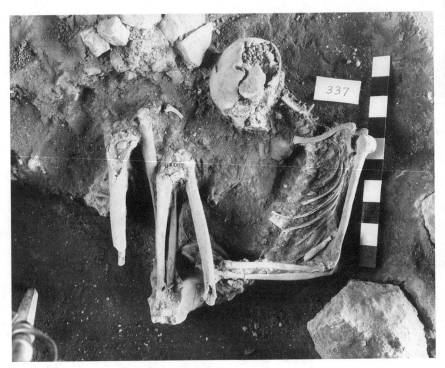

30. Burial 6 (Cat. No. 337 IV)—Squares B2 and C2

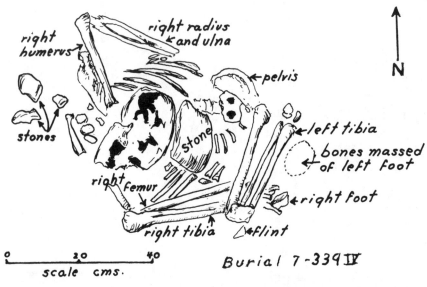

31. Burial 7 (Cat. No. 339 IV)—Squares C1 and C2

32. *Burial 7 (Cat. No. 339 IV)—Squares C1 and C2*

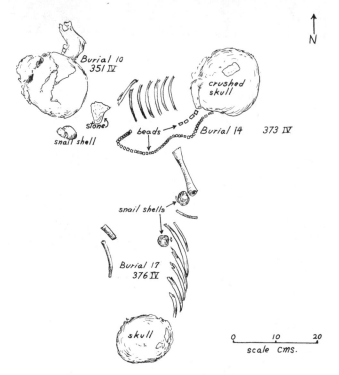

N

33. *Burials 10 (Cat. No. 351 IV), 14 (Cat. No. 373 IV), and 17 (Cat. No. 376 IV)— Square C1*

34. Burials 10 (Cat. No. 351 IV), 14 (Cat. No. 373 IV), and 17 (Cat. No. 376 IV)— Square C1

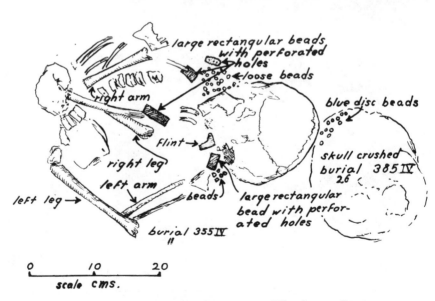

35. Burials 11 (Cat. No. 355 IV) and 26 (Cat. No. 385 IV)—Square C1

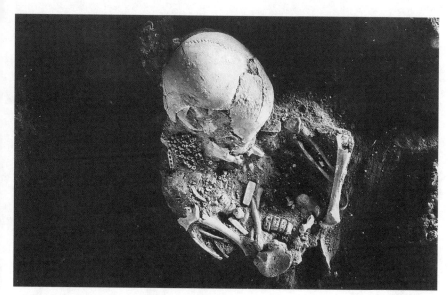

36. Burial 11 (Cat. No. 355 IV)—Square C1

37. Burials 13 (Cat. No. 372 IV), 11 (Cat. No. 355 IV), 10 (Cat. No. 351 IV), and 26 (Cat. No. 385 IV)—Square C1

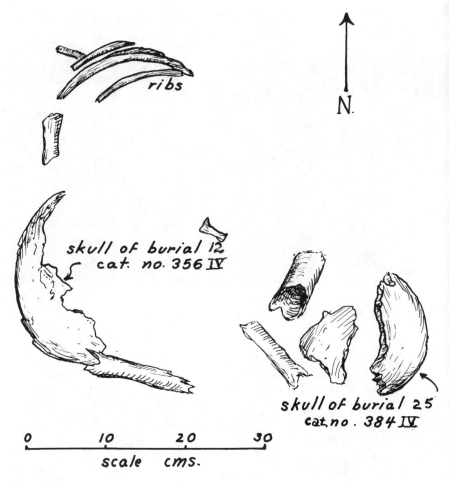

ribs

N.

skull of burial 12
cat. no. 356 IV

skull of burial 25
cat.no. 384 IV

0   10   20   30
scale   cms.

38. Burials 12 (Cat. No. 356 IV) and 25 (Cat. No. 384 IV)—Square C1

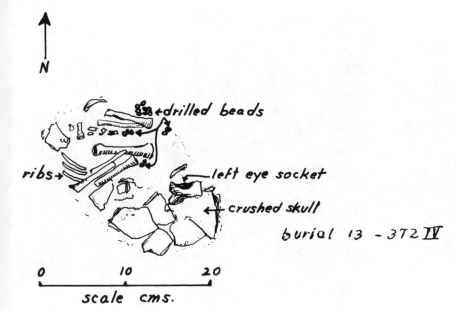

39. Burial 13 (Cat. No. 372 IV)—Square C1

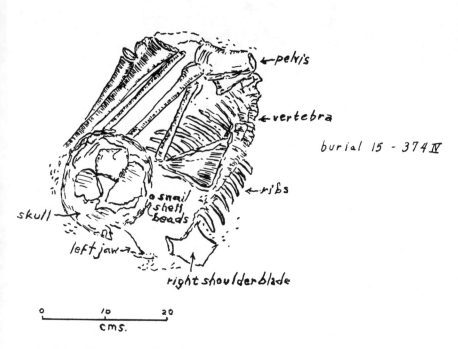

40. Burial 15 (Cat. No. 374 IV)—Squares C1 and C2

144

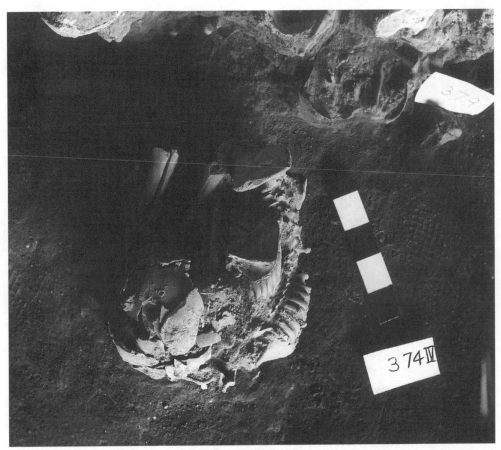

41. Burials 15 (Cat. No. 374 IV) and 20 (Cat. No. 379 IV)—Squares C1 and C2

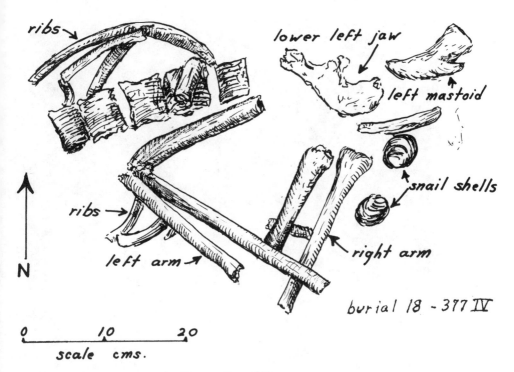

42. *Burial 18 (Cat. No. 377 IV)—Squares D1 and D2*

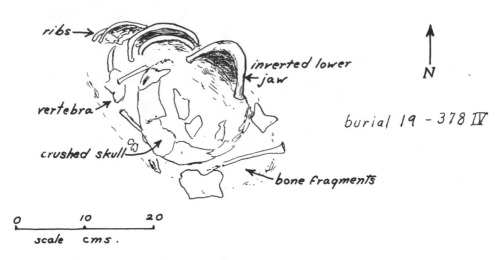

43. *Burial 19 (Cat. No. 378 IV)—Square C1*

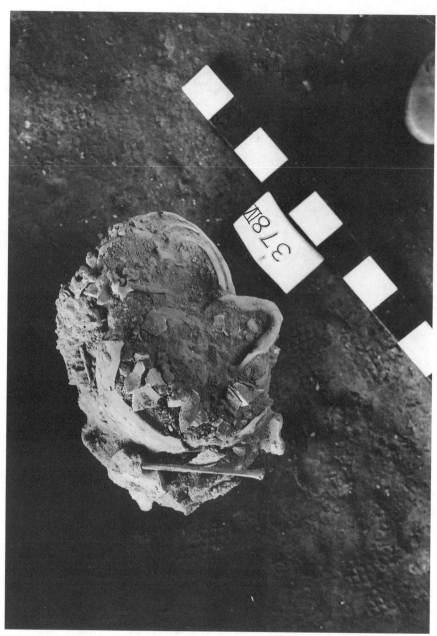

44. *Burial 19 (Cat. No. 378 IV)—Square C1*

45. Bone tools found with Burials 22 (Cat. No. 381 IV) and 24 (Cat. No. 383 IV)

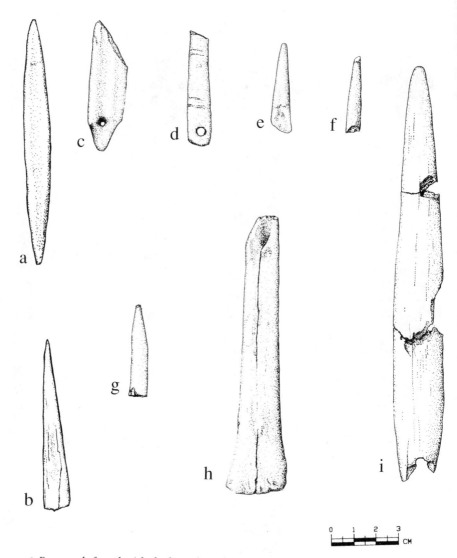

46. Bone tools found with the burials and in the cemetery fill

149

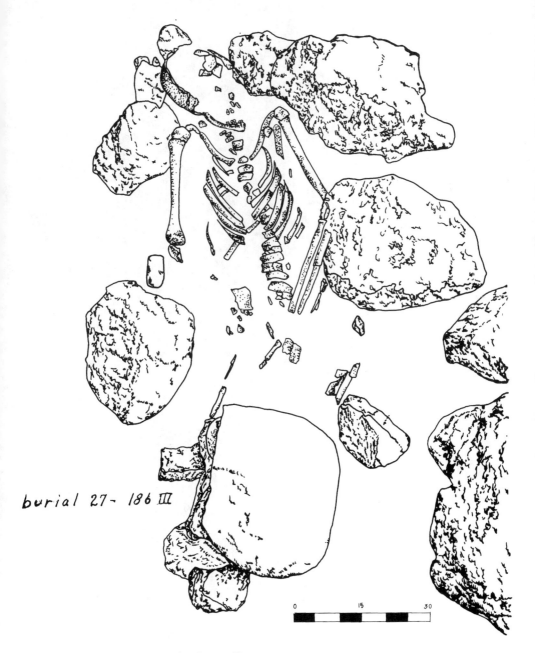

burial 27 - 186 Ⅲ

47. Burial 27 (Cat. No. 186 III)—Square D9

150

48. Burial 27 (Cat. No. 186 III)—Square D9

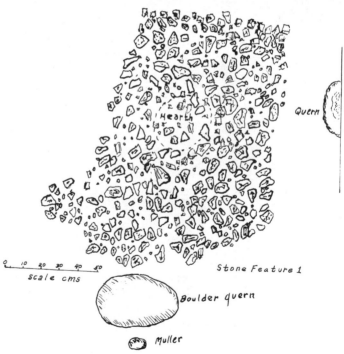

49. Stone Feature 1 (Cat. Nos. 283 IV and 293 IV)—Square B1

50. *Stone Feature 1 (Cat. Nos. 283 IV and 293 IV)—Square B1*

quern
fragment

stone feature 2 - 331 IVa

51. *Stone Feature 2 (Cat. No. 331 IV a)—Square B2*

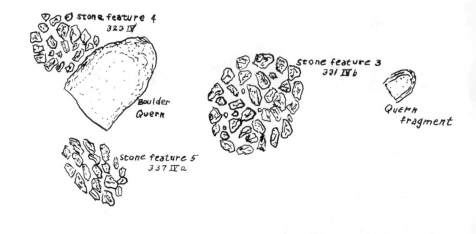

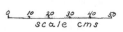

52. *Stone Features 2 (Cat. No. 331 IV a), 3 (Cat. No. 331 IV b), 4 (Cat. No. 323 IV), and 5 (Cat. No. 337 IV a)—Squares B2 and C2*

53. *Stone Feature 3 (Cat. No. 331 IV)—Square B2*

Boulder Quern

STone Feature 8

Stone Feature 9

54. *Stone Features 8 (Cat. Nos. 342 IV and 344 IV) and 9 (Cat. No. 324 IV)—Squares C3 and D3*

cat nos 342Ⅲ + 344Ⅳ
stone Feature 8

cat no 324Ⅳ
Stone Feature 9

55. Stone Features 8 (Cat. Nos.
342 IV and 344 IV) and 9
(Cat. No. 324 IV)—Square C3

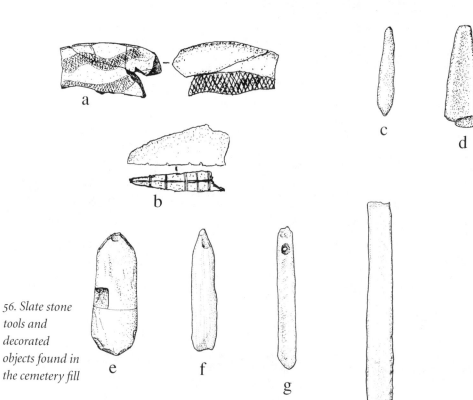

56. Slate stone
tools and
decorated
objects found in
the cemetery fill

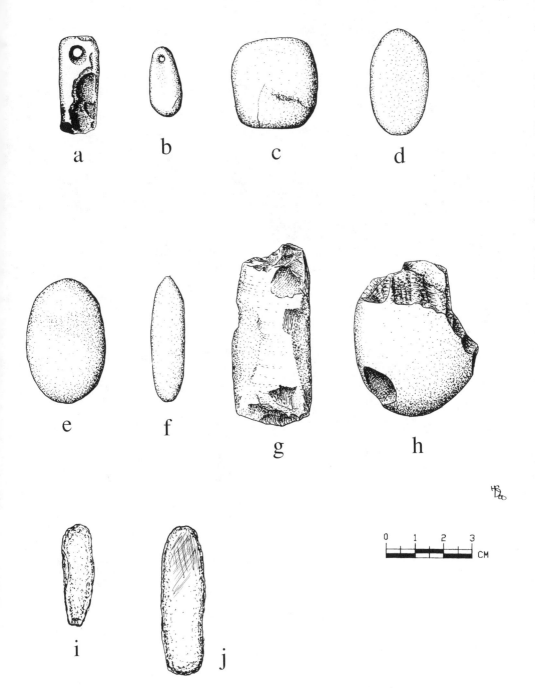

57. *Small stone pendants, shaped pebbles, chisels, and rubbers found in the cemetery fill*

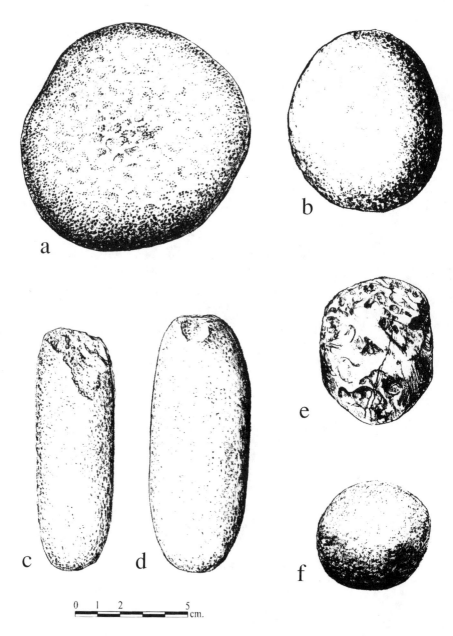

58. *Large pecked and ground stone tools found in the cemetery fill*

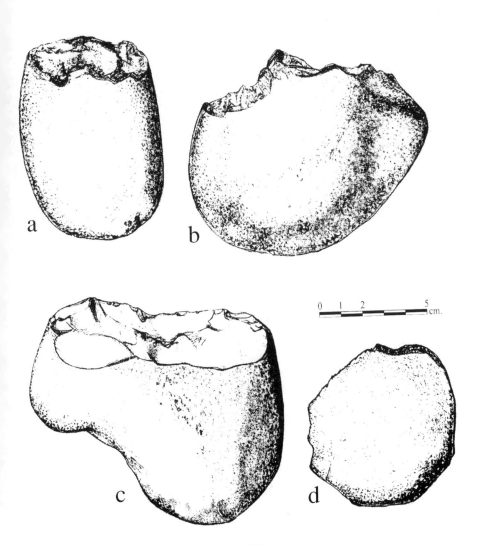

a

b

c

d

0 1 2   5
                cm.

59. *Flaked stone tools found in the cemetery fill*

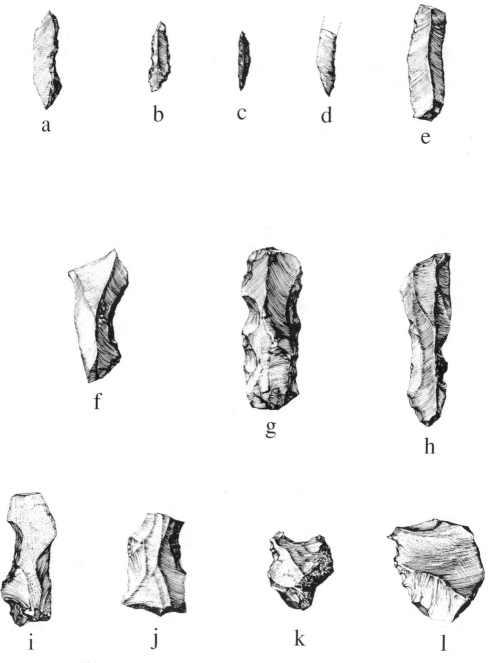

a b c d e

f

g

h

i j k l

60. Chipped stone tools from the area around Stone Feature 8 (Cat. No. 344 IV)—Squares C3 and D3

CHAPTER 9

The Shanidar Cave Proto-Neolithic Human Condition as Reflected through Osteology and Palaeopathology

ANAGNOSTIS P. AGELARAKIS

From the initiation of my archaeological career in 1975, I was involved in archaeological projects in the Old World, mostly in my homeland of Greece. Over time, I developed a specific interest and specialization in issues of human skeletal biology, palaeopathology, and palaeoenvironments, and it became my goal to provide much-needed insight on a multitude of bio-cultural aspects of the human condition in ancient Greece. As a Ph.D. candidate at Columbia University in 1985, I was prepared to continue my research on human skeletal remains recovered from Greece that spanned the Hellenic, Roman, and Byzantine time periods (Agelarakis 1983a, 1983b, 1984a, 1984b, 1986, 1986–87). At the same time, I hoped to be involved in research projects that would further enhance my understanding of the nature and ecology of disease distribution and conditions of stress among ancient human populations. Having Ralph S. Solecki as my academic advisor helped change the original plan for the subject of my doctoral dissertation; he suggested that I study the collection of Proto-Neolithic human skeletal remains (circa the eleventh millennium B.P.) that he had discovered at the cave of Shanidar in Iraq.

During the months of May and June 1985, my wife, Argyro, assisted me in Baghdad in the Iraq Antiquities Museum with the examination of the Proto-Neolithic Shanidar human skeletal collection, excavated by Ralph S. Solecki in the Zawi Chemi layer in Shanidar Cave (Layer B1), then some thirty-six years ago. The purpose of our study was initially to clarify the obvious discrepancies created by the observations of two scientists who had previously worked with this collection.[1] In fact, before our study materialized, an unknown number of interested people had evidently also examined the collection. An additional objective was to elicit information from the skeletal remains concerning dental and general palaeopathology, as well as traits of nonmetric epigenetic variation, which we felt were either absent or had not been adequately studied by the previous researchers. What follows is a summary of the study of the collection, with an emphasis on the palaeopathological features evident in this Shanidar population. For more detailed descriptions of skeletal morphological characteristics, epigenetic variation, and metric information concerning all individuals with the exception of "field catalog number 296," (or Cat. No. 296) see Agelarakis 1989. Catalog number 296 IV was included in this inventory at a later date.[2]

Background and Objectives

The Shanidar Proto-Neolithic human skeletal collection had been previously examined by two researchers, the late Juan Munizaga in 1962 and the late Denise Ferembach in 1969. Although Ralph S. Solecki, on incomplete data, reported twenty-nine exhumed skeletons (R. S. Solecki 1961), Dr. Munizaga (then assistant to T. Dale Stewart at the Smithsonian Institution) reported in 1962 a laboratory count of thirty-one individuals (report in manuscript), whereas Dr. Ferembach, of the French Centre Nationale Recherche Scientifique, was able to document only twenty-two individuals (Ferembach 1970). Given the incompatible numbers of individuals reported by the previous scholars, and considering that the Proto-Neolithic skeletal collection had not been thoroughly examined for palaeopathological manifestations and other indicators of stress, I was encouraged to undertake this investigation as the main subject of my doctoral thesis. Of course, this task required coordination between the reports of the aforementioned three researchers, as well as travel to Baghdad, Iraq, where the collection was stored.

Once in Baghdad, aided by all available information relative to the skeletal collection (Solecki's field notes, plan photographs of the skeletons in situ, and plan maps of the cave floor, as well as Munizaga's manuscript and Ferembach's publication and drawings), a sincere effort was carried out by the personnel at the Baghdad Antiquities Museum to locate the entire Proto-Neolithic skeletal collection (as it had been reported by the excavator, Ralph S. Solecki, and documented by Munizaga in his 1962 study in Baghdad, but apparently with components missing[?] prior to Ferembach's 1969 study). After several days of intense research endeavors by the museum personnel within their surface and subsurface repository areas, I was kindly invited to participate in helping to locate specific components of the human skeletal collection in question, which were considered misplaced or lost. Following zealous guided efforts, most of those missing components were located inside three of the original "tin containers," which were identified thanks to their contextual designations and the short content descriptions written on pasted paper tags in Ralph S. Solecki's handwriting. In those tin containers, the bones were still placed on cotton and straw packing, as they had been prepared for their postexcavation transportation from Shanidar Cave to the Iraq Museum.[3]

The stratigraphic and contextual integrity of the Proto-Neolithic human burials at Shanidar Cave, combined with the extreme scarcity of other contemporaneous skeletal collections from this geographic region, emphasizes the importance of this collection within the world's archaeo-anthropological prehistoric record (Agelarakis 1987–88, 1989, 1993a, 2002) at the chronological juncture of sedentism and incipient domestication. The Proto-Neolithic people of Shanidar stemmed from this transitional period, which served as a basis of transformation for the human condition, given the realization of profoundly diverse selective pressures and stress conditions—compared to hunting and gathering—as well as the subsequent distinct bio-cultural adaptations for *Homo sapiens*—that is, the initial "point of no return" to earlier cultural traditions. Emerging from such pivotal prehistoric circumstances, the Shanidar burials offer singular opportunities for the investigation of a multitude of aspects of such primal bio-cultural adaptations.

While this ancient population had been the object of extensive archaeological investigations concerning the processes of domestication and sedentism, it had received little attention relative to physical health, pathologies, and living conditions (Rathburn 1984). The results of my proposed research were expected to provide a better interpretation and understanding of this segment of the archaeological record. Furthermore, it was anticipated that the results of this work would allow for a better understanding of the processes that underlie human disease patterns and their distribution in that temporal juncture and geographic area.

Human skeletons from past populations provide the most pervasive sources of information about ancient diseases. For this reason, as much documentation and illustration of dry bone pathology must be undertaken as possible, especially since organic materials are fragile and may permanently disappear within a short time. In light of this assertion, I undertook this project in order to elucidate, at least in part, aspects of the following issues:

a. the demographic profile of the population sample involved;
b. features and characteristics of their skeletal morphology;
c. the manifestations of palaeopathological conditions and of stress (including trauma) that affected the Shanidar Proto-Neolithic population;
d. the interrelationships between the environment, subsistence patterns, and cultural adaptations;
e. the prospect of detecting, in conjunction with the rest of the archaeological record, the possibility that bio-cultural mechanisms that would normally buffer a population from the shift to new subsistence conditions had not yet adapted to the increased dependence on botanical resources at the Shanidar Proto-Neolithic.

To answer these questions I studied axial and appendicular morphology and biology, skeletal indicators of stress (including trauma), palaeo-pathological manifestations, and traits of nonmetric variation.[4] Additionally, I have augmented my research through bone isotopic and cell biological analyses that were conducted upon my return to the United States.

Skeletal Sample

Based on the fact that only a small segment (112 square meters out of the estimated 70,000 square meters) of the Proto-Neolithic village site (Zawi Chemi Shanidar) had been excavated (R. L. Solecki 1981), definite answers relative to the functional interpretation and nature of the site could not be stated at the time that I embarked on this project. Preliminary results of the archaeological record, including the cultural artifactual remains and the palaeo-environmental indicators, as well as comparative observations with contemporary settlement patterns of the local Kurdish population, could imply that the site had not functioned as a permanent village (R. L. Solecki 1981, 69). Hence, it could be suggested that the inhabitants of the site were either moving elsewhere or seeking winter shelter in the protected environment of Shanidar Cave and possibly other shelters available at the peripheries of Shanidar Valley.

In light of the above discussion, as well as the fact that the complete Proto-Neolithic cemetery at Shanidar Cave could not be excavated, it is suggested that the present human skeletal collection probably does not represent the total number of individuals to have been interred in the area during this period. Furthermore, taphonomic conditions within the rather stable speleologic environment, combined with careful excavation techniques (the skeletonized remains were exhumed by Ralph S. Solecki with the assistance of the late Dexter Perkins), provided for the good state of preservation of the human remains.

Through my analyses (Agelarakis 1989, 1993a), I was able to identify thirty-one individuals in this collection (see table 6). The majority of these individuals are, anatomically speaking, incomplete (fig. 61), given the gamut of contributing factors such as burial customs and practices, taphonomic circumstances, and postexcavation handling by a number of unknown specialists(?) who seemingly went through the collection once it arrived in Baghdad. Nevertheless, skeletal individuals represented either by cranial, dental, or postcranial remains revealed adequately preserved surfaces and osseous components for anthropological and palaeo-pathological studies, including archaeometric analyses. Considering the

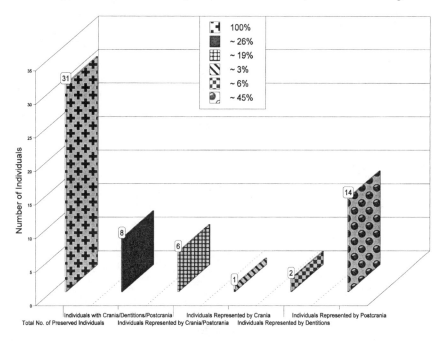

61. Skeletal preservation and representation of Proto-Neolithic individuals by cranial, dental, and postcranial remains

TABLE 6. SHANIDAR CAVE PROTO-NEOLITHIC HUMAN SKELETAL COLLECTION: DEMOGRAPHIC TABLE

Id. No.	Cat. No.	Homo Designation	Sex Assessment	Age Assessment
1	279	279 A	Indeterminate	14 to 17 years
2	295	295 A	Female	16 to 17 years
3	296	296 A	Female	>21 to <25 years
4	337	337 A	Male	30 to 35 years
5		337 B	Indeterminate	6 postnatal months (within Infancy I)
6	371	371-298 A	Female	Ca. 25 years
7		371-HBL A	Indeterminate	Infancy I
8		371-HBL B	Indeterminate	Adult
9		371-LM-379 A	Indeterminate	Adult
10		371-LMNB A	Indeterminate	Subadult/Adult
11	374	374 A	Indeterminate	Late Infancy II/early Juvenilis
12	381	381 A	Male	Ca. 20 years
13		381 B	Male	Adult
14		381 C	Indeterminate	Juvenilis/Adult
15		381 D	Indeterminate	Perinatal to 6 postnatal months
16		381 E	Indeterminate	Perinatal to 6 postnatal months
17		381-M A	Female(?)	Adult (younger than 381-M: B)
18		381-M B	Male(?)	Adult (older than 381-M: A)
19		381-M C	Indeterminate	Adult
20		381-T A	Indeterminate	Subadult to early Young Adult
21	382	382 A	Male	Ca. 25 years
22		382 B	Indeterminate	Perinatal
23	383	383 A	Male	>21 to <27 years
24		383 B	Indeterminate	9 to 12 postnatal months
25		383 C	Indeterminate	Up to 6 postnatal months
26		383 D	Indeterminate	Older than Middle/Late Adult
27	384	384 A	Female	40 to 45 yeas
28		384 B	Indeterminate	Perinatal
29	356-384	356-384 A	Indeterminate	Ca. 35 years
30		356-384 B	Indeterminate	Infancy I (younger than 356-384: C)
31		356-384 C	Indeterminate	Infancy I (older than 356-384: B)

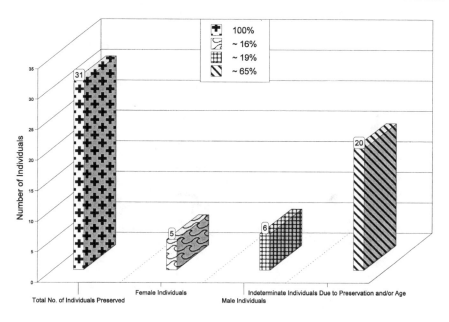

62. Aspects of demography: biological sex assessments

prospect for contributions through the study of the anthropological record, it was fortuitous that this rare collection consisted of individuals from both biological sexes (fig. 62) and a range of age groups, from Perinatal to Maturus, as presented in figure 63.

It is somewhat more beneficial to view the individuals in terms of lumped age groups as seen in figure 64 and table 7. In so doing, seven individuals were identified within the first year of life (22 percent); three individuals within Infancy I (up to six years of age) (10 percent); one individual between late Infancy II and early Juvenile (between ten and thirteen/fourteen years) (3 percent); five Juveniles (16 percent); fourteen Adults (44 percent); and one Maturus (3 percent). Adult individuals (~eighteen to forty-five years of age) constituted 44 percent of the collection, indicating the highest representation of a lumped age group and the highest prevalence of mortality in the demographics of the skeletal collection. High prevalence of mortality, with decreasing values, was also observed with the Perinatal to Infancy I age groups, which, when lumped together, constituted 32 percent of the skeletal collection. The lowest ratios observed were found within the late Infancy II to early Juvenile and Maturus age groups, respectively. It is suggested that while the low prevalence of mortality in the Infancy II to Juvenile age group might indicate a high

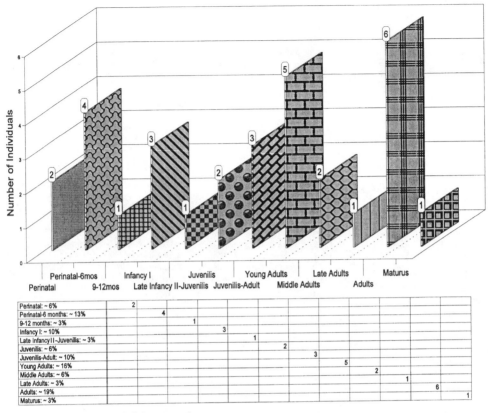

Perinatal: ~ 6%	2										
Perinatal-6 months: ~ 13%		4									
9-12 months: ~ 3%			1								
Infancy I: ~ 10%				3							
Late Infancy II–Juvenilis: ~ 3%					1						
Juvenilis: ~ 6%						2					
Juvenilis-Adult: ~ 10%							3				
Young Adults: ~ 16%								5			
Middle Adults: ~ 6%									2		
Late Adults: ~ 3%										1	
Adults: ~ 19%											6
Maturus: ~ 3%											1

63. *Aspects of demography: age assessments*

survival rate at that age juncture, as far as the Maturus age group is concerned, it reflects insignificant expectations for prolonged livelihood past Late Adulthood and Maturus years for this Proto-Neolithic population.

Overview of Morphology and Palaeopathology

Crania were lightly built, showing features and morphocharacteristics that resemble more modern aspects (fig. 65) than do those of the roughly coeval Natufian populations (Ferembach 1970) and the Mesolithic skeletal populations from Nubia, dating between the fourteenth and nineteenth millennia B.P. (Armelagos, Huss-Ashmore, and Martin 1980; Armelagos, personal communication). Furthermore, morphological features indicative of cranial artificial deformation have been documented in the cases of two relatively well-preserved crania, of a juvenile and an adult

TABLE 7. SHANIDAR CAVE PROTO-NEOLITHIC HUMAN SKELETAL
COLLECTION: AGE SUBGROUPS

Age Subgroup Category	Age in Months or Years
Perinatal	Around birth
Infancy I	Birth to 6 years
Infancy II	>6 to 12 years
Juvenilis	>12 to 16–17 years
Young Adult	18 to 25 years
Middle Adult	>25 to 35 years
Late Adult	>35 to 45 years
Maturus	>45 to 55 years

(Agelarakis 1989, 1993a; Meiklejohn et al. 1992). Examinations of the morphological characteristics of the Shanidar skeletal remains (Stewart 1979;
Krogman and Iscan 1986; Bordens and Abbott 1991) revealed well-built
skeletal bodies. Sexual dimorphism was apparent, with males manifest-
ing increased attributes of robustness and emphasized muscular imprints,

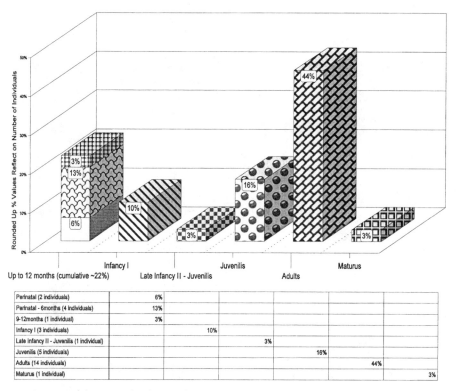

	Infancy I		Juvenilis		Maturus	
Up to 12 months (cumulative ~22%)		Late Infancy II - Juvenilis		Adults		
Perinatal (2 individuals)	6%					
Perinatal - 6months (4 individuals)	13%					
9-12months (1 individual)	3%					
Infancy I (3 individuals)		10%				
Late Infancy II - Juvenilis (1 individual)			3%			
Juvenilis (5 individuals)				16%		
Adults (14 individuals)					44%	
Maturus (1 individual)						3%

64. Aspects of demography: lumped age subgroups

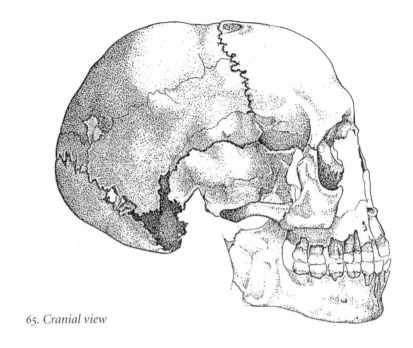

65. Cranial view

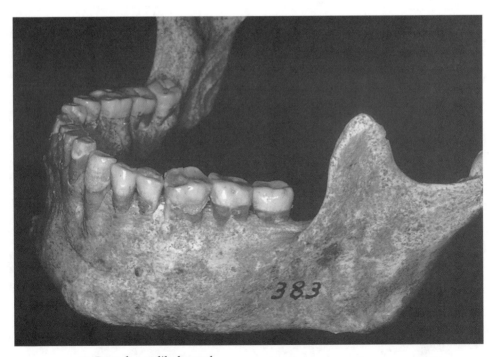

66. Dental mandibular arch

specifically in their lower extremities (Berry and Berry 1967; Levi 1972; Finnegan 1978; Huss-Ashmore 1982; Currey 1984; Currey and Alexander 1985).

Dental arches (fig. 66) were well-built, revealing tooth rows with minimal if any apparent dental crowding. Dental sizes averaged greater than the sizes of dentitions of contemporary populations. The majority of the dental surfaces revealed traits of metric and nonmetric morphological variations (Moorees 1957; Dahlberg 1963; Greene 1967; Scott and Turner 1988), with the exception of surfaces altered due to wear patterns. In examining the dental palaeopathological conditions, all preserved dental surfaces, originating from a wide range of age groups, were affected by hypoplastic enameloblastic defects (fig. 67) in the form of pitting, an observation ratio of 100 percent. Linear enamel hypoplasias affected 60 percent of individuals preserving teeth, predominantly marking the early and late childhood rings of the dental crowns, between two and four years of age. Further, all three individuals with preserved deciduous teeth revealed enameloblastic hypoplasias (fig. 68). These enameloblastic defects indicate that the affected individuals had experienced conditions of early life stress with disruptions of growth and development, caused by systemic/constitutional disturbances (Sarnat and Schour 1941; Swardstedt 1966; Grahnen 1967, 1969; Goodman and Armelagos 1984; Goodman, Armelagos, and Rose 1980; Goodman et al. 1984; Goodman and Rose 1990, 1991; Nikiforok 1981; Pindborg 1982; Rose, Armelagos, and Lallo 1978; Rose, Condon, and Goodman 1985).

Enamel microdefects (fig. 69), in the form of flaked-off enamel at the marginal rings of both incisal and occlusal surfaces, affecting all individuals with preserved teeth past the Juvenile age group (indiscriminate of sex), were classified as acquired microtraumatic conditions. These were produced by functional modification during the processes of mastication, a result of the dietary patterns and the quality of preparation of foods consumed, coupled by a suspected implication of teeth as third hands in various cultural activities. Dental wear patterns (Klatsky 1939; Brothwell 1963; Sognaes 1963; Pindborg 1970; Molnar 1971; Tomenchuck and Mayhall 1979; Lovejoy 1985) (fig. 70) indicated gradual degeneration of enamel and dentin materials conducive to age. Considering the discriminatory factor of aging, occlusal surfaces revealed wear patterns varying from unilinear horizontal conditions with obliteration of the cusp tips, showing patches of tertiary dentin, to uneven oblique planes with severe and concave occlusal surfaces. However, rarely was there exposure of the pulp cavities, exclusively due to wear.

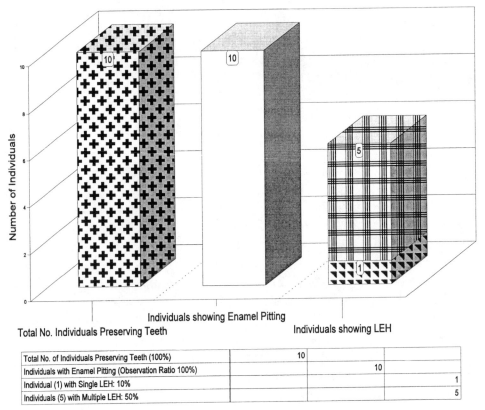

	Total No. Individuals Preserving Teeth	Individuals showing Enamel Pitting	Individuals showing LEH
Total No. of Individuals Preserving Teeth (100%)	10		
Individuals with Enamel Pitting (Observation Ratio 100%)		10	
Individual (1) with Single LEH: 10%			1
Individuals (5) with Multiple LEH: 50%			5

67. Dental enamel hypoplastic defects, pitting, and linear enamel hypoplasias (LEH)

Interproximal cervical carious lesions (Darling 1970; Mandel 1979) affected the posterior teeth of all individuals, again indiscriminately of sex, preserving teeth past the twenty-fifth year of age (fig. 71). These lesions were produced through processes of prolonged infectious lytic activities resulting in large cavities that contributed to the loss of dental material and subsequently undermined the structural integrity of occlusal surfaces. Enlarged carious cavities of dental crown surfaces were usually involved (fig. 72) in secondary infectious and inflammatory conditions, as revealed by the associated infra-bony pockets and abscesses. Local irritation caused by these infectious conditions was coupled with the advanced presence of periodontal disease (Masters and Hoskins 1964), which affected 80 percent of the individuals preserving jaws and teeth (see fig. 69), including all younger individuals, with the exception of infants.

Palaeopathological conditions observed on cranial bones (fig. 73) revealed periosteal reactive layers due to infectious and inflammatory responses at

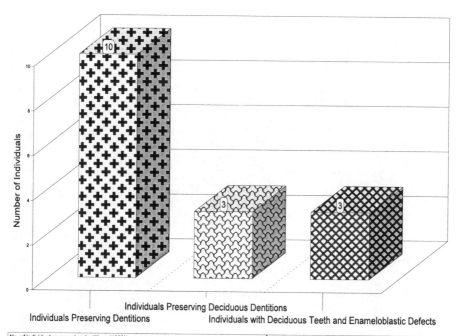

No. of individuals preserving dentitions (100%)	10		
Individuals preserving deciduous teeth (30%)		3	
Individuals with deciduous teeth and enameloblastic defects (Observation Ratio 100%)			3

68. *Dental enamel hypoplastic defects: individuals with deciduous dentitions*

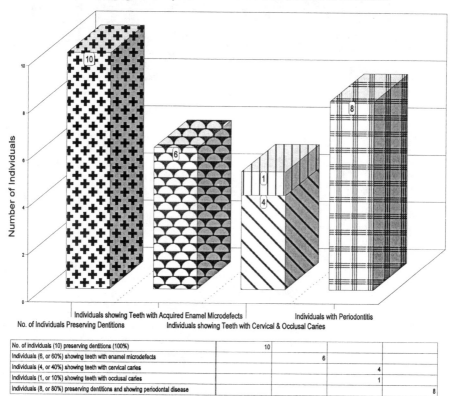

No. of Individuals (10) preserving dentitions (100%)	10		
Individuals (6, or 60%) showing teeth with enamel microdefects		6	
Individuals (4, or 40%) showing teeth with cervical caries			4
Individuals (1, or 10%) showing teeth with occlusal caries			1
Individuals (8, or 80%) preserving dentitions and showing periodontal disease			8

69. *Dental acquired enamel defects, cariogenic lesions, and periodontitis*

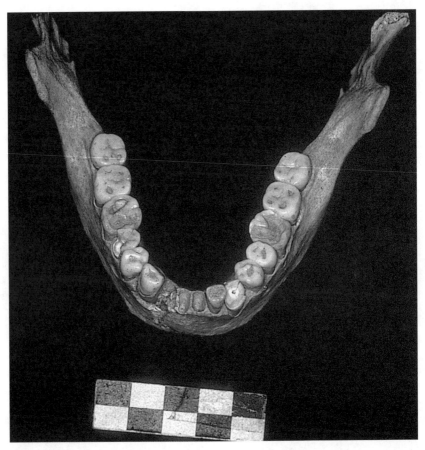

70. Dental mandibular surfaces and wear

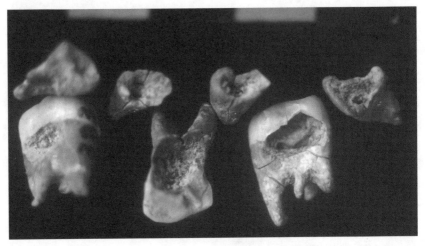

71. Inter-proximal carious lesions and wear; teeth ex situ

both ecto- and endocranial tables, affecting both females and males with a prevalence of 33 percent, coupled with a 33 percent prevalence rate of similar osseous responses just on ectocranial surfaces. Further, hyperplastic and hyperostotic osseous conditions associated with the regions of the external ear canals affected a Juvenile and a Maturus female, as well as two Adult males. These conditions were coupled with ear osteomata (fig. 74). In two of the individuals involved, one of the Adult males and the Maturus female, it is suspected that the osteomata affected their auditory capabilities in some capacity. Although the pathological causative agents for the infectious and inflammatory conditions associated with the ear canals may have varied, ranging from purulent otitis media to tuberculous otitis media (Wood-Jones 1910; Wilensky 1932, 1934), an endemic form of acquired conditions is also entertained. It is possible that the ear hyperplasias and distinct osteomata might have been organismal responses subsequent to lengthy exposures to cold stress induced by extraneous factors, that is, cold stress (Harrison 1951, 1962; Sheely 1958; DiBartolomeo 1979; Graham 1979; Filipo, Fabiani, and Barbara 1982; Kennedy 1986) from the abiotic environmental context (Agelarakis 1989, 1993a, Agelarakis and Serpanos 2002).

Relative to the sample size of this collection, there was a considerable prevalence of traumatic manifestations (Courville 1967; Hassan 1981; Trinkaus and Zimmerman 1982) that had marked primarily the crania (Stewart 1958b; Margetts 1967; Steinbock 1976) (fig. 75), followed by vertebrae and trailed by sacra (fig. 76). However, evidence of trauma was nearly systematically lacking from appendicular skeletal remains (fig. 77). These patterns were observed among a cluster of individuals, indiscriminate of sex, including one Juvenile individual and several adults, revealing a 50 percent rate of prevalence among the individuals who were represented by such osseous structures (after the exclusion of Perinatal and Infancy age groups). Multiple traumatic conditions observed on the cranial vault bones of the Juvenile, two Adult males, and one Adult female were classified as depressed fractures (fig. 78) that did not penetrate the endocranial tables. They were either well healed, indicating that the individuals had survived the injuries, or revealed active remodeling processes through the presence of periosteal reactive bone (Courville 1967; Brothwell and Sandinson 1967; Merbs 1989; Lovell 1997). The morphology of the cranial traumatic conditions, resembling ovate and/or ellipsoid depressions, combined with their exclusive anterior-superior location on the cranial vaults, may possibly represent the result of instances of malicious

TABLE 8. SHANIDAR CAVE PROTO-NEOLITHIC HUMAN SKELETAL COLLECTION: STABLE ISOTOPE RATIO ANALYSES

Geochron Lab. No.	Id. No.	Cat. No.[a]	Homo Designation	Sex Assessment	Age Assessment	13 C Apatite	13 C Gelatin	15 N Gelatin
CCNR-49423	1	279	297 A	Indeterminate	14 to 17 years	−12.1	−22.5	—
CCNR-49424	2	295	295 A	Female	16 to 17 years	−9.6	−23.4	—
CCNR-49425	4	337	337 A	Male	30 to 35 years	−11.5	−19.1	+5.4
CCNR-49426	6	371-298	371-298 A	Female	Ca. 25 years	−8.6	−19.6	+4.7
CCNR-49427	12	381	381 A	Male	Ca. 20 years	−13.0	−19.4	+5.3
CCNR-49428	21	382	382 A	Male	Ca. 25 years	−11.6	−19.5	+5.4
CCNR-49429	23	383	383 A	Male	>21 to <27 years	−12.5	−19.0	+6.0
CCNR-49430	27	384	384 A	Female	40 to 50 years	−13.7	−19.0	+16.3

[a] See table 6, page 164.

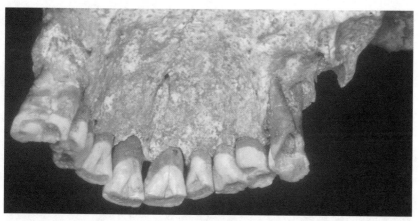

72. Maxillary Infectious-inflammatory dental conditions and periodontitis

intent, as observed with injuries caused by digging sticks, mullers, and axes used for fighting.

All individuals who exhibited traumatic conditions on their cranial vault bones, with the exception of the Juvenile individual (because of the limiting factor of preservation), also exhibited postcranial axial traumatic

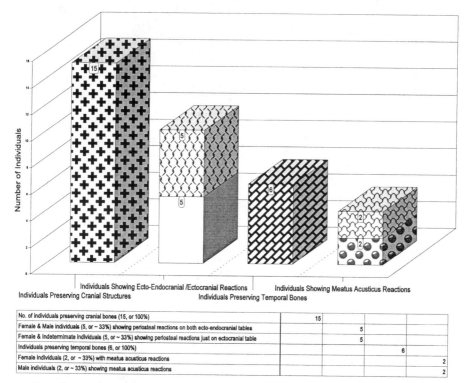

	Individuals Preserving Cranial Structures	Individuals Showing Ecto-Endocranial /Ectocranial Reactions	Individuals Preserving Temporal Bones	Individuals Showing Meatus Acusticus Reactions
No. of individuals preserving cranial bones (15, or 100%)	15			
Female & Male individuals (5, or ~ 33%) showing periosteal reactions on both ecto-endocranial tables		5		
Female & Indeterminate individuals (5, or ~ 33%) showing periosteal reactions just on ectocranial table		5		
Individuals preserving temporal bones (6, or 100%)			6	
Female individuals (2, or ~ 33%) with meatus acusticus reactions				2
Male individuals (2, or ~ 33%) showing meatus acusticus reactions				2

73. Prevalence of cranial periosteal reactions

74. Auditory osteoma

conditions that affected their vertebral columns in the form of multiple disk herniations (fig. 79), coined as Schmörl's nodes (Schmörl and Junghanns 1971). In addition, there were three cases of Adult males exhibiting cleft cervical vertebrae (fig. 80) and subsequently idiopathic scolioses of the lower spine. Such a discriminatory distribution of axial skeletal manifestations suggests the participation of these individuals in strenuous physical activities, especially in the lifting of heavy loads on their heads and shoulders (see fig. 76). The fact that nearly 50 percent of

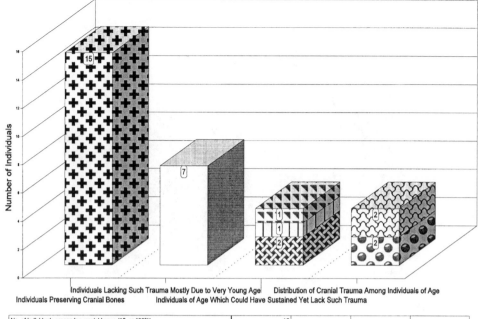

No. of individuals preserving cranial bones (15, or 100%)	15		
Individuals (7 out of 15, or ~ 47%) which could be excluded from the total sample		7	
Female individuals (2 out of 8, or 25%) lacking such trauma			2
Male individual (1 out of 8, or ~ 12%) lacking such trauma			1
Individual of indeterminate sex (1 out of 8, or ~ 12%) lacking such trauma			1
Female individuals (2 out of 8, or 25%) showing such trauma				2
Male individuals (2 out of 8, or 25%) showing such trauma				2

75. Prevalence of cranial trauma

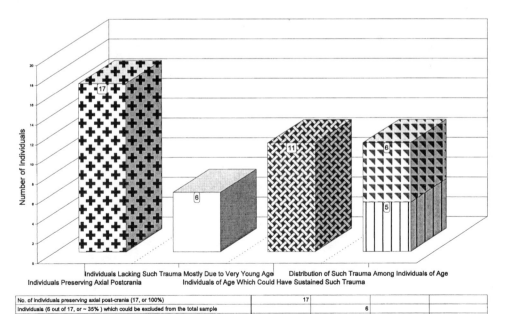

No. of individuals preserving axial post-crania (17, or 100%)	17		
Individuals (6 out of 17, or ~ 35%) which could be excluded from the total sample		6	
Individuals (11 out of 17, or ~65%) which could sustain such trauma			11
Female/Male individuals (5 out of 11, or ~ 45%) lacking such trauma				5
Female/Male individuals (6 out of 11, or ~ 55%) showing such traumatic manifestations				6

76. Prevalence of trauma affecting axial infra-cranial structures

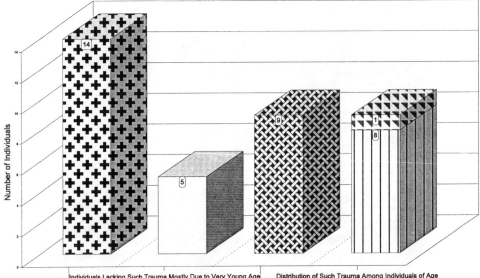

No. of individuals preserving appendicular bones (14, or 100%)	14			
Individuals (5 out of 14, or ~ 36%) which could be excluded from the total sample		5		
Individuals (9 out of 14, or ~ 64%) which could have sustained such trauma			9	
Female/Male individuals (8 out of 9, or ~ 89%) lacking such trauma				8
Male individual (1 out of 9, or ~ 11%) showing such traumatic manifestations				1

77. Prevalence of appendicular trauma

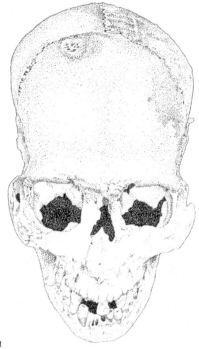

78. Cranial vault trauma

the remaining adults did not show signs of being implicated in such activities may reflect some sort of allocation and distribution of labor, possibly even occupational specialization. Furthermore, two of the adults with vertebral disk herniations, an Adult female and an Adult male, also exhibited trauma at their lower sacral segments, a result of compressed injurious incidences that had caused fracture. Periosteal layers of "woven" reactive bone observed at cranial and postcranial bone surfaces were classified as primary in the absence of any disease specific associations (Ortner and Putschar 1981).

Spondyloarthropathies (Stewart 1958a) were relatively frequent in the form of vertebral lipping and osteophytic and enthesophytic growth, as were osteoarthropathies affecting the adult individuals, who exhibited somewhat complete skeletal bodies. Finally, bone alterations suspectedly due to hemopoietic disorders (Angel 1964, 1966; Carlson, Armelagos, and Van Gerven 1974; Lallo, Armelagos, and Mensforth 1977), possibly associated with scurvy and rickets, were observed in two of the Perinatal individuals.

Bone samples from eight individuals (table 8) representing the Shanidar Cave Proto-Neolithic human skeletal collection were submitted for bone isotopic fractionation for the purpose of identifying the bone isotopic composition for dietary-pattern evaluation of these ancient peoples (Krueger 1985). I anticipated that the site-specific taphonomic conditions—in the rather stable speleologic environment—could have augmented the processes of preservation of the organic matrix component (collagen) of the human bone tissue; I was not disappointed. The bone isotopic analyses were conducted by the late H. W. Krueger. The results were intriguing, as they indicated a very good preservation of gelatin (purified collagen) for five of the samples submitted (337 A, 371-298 A, 381 A, 382 A, 383 A) and just a small amount of gelatin from the sixth individual, 383 A. The preservation of the organic matrix (collagen) of human osseous remains dating to the eleventh millennium B.P. was, at the time, one of the oldest cases of collagen preservation in the world.

Discussion

What were the reasons for such a high frequency of stress markers, trauma, and disease, as discerned through the remains of a relatively small but unique skeletal collection of the Proto-Neolithic Shanidar? It is of significant importance to consider the rest of the archaeological record prior to the screening of probabilities for competing explanatory hypotheses (Agelarakis 1992). In trying to paint a picture of the Proto-Neolithic peoples' perceived environment with broad brushstrokes, it should be noted that experimentation and innovation processes were suggested at all levels of cultural activities, as evidenced through the artifactual remains.

The Shanidar Valley is an ecotone with merging environmental components, offering a wide range of natural faunal and botanical resources for humans. The riverine environment, as well as the large cave with the nearby freshwater spring and other winter shelters within the vicinity of the valley, must have been regarded as a very desirable location for habitation. Solid multiphase architectural remains were documented for the first time ever in the Baradost, at the occupation levels of the coeval open village site of Zawi Chemi Shanidar (R. L. Solecki 1977, 1981b). Abundant tool assemblages indicate the harvesting and processing of macro botanical resources, suggestive of plant-food processing (R. L. Solecki 1972; R. L. Solecki and R. S. Solecki 1963, 1970). Tool kits further reflect an ample experimentation with bone, antler, and ivory industries and new stone-working techniques (R. S. Solecki, personal communication; R. L. Solecki 1972). Such newly introduced technologies, which reveal experimentation and innovation, argue for an increased specialization in the exploitation of broad and multifaceted available resources, reflecting changes in both systems of organization and perceived environments. In addition, the luxury and trade items found at both the cave and the village sites point out contacts and/or trade with distant territories (R. L. Solecki 1972).

Palynology indicates the presence of high frequencies of *Compositae*, suggesting fertile sediments, broken and disturbed by human activities and/or those of their animals (Leroi-Gourhan 1969, n.d.; Van Zeist and Wright 1963). Indeed, the results of the bone isotopic analyses (Krueger and Sullivan 1984; Krueger 1985) for investigations of dietary patterns indicate the people of the Proto-Neolithic cultural component relied on a nearly herbivorous C3 plant-based (Calvin) diet, as shown by both the gelatin (purified collagen) and the apatite carbon 13C values (see table 8). This is not unexpected within the optimal zone of the wild prototype of barley and wheat, as well as of woody, fruit, and flowering plants.

Archaeofaunal remains, perceived both as artifacts and ecofacts, indicate an increased cultural control over and dependence on sheep popula-

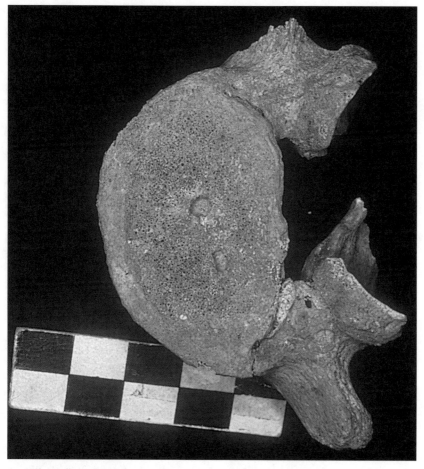

79. Schmörl's nodes

tions, leading perhaps to early domestication (Perkins 1964). This may not be unexpected within the natural habitat of such an important animal as sheep. The results of bone isotopic analyses indicate however, that both apatite and gelatin carbon parameters (average to approx. 7 o/oo) and gelatin nitrogen values (average to approx. +5 o/oo) are typical of herbivorous diets with an anticipated dietary intake of animal protein of a scale of less than 10 percent (Agelarakis 1989, 1993a). Hence, it is deduced, through the bone isotopic implications, that no substantial "harvesting" for consumption purposes of these food animals can be assumed, despite what might be reflected by the evidence provided by the archaeofaunal skeletal record.

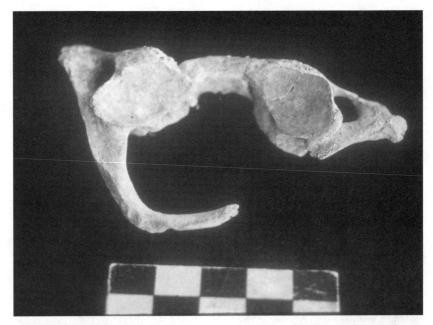

80. Cleft vertebra

With the introduction of the archaeo-anthropological aspects and perspectives of the technological and organizational capacities of these prehistoric people, it is argued that we are facing the reflections of a metamorphosis, a transitional period in our human prehistory and a point of no return to earlier cultural traditions following the beginnings of sedentism, the cultural control over cerealia, and food animals. It was a transformation of the deeply rooted ideational systems that praised the hunter, who now became the protector of a herd of animals, and from the nomadic or seminomadic gatherer's lifestyle to that of the food producer (Agelarakis 1993b).

Based on these new conditions, brought about by the changes in sociocultural, techno-economic, and ideational organizations, it is strongly suggested that varied selective evolutionary processes were initiated, which affected the Shanidar Proto-Neolithic population in light of the new lifeways and environmental settings. The traumatic conditions may reflect both intergroup struggles for dominance and territory, and markers of habitual and occupational stress (Agelarakis 1996). The early life stress conditions and subsequent manifestations of disease reflect changes in dietary patterns, living in aggregates, and the transmission of infectious diseases through a new cauldron of relationships between disease entities, vectors, and the human hosts (Selye 1956; Angel 1968, 1969a, 1969b; Rathburn 1984, Agelarakis 1993a, 1993b, 1999). It might be imagined that the new organization of life could have "thrown off" any suspected balance sustained by older cultural buffer mechanisms by presenting unexpected conditions of stress. However, most of the serious traumatic conditions, debilitating and often immobilizing as they were in my assessment, had received careful "medical" attention and support revealing a vast legacy of knowledge of treatment mechanisms and the sensitivity, care, and ability of the larger social context.

By piecing together the telltale story of the bones of these ancestors it is possible to grasp aspects of processes of their bio-cultural adaptations—the construction and acclimatization of mechanisms appropriate to the new forum of human circumstances, coupled with the relentless pursuit of manipulating, conquering, and controlling evolutionary mechanisms of nature.

Acknowledgments

I wish to express my sincere gratitude to my professors and mentors, Ralph S. and Rose L. Solecki, for advising me through my graduate years at Columbia University, and for offering me the singular opportunity to study the Proto-Neolithic human skeletons of Shanidar Cave. Further, I wish to extend my thanks to the Directorate General of Antiquities of Iraq, and to the Antiquities Museum personnel for their help and assistance. Taking this opportunity I also wish to thank Aditi Bondyopadhyay, Professor of Libraries at Adelphi University, for her kind help with many of the bibliographical references, as well as my former student Anna Konstantatos for helping edit this document from its earlier longer version. Last but not least I wish to recognize and thank my wife Argyro Agelarakis, field partner and illustrator, for her commitment to my research and for the exchange of ideas, and the pleasures of discussions on archaeological anthropology.

Notes

1. These scientists were Dr. Juan Munizaga and Dr. Denise Ferembach.
2. In the mid-1990s, Ralph S. Solecki was able to locate, identify, and ship to me the last missing remains of the collection.

3. After the completion of the laboratory work and the return from Baghdad, the Shanidar Proto-Neolithic skeletal collection was compared to the relatively coeval and geographically closely located human skeletal collection from the Iranian Early Neolithic site of Ganj-Dareh Tepe, the largest reported Neolithic sample. A total of forty-nine individuals have been identified within the Ganj-Dareh Tepe skeletal collection (circa 9,000 B.P.) from the southeast of the Iranian Zagros Mountains at the borders of the Iranian Khuzistan and Luristan. The comparative study revealed the presence, the absence, and the differences of palaeopathological conditions and indicators of stress that had affected the two populations (Agelarakis 1989).

4. Osteometric data of cranial and postcranial indices of the skeletal bodies, with the exception of the dental and vertebral measurements, are not presented in my dissertation (Agelarakis 1989). However, it should be noted that I remeasured the majority of the axial and appendicular skeletal remains of the Shanidar Proto-Neolithic collection and was in agreement with the results recorded by Ferembach (1970). My use of refined electronic calipers produced insignificant differences when compared to Ferembach's data, ranging from decimal fractions of a millimeter to a millimeter plus decimal fractions. Some of these insignificant osteometric differences may have been the result of subjective assessments of identification and location of the points used for the reading of the osteometric measurement. A further important condition for referring to Ferembach's osteometric results is the fact that it was not possible to take many of the measurements due to morphological alterations of the skeletal remains caused by conservation methods and materials used by previous workers.

APPENDIX A

Summary of the Proto-Neolithic Skeletons from Shanidar Cave

JUAN MUNIZAGA

Dr. Juan Munizaga (deceased) kindly gave permission for the publication of this appendix in a letter dated March 12, 1988.

On the suggestion of Ralph S. Solecki, T. Dale Stewart asked his col-league Juan Munizaga, who accompanied him to Baghdad in 1962, to review the Proto-Neolithic skeletal remains while Stewart worked with the Neanderthal remains. Unfortunately, the excavation records pertaining to the burials were not available to Munizaga. The extra intelligence would have cleared up some confusions. In the initial portion of his appendix, he states that he cleaned and numbered the skeletal remains, which he had removed from the twenty-nine individual packing containers in the Baghdad Museum. These cases contained the twenty-six burial units recorded at the time of excavation, plus three boxes of disturbed/partial skeletal remains. Originally, Munizaga believed that each packing case contained only a single skeleton, but he soon realized that some contained more than one individual. In Munizaga's "Summary of the Material," specifically under the subsection "According to Their Distribution in the Containers," he initially calculates that forty-five individuals were repre-sented in the collection. However, under "Distribution of the Population According to Age," he identifies thirty-one individuals (see table A1). We have carefully checked the excavation records against Munizaga's counts and have been able to revise downward his initial counts by identifying those instances when bones from the same individual were placed in more than one container (due to the disturbed, intermingled nature of some of the burials). In one particular example, Munizaga's PN 27 (Cat. No. 388 IV), the records indicate that this was a loose collection of skeletal remains

*found in the fill of Square C1. Munizaga's PN 28 (Cat. No. 339 IV), the
skeletal remains of an adult female more than forty- five years old, is out
of place in his tabulation. The skeletal remains of Munizaga's PN 29 (Cat.
No. 375 IV) were also located in container PN 16. Cat. No. 291 IV was not
a burial, as Munizaga surmised (his PN 2). On the other hand, he could
not find our Burial 3 (Cat. No. 296 IV) (his PN 4).*

*Munizaga's summary has given us a quantitative and qualitative state-
ment concerning the number of skeletal remains, their condition, and the
age groups of the individuals as he saw them in the course of his study. In
the brief time he spent with the collection, he was not able to produce
measurements on other skeletal parts, including the skulls. He did not deal
with the dentition of the individuals or make detailed analyses of the
palaeopathology, which Agelarakis was later to record in his own study.
—Ralph S. and Rose L. Solecki*

After cleaning, numbering, and restoring, which we thought was proper
to do on this occasion, the following observations were made.

a. The material was comprised in general of fragmentary and incomplete
skeletons; at times, bones of more than one individual were found in the
same burial.

b. Studied as a population, a clear predominance of subadults was observed.
This establishes the following age categories:

1. Adults

2. Adolescents (with second permanent molar)

3. Children (with first permanent molar)

4. Children with second milk molar

5. Children with first milk molar

6. Infants within six months old

These categories ought to be tested by determinations based on measurements
of the long bones (see more detailed summary).

c. As for pathology, it was observed as a scarce occurrence in the bones.

d. With regard to morphological aspects, I would like to call attention to
several scapulae that resemble those of Neanderthals.

Description of the Remains by Burial Containers
PN (Proto-Neolithic)

PN 1 (Cat. No. 279 IV)
An almost complete skeleton, lacks cranial bones. Age: adolescent (thirteen to fifteen years).

PN 2 (Cat. No. 291 IV)
Not present.

PN 3 (Cat. No. 295 IV)
Parts of the cranium. [See possible relationship to Cat. No. 279 IV (PN 1).] Age: adolescent(?).

PN 4 (Cat. No. 296 IV)
Not present.

PN 5 (Cat. No. 297 IV)
Remains of at least three individuals, A, B, and C.

A: An almost complete skeleton, cranium and face in the same condition. Age: six or seven years (first molar).
B: Remains of cranial bones. Age: newborn.
C: Calcaneum and metacarpal bones. Age: adult.

PN 6 (Cat. No. 298/371 IV)
An almost complete female skeleton, with face and cranium in similar condition. Age: adult, over thirty years.

PN 7 (Cat. No. 337 IV)
An almost complete male skeleton, with face and cranium in similar condition. Age: adult, over twenty-six years.

PN 8 (Cat. No. 347 IV)
Only some fragmentary long bones. Age: child(?).

PN 9 (Cat. No. 350 IV)
Remains of three individuals, A, B, and C.

A: We have only one femur of the skeleton, incomplete cranium, mandible lacking in the face. Age: adolescent with second molar. [See Cat. No. 380 IV (PN 21).]

B: No skeleton, cranium very fragmentary but almost complete, in the face mandible lacking. Age: one year(?). [See Cat. No. 380 IV (PN 21).]

C: No skeleton, cranium fragmentary and incomplete. Age: half a year(?). [See Cat. No. 380 IV (PN 21).]

PN 10 (Cat. No. 351 IV)

Skeleton absent, cranium almost complete with face and mandible. Age: first milk molar.

PN 11 (Cat. No. 355 IV)

Remains of two individuals, A and B.

A: Skeleton without lower extremities, cranium fragmentary and incomplete, face complete. Age: first milk molar.

B: Isolated bones, crest of ilium, part of a radius. Age: over twenty-three years.

PN 12 (Cat. No. 356 IV)

Remains of two individuals, A and B.

A: Only fragmentary bones of skeleton, cranium very incomplete, without a face. Age: about one year(?).

B: Very incomplete skeleton without cranium or face (ulna, 10.0 centimeters; fibula, 19.9 centimeters). Two individuals(?). Age: ?

PN 13 (Cat. No. 371 IV). See PN 6 (Cat. No. 298 IV)

PN 14 (Cat. No. 372 IV)

Skeleton incomplete, cranium fragmentary but almost complete, same with face. Age: first milk molar.

PN 15 (Cat. No. 373 IV)

Almost complete skeleton, cranium fragmentary and incomplete, the same with the face. Age: first milk molar.

PN 16 (Cat. No. 375 IV)

Skeleton very incomplete and fragmentary, same with face and cranium. Age: second milk molar.

PN 17 (Cat. No. 376 IV)
Remains of two individuals, A and B.

A: Very incomplete skeleton, cranium complete but fragmentary, face incomplete. Age: second milk molar erupting.
B: Only the tibia and fragments of the vertebrae. Age: adult.

PN 18 (Cat. No. 377 IV)
Male(?). Very incomplete skeleton, of the cranium only part of the mastoid, of the face only the ramus. Age: adult.

PN 19 (Cat. No. 378 IV)
Almost complete skeleton, face and cranium almost complete. Age: second milk molar.

PN 20 (Cat. No. 379 IV)
Skeleton almost complete, cranium and face fragmentary and incomplete.
Age: newborn.

PN 21 (Cat. No. 380 IV)
Remains of at least four individuals, A, B, C, and D.

A: Of the skeleton, only a head of a femur is present, fragments of the cranium
   fit "B" of Cat. No. 350 IV (PN 9). Age: one year(?).
B: Part of the cranium, which seems to go with "C" of Cat. No. 350 IV (PN 9).
C: Bones of an adult.
D: Tibia of an adolescent [may correspond to "A" of Cat. No. 350 IV (PN 9)].

PN 22 (Cat. No. 381 IV)
Skeleton almost complete, cranium very incomplete and without face.
Age: adult.

PN 23 (Cat. No. 382 IV)
Remains of three individuals, A, B, and C.

A: Almost complete skeleton, cranium fragmentary but almost complete. Face
   complete. Age: adult.
B: Only tibia remains of skeleton, cranium very incomplete. Face missing. Age:
   newborn.
C: Only a fragment (of cranium frontal?). Age: adolescent (?).

PN 24 (Cat. No. 383 IV)
Remains of three individuals, A, B, and C.

A: Skeleton very incomplete, cranium incomplete, face complete. Age: adult.
B: Only two fragments of the parietals. Age: child(?).
C: Only some fragments of cranium. Age: about six months(?).

PN 25 (Cat. No. 384 IV)
Remains of two individuals, A and B.

A: Almost complete skeleton, fragments of cranium, face lacks mandible. Age: adult.
B: Only right half of mandible. Age: newborn.

PN 26 (Cat. No. 385 IV)
Remains of three individuals, A, B, and C.

A: No skeleton, almost complete face and cranium, lacks mandible. Age: newborn.
B: Fragments of cranial bones that belong to Cat. No. 373 IV (PN 15).
C: Cuboids of an adult.

PN 27 (Cat. No. 388 IV)[1]
Remains of three individuals, A, B, and C.

A: Very incomplete skeleton. Cranium very fragmentary but almost complete. Face incomplete. Age: with first milk molar.
B: Very incomplete skeleton. Cranium almost complete without face. Age: probably older than A.
C: Very incomplete skeleton. Only fragments of the cranium frontal. Face missing. Age: adult(?).

PN 28 (Cat. No. 339 IV)
Female skeleton almost complete. Cranium in fragments and incomplete. Lacks concha of occipital bone. Face fragmentary but complete. Age: adult more than forty-five years.

PN 29 (Cat. No. 375 IV)[2]
Incomplete skeleton. Skull incomplete and fragmented. Face incomplete and fragmented. Age: with second milk molar.

Summary of the Material

According to Their Distribution in the Containers

Of the twenty-nine burials that are listed here, it was impossible to rel-
egate the skeletal remains corresponding to Cat. Nos. 291 IV and 296 IV.
There is also a confusion between Cat. Nos. 298 IV and 371 IV, since they
correspond to the remains of a single individual stored under these two
numbers in one container.[3]

For these reasons, it seems that in actuality we have only twenty-six
burials. Of these, fifteen have remains of only one individual and eleven
have remains of more than one individual. We can therefore schematize
the distribution of the individuals in the burials in the following manner:

a. with remains of one individual: fifteen
b. with remains of two individuals: four
c. with remains of three individuals: six
d. with remains of four individuals: one

In the containers in which there were remains of more than one individual, it was possible to find bones that belonged to individuals from
other burials, as occurred in the following cases.

Container Cat. No. 350 IV related to Cat. No. 380 IV
Container Cat. No. 385 IV related to Cat. No. 373 IV

Distribution of the Population According to Age (Table A1)

According to the categories previously mentioned, the population was
distributed in the following way.

Furthermore, it is of interest to point out that although the bony tissue
was in good condition, the bones and the skeletons appeared to be, unex-
pectedly, in large part incomplete. In order to estimate the percentage of
conservation, we may take the presence or absence of the bones of the
upper and lower extremities as a base, as may be seen in table A2.

The estimated percentage of the conservation of the bones in a population of twenty-eight skeletons, and therefore of fifty-six paired bones, is
grouped in the manner shown here.

From the analysis of these figures we deduce that only 47.7 percent of
the skeletal remains were preserved and that the lower extremities were

TABLE A1. DISTRIBUTION OF THE POPULATION ACCORDING TO AGE

Age Grade	Age Relatively Certain	Age Hypothetical	Total
Adults	8	—	8
Adolescents	2	1	3
Children	3	1	4
Children with Second Milk Molar	3	—	3
Children with First Milk Molar	7	—	7
Newborn, up to Six Months	5	1	6
Total	28	3	31

present in a larger proportion than the upper extremities (51.1 percent and 45.0 percent, respectively). I did not observe any variation in conservation from the left and right sides of the skeletons, since both the right and left extremities are preserved up to 47.0 percent. On the other hand, the degree of destruction of the bones can be estimated through the number of incomplete bones found. From this point of view, of some 187 bones of the upper and lower extremities recovered in the cemetery, 57.7 percent appear to be whole and in good condition. The percentage amount varies very little if one considers the bones in an individual manner.

From the former, one deduces that the type of disturbance that the cemetery had undergone was homogenous throughout the extension of the excavation area.

TABLE A2. THE SKELETONS OF THE PROTO-NEOLITHIC PERIOD OF SHANIDAR CAVE

Type of Bone	Number of Bones Found			Percentage of Bones Conserved
	Left	Right	Total	
Clavicle	7	11	18	32.14
Humerus	20	12	32	57.32
Cuboid	12	15	27	48.21
Radius	12	12	24	42.14
Femur	18	16	34	60.71
Tibia	14	12	26	46.42
Fibula	10	16	26	46.42
Totals	93	94	187	47.70

Pathology

 a. Osteoporosis simetrica (Cat. No. 278 IV)
 b. Perforated scapula at the inferior angle (Cat. No. 339 IV)
 c. Fontanella bregmetica pathology(?) (Cat. No. 355 IV)

In general, the dentition is in good condition; pathology is rarely seen.

Morphological Characteristics

Scapulae that show traces of Neanderthalism in the eje axial: three out of five cases observed (Cat. Nos. 298 IV, 38l IV, and 382 IV).

If we take as a base the distinctions of the morphological elements that, according to T. Dale Stewart, characterize the Neanderthals of Shanidar, we see that we meet them in the face, the mastoid region, and the waist of the scapula and pelves (Stewart 1977). From this viewpoint, the rest of the bones that I have analyzed present no morphological characteristics that suggest Neanderthal connections, with the exception of the waist of the scapula. The latter presents the following characteristics.

a. The axilar border of the scapula. Out of the five individuals whose axillary borders of the scapula were preserved, in three of them the pattern of the furrows could be clearly determined; two present dorsal furrows (Cat. Nos. 381 IV and 382 IV), and one presents two furrows (Cat. No. 339 IV). The remainder (Cat. Nos. 377 IV and 384 IV) are much too incomplete to make a diagnostic analysis, although Cat. No. 377 IV possibly has a dorsal furrow. In general, the pattern of the furrows corresponds much better with Chancelade.

b. Glenoid cavities in the scapula. Although relatively narrow, they do not present an angulation of the vertical axis such as is found in the Neanderthal. Dr. D. Ferembach obtained measurements on only two adults (Cat. Nos. 371 and 298 IV), whose indices run 71.0 and 71.4, respectively.[4]

c. Clavicles. Eighteen clavicle bones were recovered, half of them incomplete. But the remaining permit an appreciation of their morphological variability. Among the clavicles of the children is found an extreme variability with regard to the curvature of the body. At least one very rectilinear occurrence is distinguished.

From the point of view of the morphology of the narrowness of the scapula, the characteristics of the position of this population in antiquity are rather like those of the population of the Upper Palaeolithic, since the range of variation of the characteristics is in the range of the upper limit of the Neanderthals and the lower limit of the Palaeolithic. It agrees with the values that Dr. Trinkaus (1983) extracted in his study of the Shanidar Neanderthals. One ought to point out the variability of the curvature of the clavicle, whose upright bodies one finds also in the Shanidar Neanderthals.

Measurements of the Long Bones of Subadults among the Proto-Neolithic Human Remains from Shanidar Cave, Iraq

Following is an explanation of the elements.

a. The first number is simply the number of the order in this list.
b. The second number is the Cat. No. of the burial, or collection of bones.
c. The letter that follows the Cat. No. in some cases indicates that the burial contains more than one individual and that the measurements given correspond to the individual of the same letter that appears in the description of material in general. For example, 378 IV A = 378 IV (number of grave); "A" (separates out one particular skeleton from several in the burial).

1. Cat. No. 297 IV A (six to seven years old)

	Right	Left
Humerus	—	18.5
Ulna	—	17.9
Radius	18.2	18.1
Femur	25.9	—
Tibia	21.2	21.5
Clavicle	—	9.0

2. Cat. No. 350 IV A (twelve years?)

	Right	Left
Femur	26.1	—

3. Cat. No. 355 IV A (with first milk molar)

	Right	Left
Cuboid	9.1	9.1
Radius	8.0	8.1
Femur	—	13.8

4. Cat. No. 356 IV A, B

	A		B	
	Right	Left	Right	Left
Cuboid	—	—	10.4	—
Tibia	—	10.3	—	—
Fibula	—	—	19.9	—

5. Cat. No. 372 IV

	Right	Left
Humerus	6.1	—
Cuboid	5.5	—
Radius	—	4.9
Femur	—	6.8
Fibula	5.5 (right?)	—

6. Cat. No. 373 IV

	Right	Left
Humerus	9.3	9.4
Cuboid	8.3	8.1
Radius	—	7.2
Femur	—	11.6

7. Cat. No. 374 IV

	Right	Left
Humerus	19.2	—
Cuboid	16.5	16.7
Radius	14.7	14.6
Femur	—	26.2
Tibia	22.3	21.9
Fibula	—	21.4
Clavicle	9.0	—

8. Cat. No. 375 IV

	Right	Left
Humerus	11.2	—

9. Cat. No. 376 IV B

	Right	Left
Humerus	—	9.1
Femur	—	11.7
Tibia	—	9.4
Fibula	9.5	9.1

10. Cat. No. 378 IV A

	Right	Left
Femur	—	17.5
Clavicle	7.0	—

11. Cat. No. 379 IV A, B

	A		B	
	Right	Left	Right	Left
Humerus	—	6.9	—	7.0
Cuboid	6.3	—	—	—
Radius	5.6	5.6	—	—
Femur	8.2	8.2	—	—
Tibia	7.1	7.1	—	—
Fibula	6.8	6.7	—	—
Clavicle	4.5	4.4	—	—

12. Cat. No. 380 IV D

	Right	Left
Tibia	20.7	—
Fibula	20.3	—

13. Cat. No. 383 IV B

	Right	Left
Femur	—	14.5

14. Cat. No. 388 IV A, B

	A		B	
	Right	Left	Right	Left
Femur	—	—	—	9.1
Tibia	11.7	—	—	—

Notes

1. R. L. and R. S. Solecki note: PN 27 was not a burial. These human skeletal remains were collected loose in Square C1.
2. R. L. and R. S. Solecki note: PN 29 is the same as PN 16. It is not known how two separately numbered containers held the remains of the same individual.
3. R. L. And R. S. Solecki note: This is correct. The skeletal remains of this individual were given two different catalog numbers in the field during excavation in the course of recording.
4. R. L. and R. S. Solecki note: These catalog numbers pertain to a single burial.

APPENDIX B

Beads and Pendants from the
Proto-Neolithic of Shanidar Cave and
Zawi Chemi Shanidar Village

PETER FRANCIS, JR.

A selection of ornaments and related artifacts at Columbia University, from the excavations at Shanidar Cave and Zawi Chemi Shanidar Village conducted by Ralph S. Solecki and Rose L. Solecki, was examined with emphasis on the manufacturing techniques used for them. The results have been divided into three sections: (1) the stone beads from Shanidar Cave, (2) the bone beads from Zawi Chemi Shanidar, and (3) the methods used to perforate artifacts at Zawi Chemi.[1] In this appendix the author has added a lowercase letter to some catalog numbers assigned by the excavators to excavation units. These letters were added arbitrarily for convenience to distinguish different artifacts with the same number.

Stone Beads from Shanidar Cave

Stone and bone beads and pendants of teeth were found at Shanidar Cave. Forty-six stone beads from the site were examined. Forty-three are small disc beads, eighteen from a child burial (Cat No. 373 IV, Burial No. 14), and two others were found at the same level. Another twenty-five were similar beads found scattered through Level B. One bead was found with a child in Burial No. 3, in Square C1.

Burial No. 14, of a child, contained a number of stone beads, most of which were included in a single necklace. Eighteen disc beads of pink calcite (Cat. No. 373 IV) that were on the necklace had been ground to shape individually and perforated afterward. Only four have slightly eccentric or off-center perforations, which suggests that the beads were drilled with the help of a mechanism, such as a bow drill. The drill bit used for them was of flint or a similar stone.

They are tabulated in table B1.

Twenty-five pink calcite disc beads similar to those in Burial No. 14 were stray finds scattered throughout Square B1 (Cat. No. 427 IV). On average they are somewhat smaller than the ones from the burial (average diameter 0.42 centimeters, compared to 0.48 centimeters; average length 0.23 centimeters, compared to 0.26 centimeters; average aperture 0.169, compared to 0.178) and are generally more rectangular in profile. They were made in the same manner and are otherwise similar enough to be assumed to have been employed in the same fashion. They are tabulated in table B2.

One other bead of pink calcite from the burial horizon of Burial No.14 is barrel shaped (Cat. No. 331 IV) and slightly beveled at one end. Its diameter is 1.12 centimeters, length 1.25 centimeters, and bores 0.25 centimeters at one end and 0.22 centimeters at the other; it was drilled from both sides. The bead has been well polished and retains few marks of abrasion.

TABLE B1. PINK CALCITE DISC BEADS FROM SHANIDAR CAVE (CAT. NO. 373 IV)

Bead	Diameter (cm)	Length (cm)	Profile	Remarks
a	0.54	0.44	Slightly rounded (barrel)	
b	0.56	0.34	Slightly rounded	Slightly beveled
c	0.50	0.39	Slightly rounded	
d	0.45	0.33	Slightly rounded	Slightly beveled
e	0.49	0.23	Straight	Slightly beveled
f	0.46	0.23	Straight	
g	0.49	0.30	Straight; wedge shape	
h	0.45	0.16	Straight	Eccentric bore
i	0.44	0.27	Straight; slightly wedge	Eccentric bore
j	0.44	0.23	Straight; wedge shape	Eccentric bore
k	0.45	0.14	Straight; wedge shape	Eccentric bore
l	0.45	0.22	Straight	
m	0.45	0.21	Straight; slightly wedge	
n	0.48	0.26	Straight	
o	0.47	0.25	Straight	
p	0.46	0.13	Straight	Edges chipped
q	0.46	0.24	Straight; very wedge shaped	
r	0.45	0.19	Straight; slightly wedge	

A loose find in the burial horizon of the same burial was a triple spacer bead of jadeite (Cat. No. 293 IV [a]) (fig. 27 [a]). It has three parallel perforations, no doubt to accommodate three strands of beads. It is lenticular in section and rectangular in profile. Its length (the axis of perforation) is 1.19 centimeters, its major diameter is 2.19 centimeters, and its minor diameter is 0.78 centimeters. Bores at their apertures: middle bore 0.33 by 0.33 and 0.41 by 0.36 centimeters, bore at one end 0.30 by 0.32 and 0.20 by 0.23 centimeters, at the other 0.30 by 0.27 and 0.29 by 0.28 centimeters.

This is one of the earliest known spacer beads. Others found in Shanidar burials were left in the Baghdad Museum and were unavailable for study. One burial (Burial No. 11, Cat. No. 355 IV), had a quadruple-holed spacer bead. A spacer bead was found at Karim Shahir, roughly coeval with

TABLE B2. PINK CALCITE DISC BEADS FROM SHANIDAR CAVE (CAT. NO. 427 IV)

Bead	Diameter	Length	Side	Remarks
a	0.40	0.19	Straight	
b	0.47	0.25	Straight	
c	0.46	0.26	Straight	
d	0.50	0.47	Straight	
e	0.46	0.22	Straight	
f	0.38	0.20	Straight; slightly wedge	
g	0.35	0.22	Straight	
h	0.44	0.28	Straight	Eccentric bore
i	0.48	0.30	Straight	
j	0.48	0.30	Straight; slightly wedge	
k	0.43	0.13	Straight	
l	0.42	0.19	Straight	
m	0.46	0.12	Straight; slightly wedge	
n	0.48	0.41	Straight; slightly wedge	
o	0.44	0.25	Straight	
p	0.48	0.27	Slightly curved	
q	0.45	0.17	Straight; slightly wedge	
r	0.40	0.30	Straight; slightly wedge	
s	0.42	0.16	Straight	
t	0.43	0.15	Straight	
u	0.37	0.23	Curved; slightly wedge	
v	0.31	0.12	Straight	
w	0.28	0.11	Straight	
x	0.34	0.22	Curved	
y	0.35	0.25	Curved	

Shanidar Cave (Braidwood and Howe 1960, pl. 23.10), and at Level IV at Çatal Hüyük (ca. 7900 B.P.), and evidence for multiple strands was found at lower levels (Mellaart 1964, 95), but multistrand necklaces as early as the Upper Paleolithic are known without spacers.

In another child burial, in Square C1, a single green bead of a jadelike stone was uncovered (Burial No. 9, Cat. No. 350 IV). Fine striae on its surface indicate that it had been ground to shape against a flat surface in an oblique direction across the surface of the bead, and the ends ground flat. Fairly large chips or flakes had been removed from around both apertures, perhaps due to wear. The chipped area had been reground, but the regrinding was not as finely done as the original grinding. Length 3.97 centimeters, major diameter 2.41 centimeters, minor diameter 0.93 centimeters, bores 0.43 and 0.31 centimeters. Bored from both sides.

The shape of the bead, with a lenticular section and double convex profile, is relatively easy to fashion, consisting of two curved and two flat surfaces. It has enjoyed cycles of popularity, although this example is certainly an early one. It was popular at Çatal Hüyük, but at Haçilar only one was uncovered in Level III, circa 7450 B.P. (Mellaart 1970, 159). In the 'Amuq sequence, lenticular sections are found on "double-ax" beads, including a degenerate form, in Phase A, dated roughly from 7500 ± 500 B.P. (Braidwood and Braidwood 1960, fig. 36.5–7).Only one was found in Phase B, but ten were found in Phases E through H, spanning the sixth millennium B.P., and none thereafter (Braidwood and Braidwood 1960, figs. 67.7.160.17, 166.12–13, 252.17–21, 296.14, 296.16, and 378.6).

The material of the spacer and the lenticular double convex bead is noteworthy. They are both jade, the spacer having been identified as jadeite, one of the distinct mineral species called jade (the other one is nephrite). Jade is widespread in small amounts, commonly found in secondary riverine deposits. Although the mineralogical literature does not indicate the existence of jade in the region, small deposits may have been overlooked or anciently exhausted.

Jade use began in the Neolithic; ground celts and ax heads are known from several sites in Europe (Bauer [1904] 1968, 460), China (Needham 1959, 666), and Egypt (Lucas and Harris 1962, 396). Five nephrite celts were reported from the Halaf Phase at Judaideh (Braidwood and Braidwood 1960, 95, 96, fig. 65.1–2). Aside from the Shanidar pieces, however, the earliest jade beads may be a comma-shaped pendant, recalling but not likely related to the Korean *gokuk* and Japanese *magatama*, from Kurdu, Phase E, circa 6000 to 5500 B.P. (Braidwood and Braidwood 1960, fig. 166.16), and a bead from Judaideh, Phase H (Braidwood and Braidwood 1960, 390).

The toughness of jade; the length of the perforations, especially of the lenticular double convex bead; and the circularity of their apertures (although the apertures of the spacer are rather eccentric) point to drilling done with mechanical aid, such as a bow drill.

Bone Beads from Zawi Chemi Shanidar

The available Zawi Chemi Shanidar material is primarily bone, the most common objects being beads made by sectioning long bones. R. L. Solecki (1981, 49–50) has divided these into three subtypes. Those in Subtype A (R. L. Solecki 1981, pl. 10s) are tubular beads, mostly of bird bone; forty-one examples were recovered. Those in Subtype B (R. L. Solecki 1981, pl. 10t) are similar tubular beads but with flattened sections; seven were recovered. Those in Subtype C (R. L. Solecki 1981, pl. 10r,u) are larger, circular barrel or elliptical barrel beads from mammal bones; eleven specimens were recovered.

The following examples of Subtype A (thin tubular beads with round cross sections, mostly of bird bones) were examined.

Cat. No. 31a IV. Protobead. Diameter 0.70 centimeters, length 3.04 centimeters.

Cat. No. 31b IV. Bead fragment. Length 1.89 centimeters, width 0.67 centimeters. Fire darkened.

Cat. No. 31c IV. Bead fragment. Length 1.93 centimeters, width 0.69 centimeters. Fire darkened.

Cat. No. 34a IV. Bead, broken in half lengthwise. Width 0.65 centimeters, length 1.91 centimeters. Fire darkened.

Cat. No. 34b IV. Bead fragment. Width 0.58 centimeters, length 1.26 centimeters.

Cat. No. 50a IV. Bead. Diameter 0.67 centimeters, length 2.96 centimeters. Fire darkened.

Cat. No. 50b IV. Bead fragment. Remaining width 0.44 centimeters, length 2.40 centimeters. Fire darkened.

Cat. No. 53 IV. Bead. Diameter 0.44 centimeters, length 2.66 centimeters.

Cat. No. 68a IV. Protobead. Width 0.62 centimeters, length 2.39 centimeters. Fire darkened.

Cat. No. 68b IV. Bead. Diameter 0.39 centimeters, length 1.69 centimeters. Fire darkened.

Cat. No. 72 IV. Bead fragment. Width 0.76 centimeters, length 1.37 centimeters. Fire darkened.

Cat. No. 76 IV. Protobead. Diameter 0.40 centimeters, length 0.72 centimeters.

Cat. No. 77 IV. Protobead, broken in half lengthwise. Width 0.76 centimeters, length 1.86 centimeters.

Cat. No. 80a IV. Protobead, slightly elliptical in section. Diameter 0.78 centimeters, length 2.85 centimeters.

Cat. No. 80b IV. Bead fragment. Width 0.37 centimeters, length 0.83 centimeters.

Cat. No. 82 IV. Protobead, broken, with a center section missing, fire darkened. Diameter 0.76 centimeters, length 3.71 centimeters.

Cat. No. 88a IV. Protobead. Diameter 0.57 centimeters, length 2.61 centimeters. Fire darkened.

Cat. No. 88b IV. Bead, broken in half lengthwise. Width 0.44 centimeters, length 2.34 centimeters.

Cat. No. 88c IV. Tubular bead, broken in half lengthwise. Width 0.77 centimeters, length 1.97 centimeters. Fire darkened.

Not all the beads of Subtype A are finished. Some are only tubes that have been sectioned from the raw bone, and others show evidence of intermediate steps in the bead-making process. If they are arranged in a series beginning with unmodified bone sections and ending with finished beads, it is possible to discern the steps in their manufacturing. Because the steps often overlap, it can be seen that in nearly all cases beads of this type were made in a definite sequence, as follows.

1. The bone was segmented with a tool with a wedge-shaped working edge that was drawn back and forth against it, no doubt a flint blade used as a saw. The bone was sawed at one spot and then turned and worked at another spot to form a deep notch around the circumference. A piece of bone with two grooves, apparently cut so as to be divided into three segments, was found at Zawi Chemi, although it was not available for examination (R. L. Solecki 1981, pl. 10v).

2. The segments were snapped off the bone. After the notch was cut around the bone, the pieces were detached by bending the bone until it broke. Cat. No. 88a IV is an example of such a segment not further modified.

TABLE B3. STEPS IN THE MANUFACTURE OF THIN BONE BEADS (SUBTYPE A)

(Season IV)	88a	31a	50a	31b	76	82	68a	88b	34a	50b	77	53	80a	72	68b	88c	80b	34b	31c
Ends cut; not further modified	x	x	x	x	x	x	x												
Interior still filled	x																		
Longitudinal striae		x	x	x	x	x		x	x	x	x	x	x	x					
Striae encircling the ends			x	x	x	x	x			x	x			x					
One end only smoothed								x	x	x	x								
Both ends smoothed												x	x	x	x	x	x	x	x
Complete exterior polished															x	x	x	x	x
Interior reamed or worn smooth																x	x	x	x

3. The surface was ground to give the segment a smooth, tubular shape. It was ground laterally, up and down the length of the segment, as evidenced by long striae parallel to the perforation on the bead. Cat. No. 31a IV represents only this stage.

4. The ends were roughly ground in preparation for smoothing them. This grinding left encircling striae around each end. These are to be seen on Cat. Nos. 68a IV (which did not first go through step 3), 76 IV, 31b IV, 50a IV, and 82 IV.

5. One end was smoothed. This was also a grinding operation, but it must have been done with a stone or abrasive that was finer than that used for steps 4 and 5, as this stage left a polish on the end. Cat. Nos. 88b IV, 34a IV, 77 IV, and 50b IV exhibit this stage.

6. The other end was smoothed. In two cases this was done either without the initial rough grinding (step 4) or each end was individually rough and fine ground separately (see Cat. Nos. 88b IV and 34a IV). Cat. Nos. 53 IV, 72 IV, and 80a IV illustrate this step.

7. The entire surface was polished. Cat. No. 68b IV represents only this step.

8. The interior was worn smooth. This may have been done by the bead maker using some sort of reamer. Alternately, smooth interiors may be the result of the action of the string on which a bead was worn. Cat. Nos. 88c IV, 80b IV, 34b IV, and 31c IV exhibit this effect.

The beads of Subtype B are similar to those of Subtype A, except that the bones from which they were made were flat in cross section. Three of these beads were available for examination.

Cat. No. 36a IV. Both ends are flat and do not appear to have been cut (R. L. Solecki 1981a, pl. 10t). There is no sign of abrasion. This may be a naturally sectioned bone rather than a protobead. Diameter 0.85 centimeters, length 1.83 centimeters.

Cat. No. 90 IV. Both ends have been cut only. The surface has longitudinal abrasion marks and some cross-cut marks where a longitudinal ridge in the bone was being smoothed. Diameter 0.54 centimeters, length 1.63 centimeters.

Cat. No. 36b IV. Both ends have been smoothed, and the bead has been lightly polished. Diameter 0.59 centimeters, length 1.18 centimeters.

Except for Cat. No. 36a IV, which may not be a protobead, these beads fit the pattern noted above for the manufacturing of Subtype A beads.

The beads of Subtype C were made from larger mammal bones and are barrel shaped. Some are slightly elliptical in section due to the shape of the bone used. Judging from the few examples here, the process for making these beads appears to have been similar to that noted for Subtypes A and B, except that an additional step, the cleaning of the marrow cavity, was necessary. This was apparently done after the protobeads were sectioned from the bone. The interiors may have also been further reamed when the beads were finished, but not enough examples are present to determine this (see table B4). The beads of Subtype C are as follows.

Cat. No. 82 IV. A fragment of a protobead with an elliptical section. Neither end is smoothed. There are longitudinal striae on the surface, and the marrow cavity is still rough. This specimen was broken lengthwise into three or more parts; two have been recovered and glued together. Diameter 1.60 centimeters, length 1.95 centimeters.

Cat. No. 72a IV. A bead with an elliptical section, which is not quite finished (R. L. Solecki 1981, pl. 10r). The bead has been smoothed at one end only; the other end has only been lightly ground. Abrasion runs laterally and across the squarish edges of the bone. Major diameter 1.58 centimeters, minor diameter 0.90 centimeters, length 1.82 centimeters.

Cat. No. 72b IV. A finished bead that is broken in half lengthwise. Both ends are smoothed, and it is highly polished. The perforation has either been reamed or polished through string wear. Diameter 1.58 centimeters, length 1.78 centimeters.

Cat. No. 88 IV. A finished bead fragment that is broken in half lengthwise. Both ends are smoothed, the surface is polished, and the interior is smooth. Diameter 1.02 centimeters, length 1.37 centimeters.

Cat. No. 98 IV. A barrel bead, rounded in profile (R. L. Solecki 1981, pl. 10u). This is a finished bead that has been lightly polished. The ends are smoothed, but neither is perfectly flat. The interior is smooth. Diameter 1.20 centimeters, length 1.82 centimeters.

Bone beads were widespread in the early Neolithic. Thin, tubular beads similar to Subtype A were found at Jarmo (Braidwood and Howe 1960, 48), a flat barrel bead similar to Subtype C was found at Gird Ali Agha (Braidwood and Howe 1960, 38), and bone beads were recovered from Karim Shahir (Braidwood and Howe 1960, 53). A more elaborate example with incised zonal decorations was found at Judaidah circa 7500 ± 500 B.P.

TABLE B4. STEPS IN THE MANUFACTURE OF BARREL BONE BEADS (SUBTYPE C)

Season IV	82	72a	72b	88	98
Ends cut; not further modified	x				
Interior still rough	x				
Longitudinal striae	x	x			
Striae encircling the ends		x			
One end only smoothed		x			
Both the ends smoothed			x	x	x
Exterior completely polished			x	x	x
Interior reamed or worn smooth			x	x	x

(Braidwood and Braidwood 1960, 67, fig. 38.9). A workshop for making bone beads was uncovered at Beidha, near and roughly contemporary with Jericho (Kirkbride 1966, 203–204).

Other Perforated Objects from Zawi Chemi: Ornaments

Six other ornaments, three of stone, one of tooth, and two of bone, were examined. These ornaments and the bone tools described in the following section were studied with particular emphasis given to their method of perforation. The characteristics of the perforations noted are: the shape of the aperture, the centering of the interior of the bore in relation to the aperture, the shape of the bore when viewed lengthwise, and the nature of the inside surface of the bore (see table B5).

A red deer (*Cervus elaphus*) canine (Cat. No. 53 IV) was perforated for use as a pendant (R. L. Solecki 1981, pl. 11h). There has been a long association between red deer and humans, leading to speculations about early herding or at least conscious selection in killing deer (Jarman 1972). Deer canine pendants were used in Europe and the Middle East as early as the Upper Paleolithic (Leroi-Gourhan 1968, 274); the corpus of Upper Paleolithic material presented by Müller-Karpe (1966) shows ninety-three specimens recorded at six sites. Pendants cut from bone in a shape apparently derived from deer canines were a conspicuous feature of Natufian necklaces at Mount Carmel (Garrod and Bate 1937, 39–40). At Zawi Chemi, red deer provided the bulk of meat in the early stages (R. L. Solecki 1981a, 68), but there is no indication of incipient herding. Thickness at perforation 0.40 centimeters, maximum thickness along axis of perforation 0.69 centimeters, length 2.07 centimeters, width 0.95 centimeters.

A wing-shaped object (Cat. No. 91 IV) with a slightly convex cross section was made from a sliver of a large bone (R. L. Solecki 1981, pl. 10q). In the center is a section somewhat wider than the rest of the object, bored with two perforations. From either side of this section extend two slightly tapering "wings." The surface is polished, but there are two grooves running through one perforation. Thickness at perforation 0.35 centimeters, length 3.82 centimeters, width 1.34 centimeters. R. L. Solecki (1981, 49) suggests that this was a pendant but said that the lines running through the perforation would not be explained by that function. The lines may have been scraped accidentally or postdispositionally; they were made after the object was perforated, and there are a number of shallow lines near and parallel to them. It is likely that the object was an ornament, but worn flat against the body rather than as a pendant. It seems to be without parallels.

A second bone object (Cat. No. 65 IV) may be a variant of the "wing-shaped object" just discussed, although it is fragmentary (R. L. Solecki 1981, pl. 10ee). It was also made from a sliver of a large mammal bone, with three small perforations in a row at what would correspond to the center section. One "wing" is broken and the other completely absent. At the base of the center section is a triangular appendage that has been purposely ground to shape. The object is not polished. Thickness at perforation 0.27 centimeters, length 2.43 centimeters, width 1.28 centimeters.

An ovate-shaped disc pendant of white marble with two perforations at one end (Cat. No. 64 IV) represents the most common pendant type at Zawi Chemi Shanidar, where seven were recovered (R. L. Solecki 1981, 42, pl. 8a–c). The specimen (R. L. Solecki 1981, pl. 8c) is broken at the perforations and has been somewhat repaired. The back has a dark incrustation. The face of the pendant has small abrasion lines running in various directions, indicating that it was smoothed by a circular motion against a flat surface (Francis 1982, 714). Length 3.78 centimeters, width 3.07 centimeters, thickness at perforation 0.36 centimeters, maximum thickness 0.76 centimeters.

Double perforations at one end of a flat pendant are found on tab-shaped shell pendants from Jarmo, where the perforations were said to give the effect of two eyes (Braidwood and Howe 1960, 46). A mother-of-pearl pendant from Haçilar closely resembles the Zawi Chemi Shanidar specimens, except for a third perforation at the bottom (Mellaart 1970, fig. 176.7). Whether the two perforations were meant to resemble eyes, were only used so that the pendant would lay flat against the body, or for both reasons remains speculative.

Two pendants were made from what appear to be naturally formed river pebbles. One (R. L. Solecki 1981, pl. 8h) is an irregular, elongated, flat brown stone, broken at the end opposite the perforation (Cat. No. 72 IV), and the other (R. L. Solecki 1981, pl. 8e) is similar to a plumb bob in shape (Cat. No. 94 IV). Hole, Flannery, and Neely (1969, 233) note pendants made from natural pebbles from Ali Kosh, Tape Asiab, and Karim Shahir, the latter resembling Cat. No. 72 IV (Braidwood and Howe 1960, fig. 23.14). The measurements for Cat. No. 94 IV are: length 5.38 centimeters, thickness at perforation 1.00 centimeters, width at perforation 0.72 centimeters, maximum width of pendant 1.19 centimeters. The measurements for Cat. No. 72 IV are: length 2.82 centimeters, width 1.05 centimeters, thickness 0.47 centimeters, thickness at perforation 0.47 centimeters.

Perforated Tools from Zawi Chemi Shanidar

Eight other objects, seven of bone and two of ivory, were examined to determine their method of perforation. All of them are broken, and four are so fragmentary that their final forms cannot be discerned. Several of them have incised decorations.

Four of the bone objects have a pointed ovate shape with a perforation at one end, resembling pendants. However, R. L. Solecki (1981, 47, 52) notes that the outstanding feature of the forty-five such artifacts at Zawi Chemi is a high polish restricted to their pointed ends, indicating that they were tools whose precise uses(s) are not known (R. L. Solecki 1981, 47, 52). While it is possible that some of these tools were occasionally worn as pendants, just as spindle whorls are sometimes worn as beads, no evidence of that has been found.

Because our interest in these objects involves their perforation technique, only brief descriptions of them will be given.

> Cat. No. 75 IV was made from the end of a *Cervus elaphus* metapodial. A similar object with an illegible number was made from the end of a bone of perhaps bear or lion, but certainly not deer, sheep, or goat. Their functions are unknown. They both have biconical perforations

that are not well centered, but the spongy nature of the material makes it difficult to examine their interiors.

Cat. No. 88a IV is a fragment of ivory. The perforation has been drilled from the nonenamel side only, and near it are two shallow depressions where attempts at perforating were made. There may have been a second perforation adjacent to the one remaining. The perforation is conical, fairly well centered, and deeply grooved on the interior. It is broken, and the apertures could not be measured. Length of perforation: 0.42 centimeters.

Cat. No. 88b IV is a fragment of ivory with one complete and one broken perforation. Both are off-center and slightly biconical and are polished or worn smooth inside.

Cat. No. 61 IV is a flat object made from the splinter of a large bone (R. L. Solecki 1981, pl. 10aa). The perforation is biconical and fairly well centered. It is broken, and its thinness makes it difficult to determine whether it is grooved inside. Length of perforation: 0.18 centimeters.

Cat. No.123 IV is a fragment of a similar object with two perforations (R. L. Solecki 1981, pl.10bb).

Cat. No. 135 IV is a flat pointed bone or ivory object with one broken perforation (R. L. Solecki 1981, pl. 10l).

Cat. No. 58 IV is an elongated ovate bone object with two perforations (R. L. Solecki 1981a, pl. 10k).

A total of fourteen objects with twenty-one perforations are examined and tabulated in tables B5 and B6. Table B5 notes the longitudinal shapes, the shapes of the apertures, the centering of the apertures, and the condition of the inside walls of the perforations. Table B6 presents measurements of the perforation lengths, the major and minor diameters of the apertures, and the width of the center of the bore. It also includes the "tapering index," a number computed by subtracting the width of the center of the bore from the smallest aperture radius, dividing the remainder by the aperture radius, and dividing this figure by half the length of the perforation (the assumption being that the center of the bore is in the center of the object). A perforation that loses half its diameter in one unit (centimeter) would have an index of 0.5. The larger the index, the more tapered the perforation is. A perforation with a tapering index of 2.0 was computed for some of the perforations.

These twenty-one perforations share many characteristics. All but one

TABLE B5. PERFORATION CHARACTERISTICS AT ZAWI CHEMI

No.(IV)	Material	No. of Perfs.	Complete Perfs.	Profile	Aperture 1	Aperture 2	Shape	Centered?	Deep Grooves?
53	Tooth	1	1	Bicone	0.39 x 0.32	0.42 x 0.36	Elliptical	No	Yes
58	Bone	2	0	Bicone	—	—	Elliptical	No	Yes
				Bicone	—	—	Elliptical	No	Yes
61	Bone	1	0	Bicone	—	—	?	Yes	Yes
64	Marble	2	1	Bicone	0.57 x 0.47	—	Elliptical	No	?
				Bicone	—	—	?	No	?
65	Bone	3	1	Bicone	0.32 x 0.32	0.37 x 0.35	Circular	Yes	Yes
				Bicone	—	—	Elliptical	No	Yes
				Bicone	—	—	Elliptical	No	Yes
72	Stone	1	1	Bicone	0.41 x 0.38	0.43 x 0.37	Elliptical	No	Yes
75	Bone	1	1	Bicone	0.51 x 0.48	0.62 x 0.42	Elliptical	No	?
?	Bone	1	1	Bicone	0.64 x 0.54	0.65 x 0.49	Elliptical	No	?
88a	Tooth	1	0	Conical	—	—	Circular	Yes	Yes
88b	Ivory	2	1	Bicone	0.39 x 0.37	0.46 x 0.42	Elliptical	No	No?
				Bicone	—	—	?	No	No?
91	Bone	2	2	Bicone	0.37 x 0.35	0.40 x 0.49	Circular	Yes	Yes
				Bicone	0.48 x 0.42	0.46 x 0.37	Elliptical	No	Yes
94	Stone	1	1	Bicone	0.80 x 0.72	0.86 x 0.76	Elliptical	Yes	Yes
123	Bone	2	2	Bicone	0.24 x 0.24	0.28 x 0.25	Circular	No	Yes
				Bicone	0.45 x 0.34	—	Elliptical	Yes	Yes
135	Bone/ivory	1	0	Bicone	—	—	Elliptical	No	No?

213

TABLE B6. TAPERING INDICES OF ZAWI CHEMI PERFORATIONS

No. (IV)	Material	No. of Perfs.	Complete Perfs.	Length (cm)	Smallest Aperture	Center Bore	Tapering Index
53	Tooth	1	1	0.40	0.32	0.18	2.19
58	Bone	2	0	0.34	—	—	
61	Bone	1	0	.018	—	—	
64	Marble	2	1	0.36	0.47	0.37	1.18
65	Bone	3	1	0.27	0.32	0.14	4.17
					—	—	
72	Stone	1	1	0.47	0.37	0.18	2.34
75	Bone	1	1	0.88	0.42	0.38	0.22
?.	Bone	1	1	0.96	0.49	0.30	0.81
88a	Tooth	1	0	0.42	—	—	
88b	Ivory	2	1	0.37	0.37	0.27	1.46
					—	—	
91	Bone	2	2	0.35	0.35	0.23	1.96
					0.37	0.27	1.54
94	Stone	1	1	1.00	0.72	0.25	1.34
123	Bone	2	2	0.37	0.24	0.16	1.80
				0.28	0.34	0.24	2.10
135	Bone/ivory	1	0	0.45	—	—	

are biconical in shape, indicating that they had been drilled from both sides of the material. The exception is a piece of ivory not drilled through the tough enamel surface. The tapering index on twelve of the perforations indicates quite conical bores, with only the two bone ends having an index of less than 1.0. The average index, excluding these two samples, was 2.01—that is, bores lose half their width in 0.25 centimeters.

Only three perforations have circular apertures, and each was on an object with other perforations with elliptical apertures. The three with circular apertures were well centered, while only two with elliptical apertures and two broken ones were well centered; the shapes of apertures on broken perforations could not be determined. The eccentricity of perforation apertures indicates a drill rotated by hand, producing a typical "wobble" in the bore (Semenov 1964, 18; Gwinnett and Gorelick 1979, 20–21), rather than a drill mechanically rotated such as with a bow, which leaves a more circular bore.

There are deep grooves on the interior perforation walls of all but seven specimens. The ones that do not show such grooves are either of material that does not retain them well (spongy bone ends, marble) or are ivory pieces whose perforations appear to be heavily worn from use. These grooves indicate a hard stone drill, perhaps of flint (Gorelick and Gwinnett 1981, 25; Gwinnett and Gorelick 1982, 90).

Flint Borers at Zawi Chemi Shanidar

A large number of borers were found at Zawi Chemi, and complete ones were measured to try to determine which subtypes had been used to perforate which classes of objects. The tapering indices (TIs) of the borers were computed by measuring the greatest width of the borers as close to their tips as possible and also 0.25 and 0.50 centimeters up their lengths. The results are in table B7.

When the tapering indices of the borers in table B7 are compared with those of the perforated objects in table B6 some conclusions may be drawn, especially about ornaments or tools with low TIs. The lowest indices, those of the two bone ends (TI 0.81 and 0.22), are consistent with those of double-backed parallel-sided borers (TI at 0.50, 0.79, and 0.80). The large stone pendant (TI 1.22) is most consistent with double-backed, double-backed triangular, and double-backed elongated borers at 0.50 centimeters, but not with most microlithic borers. The marble pendant (TI 1.18) could only have been bored with the double-backed parallel-sided borers or the microlithic borer alternately backed on one side, among the tools measured.

The flatter objects of bone and ivory, with an average TI of 2.21 and a range of 4.16 to 1.54, could have been bored by several of the recognized tool groups. Microlithic double-backed borers, by far the most common microlithic borer subtype (R. L. Solecki 1981, 11), have average TIs of 2.33

TABLE B7. FLINT BORERS FROM ZAWI CHEMI

	No. (IV)	Width at Tip	Width at 0.25	TI	Width at 0.50	TI
Microlithic Double-Backed Borers						
	31	0.10	0.28	1.68	0.37	1.46
	54a	0.19	0.31	1.83	0.35	1.00
	54b	0.13	0.35	2.51	0.39	1.33
	80	0.18	0.35	1.94	0.48	1.25
	127	0.17	0.38	2.21	0.55	1.38
	—	0.11	0.31	3.87	0.45	1.51
Microlithic Alternately Backed Borer						
	80 or 89	0.14	0.40	2.60	0.60	1.53
Microlithic Borer, Alternately Backed on One Side	80	0.18	0.23	0.87	0.36	1.00
Microlithic Notched Bore	80	0.16	0.32	2.00	0.34	1.00
Double-Backed Borers						
	74	0.18	0.31	1.68	0.45	1.20
	80	0.21	0.41	1.66	0.49	1.14
	88	0.13	0.35	2.51	0.49	1.47
Double-Backed Elongated Borers						
	70	0.19	0.28	1.29	0.42	1.10
	91	0.15	0.29	1.93	0.48	1.38
		0.13	0.28	2.14	0.38	1.32
Double-Backed Triangular Borers						
	79	0.14	0.24	1.66	0.39	1.28
	91	0.16	0.37	2.27	0.54	1.41
Double-Backed Parallel-Sided Borers						
	8	0.21	0.29	1.10	0.35	0.80
	91	0.23	0.25	0.32	0.38	0.79
Double-Backed Borers, Alternately Backed on One Side	91	0.12	0.35	2.63	0.43	1.91
Alternately Backed Borers						
	65	0.17	0.27	2.52	0.34	1.00
	87	0.10	0.28	2.57	0.46	1.57

and a range of 3.87 to 1.66. As a group, they are closest to the bored objects. All microlithic borers have a TI average of 2.17 and a range of 3.87 to 0.87, while all regular borers have a TI average of 2.08 and a range of 2.63 to 1.29. Three subtypes could be eliminated: the double-backed parallel-sided borers, the microlithic borers alternately backed on one side, and the double-backed elongated borers, all with TIs too small for the perforated objects, although the sample size is also small.

Summary and Conclusions

The beads and pendants from Shanidar Cave burials and Zawi Chemi Shanidar village are very different. Those from Shanidar Cave are made from colorful stones that had been carefully shaped and probably drilled with a mechanical device such as a bow drill. Several (spacers and the lenticular double convex bead) are made of a very hard and uncommon stone, which in one case had been reground so that its life could be extended. By contrast, those from Zawi Chemi Shanidar are of more prosaic and less colorful materials: organic materials and common stones. They are not as elaborately shaped and were drilled without mechanical aid. In some cases it has been possible to determine which borer subtype was used to perforate them or to eliminate certain groups. More studies along these lines appear to be a promising area of future research.

Since the two sites were apparently occupied by the same people, the striking difference between the beads calls for an explanation. It is not likely that more colorful beads or those with more work expended upon them were worn only at the cave, nor that they were exclusively used for burials, especially as most were of infants and children. The difference appears to confirm the hypothesis that beads uncovered from an occupation site are on the average less attractive and valuable than those used at the site during its occupation; more valued beads worn at Zawi Chemi Shanidar would have been lost less often than common ones, while broken examples were probably discarded (Francis n.d.).

While there is no evidence for bead making at Shanidar Cave, there is evidence of the use of beads, with the earliest known example of multiple-strand necklaces held apart by spacers. The lenticular double convex bead is also an early example of this style of bead, while it and the spacers demonstrate the earliest known uses of jade for beads.

The bone beads of Zawi Chemi Shanidar of Subtypes A, B, and C were made by sectioning long bones. Enough examples were present to reconstruct the process for making these beads. They were grooved around the circumference, snapped off, then ground longitudinally and around the ends. The ends and finally the lengths of the beads were polished. Several finished beads have very smooth perforations, either because they were finished by the bead maker or because they were worn smooth on a string.

No workshop area for these beads was found at Zawi Chemi, but the process may be compared to that used at a bead maker's workshop discovered at Beidha. There a long tibia bone was found that had been grooved into nineteen sections in preparation for being broken apart into bead-sized segments, which were to be further ground and polished with pumice and black hematite. The bead maker worked on flat stone slabs laid on the ground (Kirkbride 1966, 203–204). Leather may also have been used for the final polish.

Acknowledgments

The author is most grateful to those who assisted in the present work. Ralph S. and Rose L. Solecki have kindly allowed me to study their material and have rendered extraordinary help in the course of this study. John Sanders of the Department of Geology, Barnard College, identified the material of the stone beads from Shanidar Cave. John A. Gwinnett of the School of Dental Medicine, State University of New York at Stony Brook, and Leonard Gorelick of Great Neck, New York, assisted in the identification of drilling-bit materials.

Notes

1. R. L. and R. S. Solecki note: The bone beads from Zawi Chemi Shanidar studied by Peter Francis Jr. are deposited with the U. S. national Museum, Smitsonian Institution. No bone beads were found in the Proto-Neolithic cemetery. The Zawi Chemi Shanidar bone beads were briefly described by R. L. Solecki (1981) in her report.

REFERENCES

Agelarakis, A. 1983a. Palaeopathological conditions on human skeletal remains from the fourth century B.C., Abdera. *Archaeological Report* [archival]. Prehistoric and Classical Museum of Kavala, Greece.

———. 1983b. Physical anthropology, palaeopathology, and dietary patterns of the Middle and Late Byzantine sites at Polystylon Abdera. *Archaeological Report* [archival]. Twelfth Byzantine Ephoreia of Kavala, Greece.

———. 1984a. Palaeoenvironmental and palaeopathological conditions of the human skeletal remains of the fifth century B.C. cemetery in Abdera, Greece. *Archaeological Report* [archival]. Prehistoric and Classical Museum of Kavala, Greece.

———. 1984b. Palaeopathological and palaeoenvironmental conditions at the seventh century B.C. burial ground in Abdera, Greece. *Archaeological Report* [archival]. Prehistoric and Classical Museum of Komotini, Greece.

———. 1986. Analyses of cremated human skeletal remains dating to the seventh century B.C., Chios, Greece. *Horos: Ena Archaeognostiko Periodiko* 5 (4): 145–53.

———. 1986–87. Report on the main burial of the Mycenaean human skeletal remains excavated from Archontiki Site, Psara, Greece. *OSSA: International Journal of Skeletal Research* 5 (13): 3–11.

———. 1987–88. Proto-Neolithic human skeletal remains in the Zawi-Chemi layer in Shanidar cave. *Sumer* 5 (1–2): 7–16.

———. 1989. "The paleopathological evidence, indicators of stress of the Shanidar Proto-Neolithic and the Ganj Dareh early Neolithic human skeletal collections." Ph.D. diss., Columbia University. Ann Arbor: University Microfilms International.

———. 1992. Stress and adaptability observed among the Proto-Neolithic human population of the Shanidar cave. Paper presented at the 3rd International Congress on Human Paleontology, August 23–28, 1992, Jerusalem, Israel.

———. 1993a. The Shanidar cave Proto-Neolithic human population: Aspects of demography and paleopathology. *Human Evolution* 8 (4): 235–53.

———. 1993b. Paleopathology and manifestations of stress at the dawn of sedentary life: The *Homo sapiens* population of the Shanidar cave. Paper presented at the 20th Annual Meeting of the American Paleopathology Association, 13–14 April, 1993, Toronto, Canada.

———. 1996. The archaeology of human bones: Prehistoric copper producing peoples in the Khao Wong Prachan Valley, Central Thailand. In *The Indo-Pacific Prehistory: The Chang Mai Papers*, ed. P. Bellwood. *IPAA Bulletin* 5 (14): 133–39.

———. 1999. The Proto-Neolithic human population of Shanidar cave. Paper presented at the 64th Annual Meeting of the Society for American Archaeology, March 24–28, 1999, Chicago, Illinois.

Agelarakis, A., and Y. Serpanos. 2002. Inner ear palaeopathological manifestations, causative agents, and implications affecting the Proto-Neolithic *Homo sapiens* population of Shanidar cave, Iraq. *Human Evolution* 5 (17): 247–52.

Anati, E. 1963. *Palestine before the Hebrews.* New York: A. Knopf.

Angel, J. L. 1964. Osteoporosis: Thalassemia? *American Journal of Physical Anthropology* 22: 369–74.

———. 1966. Porotic hyperostosis or osteoporosis symmetrica. In *Diseases in antiquity,* ed. D. R. Brothwell and A. T. Sandison. Springfield, Ill.: C. C. Thomas.

———. 1968. Ecological aspects of paleodemography. In *The skeletal biology of earlier human populations,* ed. D. R. Brothwell. Symposia for the Study of Human Biology, no. 8. Oxford: Pergamon Press.

———. 1969a. The bases of paleodemography. *American Journal of Physical Anthropology* 30: 427–37.

———. 1969b. Paleodemography and evolution. *American Journal of Physical Anthropology* 31: 343–53.

———. 1971. *The people of Lerna.* Washington, D.C.: Smithsonian Institution Press.

Armelagos, G. J., R. Huss-Ashmore, and D. Martin. 1980. Morphometrics and indicators of dietary stress in prehistoric Sudanese Nubia. *MASCA Journal* 2: 22–26.

Bar-Yosef, O. 1991. The archaeology of the Natufian Layer at Hayonim Cave. In *The Natufian Culture in the Levant,* ed. O. Bar-Yosef and F. Valla. Ann Arbor: International Monographs in Prehistory.

———. 1998. The Natufian culture in the Levant: Threshold to the origins of agriculture. *Evolutionary Anthropology* 6 (5): 159–77.

Bar-Yosef, O., and A. Belfer-Cohen. 1992. From foraging to farming in the Mediterranean Levant. In *Transitions to agriculture in prehistory,* ed. A. B. Grebauer and T. D. Price. Madison: Prehistory Press.

Bar-Yosef, O., and N. Goren. 1973. Natufian remains in Hayonim Cave. *Paleorient* 1: 49–68.

Bar-Yosef, O., and R. Meadow. 1995. The origins of agriculture in the Near East. In *Last hunters, first farmers: New perspectives on the transition to agriculture,* ed. T. D. Price and A. B. Gebauer. School of American Research Advanced Seminar Series. Santa Fe: School of American Research Press.

Bauer, M. [1904] 1968. *Precious stones.* London: Charles Griffin and Co. Reprint, 2 vols, New York: Dover Publications.

Belfer-Cohen, A. 1990. The Natufian graveyard at Hayonim Cave. In *Préhistoire du Levant: Processus des changements culturels: Hommage a Français Hours. Paléorient* [Spec. ed.]: 297–308. Working paper, Colloque International du Centre National de la Recherche Scientifique, May 30–June 4, 1988, Maison de l'Orient Mediterranéen, Lyon, France.

———. 1991a. Art items from Layer B, Hayonim Cave: A case study of art in a Natufian context. In *The Natufian Culture in the Levant,* ed. O. Bar- Yosef and F. Valla. Ann Arbor: International Monographs in Prehistory.

———. 1991b. The Natufian in the Levant. *Annual Review of Anthropology* 20: 167–86.

———. 1991c. New biological data for the Natufian populations in Israel. In *The Natufian Culture in the Levant,* ed. O. Bar-Yosef and F. Valla. Ann Arbor: International Monographs in Prehistory.

———. 1995. Rethinking social stratification in the Natufian culture: The evidence from the burials. In *The archaeology of death in the Near East,* ed. S. Campbell and A. Green. Oxbow Monographs, no. 51. Oxford, England: Oxbow Publishing.

Belfer-Cohen, A., and E. Hovers. 1992. In the eye of the beholder: Mousterian and Natufian burials in the Levant. *Current Anthropology* 33 (4): 463–71.

Berry, C., and J. Berry. 1967. Epigenetic variation in the human cranium. *Journal of Anatomy* 101: 370–90.

Bordens, K. S., and B. B. Abbott. 1991. *Research design and methods.* 2d ed. Toronto: Mayfield Publishing.

Boyd, B. 1995. Houses and hearths, pits and burials: Natufian mortuary practices at Mallaha (Eynan), upper Jordan Valley. In *The archaeology of death in the Near East,* ed. S. Campbell and A. Green. Oxbow Monographs, no. 51. Oxford, England: Oxbow Publishing.

Braidwood, R. J., and L. S. Braidwood. 1960. *Excavations on the plain of Antioch I: The earlier assemblages, phases A–J.* Chicago: University of Chicago Press.

Braidwood, R. J., and B. Howe. 1960. *Prehistoric investigations in Iraqi Kurdistan.* The Oriental Institute of the University of Chicago Studies in Ancient Oriental Civilization, no. 31. Chicago: University of Chicago Press.

Broecker, W. S. 1987. The biggest chill. *Natural History Magazine* 10: 74–82.

Broecker, W. S., J. P. Kennett, B. P. Flower, J. T. Teller, S. Trumbore, G. Bonani, and W. Wolfi. 1989. Routing of meltwater from the Laurentide Ice Sheet during the Younger Dryas cold episode. *Nature* 341: 318–21.

Brothwell, D. R. (ed.). 1963. The macroscopic dental pathology of some earlier populations. In *Dental Anthropology.* New York: Pergamon Press.

Brothwell, D. R., and A. T. Sandison, eds. 1967. *Diseases in antiquity: A survey of the diseases, injuries, and surgery of early populations.* Springfield, Ill.: C. C. Thomas.

Byrd, B. F. 1991. Beidha: An early Natufian encampment in southern Jordan. In *The Natufian culture in the Levant,* ed. O. Bar-Yosef and F. Valla. Ann Arbor: International Monographs in Prehistory.

Byrd, B. F., and C. M. Monahan. 1995. Death, mortuary ritual, and Natufian social structure. *Journal of Anthropological Archaeology* 14 (3): 251–87.

Çambel, H., and R. J. Braidwood. 1980. The joint Istanbul–Chicago University prehistoric research project in southeastern Anatolia: Comprehensive view: The work to date, 1963–1972. In *Prehistoric Research in Southeastern Anatolia I,* ed. H. Çambel and R. J. Braidwood. Istanbul: University of Istanbul, Faculty of Letters Press.

Campana, D. V. 1979. An analysis of the use-wear patterns on Natufian and Proto-Neolithic bone implements. Ph D. diss., Columbia University. New York: University Microfilms International.

Carlson, D. S., G. J. Armelagos, and D. P. Van Gerven. 1974. Factors affecting the etiology of *Cribra orbitalia* in prehistoric Nubia. *Journal of Human Evolution* 3: 405–410.

Courville, C. B. 1967. Cranial injuries in prehistoric man. In *Diseases in antiquity: A survey of the diseases, injuries, and surgery of early populations,* ed. D. R. Brothwell and A. T. Sandison. Springfield, Ill.: C. C. Thomas.

Crowfoot, G. M. 1954. Textiles, basketry, and mats. In *A History of Technology,* vol. 1, ed. C. Singer, E. J. Holmyard, and A. R. Hall. New York and London: Oxford University Press.

Currey, J. D. 1984. *The mechanical adaptations of bones.* Princeton: Princeton University Press.

Currey, J. D., and R. Alexander. 1985. The thickness of walls of tubular bones. *Journal of Zoology* 206: 453–68.

Darling, A. I. 1970. Dental caries. In *Thoma's oral pathology,* ed. R. J. Gorlin and H. M. Goldman. Saint Louis: C. V. Mosby.

DiBartolomeo, J. 1979. Exostoses of the external auditory canal. *The annals of otology, rhinology, and laryngology* (suppl. 61) 88: 1–17.

Driver, H. E., and W. C. Massey. 1957. Comparative studies of North American Indians. *Transactions of the American Philosophical Society* 47 (2): 165–456.

Ferembach, D. 1970. Etude anthropologique des ossements humains Proto-Neolithique de Zawi-Chemi Shanidar (Iraq). *Sumer* 26: 21–64.

Fiedel, S. J. 1979. Intra- and inter-cultural variability in Mesolithic and Neolithic mortuary practices in the Near East. Ph D diss., University of Pennsylvania. Ann Arbor: University Microfilms International.

Filipo, R., M. Fabiani, and M. Barbara. 1982. External ear canal exostosis: A physio-pathological lesion in aquatic sports. *Journal of Sports Medicine and Physical Fitness* 22: 329–39.

Finnegan, M. 1978. Non-metric variation of the infracranial skeleton. *Journal of Anatomy* 125: 23–37.

Francis, P., Jr. 1982. Experiments with early techniques for making whole shells into beads. *Current Anthropology* 23 (4): 713–14.

———. n.d. From the systemic context to the archaeological: The case of lost beads. Manuscript on file, Center for Bead Research.

Garrod, D. A. E. 1930. The Palaeolithic of southern Kurdistan: Excavations in the caves of Zarzi and Hazer Merd. *Bulletin of the American School of Prehistoric Research* 6: 8–43.

———. 1942. Excavations at the cave of Shukbah, Palestine, 1928. *Proceedings of the Prehistoric Society for 1942* 8: 1–20.

Garrod, D. A. E., and D. M. A. Bate. 1937. *The Stone Age of Mount Carmel: Excavations at the Wady El-Mughara,* vol. 1. Oxford: Clarendon Press.

Goodman, A. H., and G. J. Armelagos. 1988. Childhood stress and decreased longevity in a prehistoric population. *American Anthropologist* 90 (4): 936–44.

Goodman, A. H., G. J. Armelagos, and J. C. Rose. 1980. Enamel hypoplasias as indicators of stress in three prehistoric populations from Illinois. *Human Biology* 52: 515–28.

Goodman, A. H., D. L. Martin, G. J. Armelagos, and G. Clarl. 1984. Indicators of stress from bones and teeth. In *Paleopathology at the origins of agriculture,* ed. M. N. Cohen and G. J. Armelagos. New York: Academic Press.

Goodman A. H., and J. C. Rose. 1990. Assessment of systemic physiological perturba-tions from dental enamel hypoplasias and associated histological structures. *Yearbook of Physical Anthropology* 33: 59–110.

———. 1991. Dental enamel hypoplasias as indicators of nutritional status. In *Advances in dental anthropology,* ed. M. A. Kelley and C. S. Larsen. New York: Wiley-Liss.

Gorelick, L., and J. A. Gwinnett. 1981. The origin and development of the ancient Near Eastern seal: A hypothetical reconstruction. *Expedition* 23 (4): 17–30.

———. 1987. A history of drills and drilling. *The New York State Dental Journal* 53 (1): 35–39.

Graham, M. 1979. Osteomas and exostoses of the external auditory canal. *The Annals of Otology, Rhinology, and Laryngology.* 88: 566–72.

Grahnen, H. 1967. Maternal diabetes and changes in the hard tissues of primary teeth, I: A clinical study. *Odontologisk revy* 18: 162–257.

———. 1969. Neonatal asphyxia and mineralization defects of the primary teeth. *Caries Research* 3: 301–307.

Gwinnett, J. A., and L. Gorelick. 1979. Ancient lapidary: A study using scanning electron microscopy and functional analysis. *Expedition* 22 (1): 17–32.

———. 1982. Authenticity analysis of two stone statuettes in the Mildenberg Collection. *MASCA Journal* 2: 88–90.

Harlan, R., and D. Zohary. 1966. Distribution of wild wheats and barley. *Science* 153: 1074–80.

Harrison, D. 1951. Exostoses of the external auditory meatus. *Journal of Laryngology and Otology* 65: 704–14.

———. 1962. The relationship of osteomata of the external auditory meatus to swimming. *Annals of the Royal College of Surgeons of England* 31: 187–201.

Hassan, F. A. 1981. *Demographic archaeology.* New York: Academic Press.

Helbaek, H. 1959. Domestication of food plants in the Old World. *Science* 136: 365–72.

———. 1963. Textiles from Çatal Hüyük. *Archaeology* 16 (1): 39–46.

Henry, D. O., A. Leroi-Gourhan, and S. J. M. Davis. 1981. The excavation of Hayonim Terrace: An examination of the terminal Pleistocene climatic and adaptive changes. *Journal of Archaeological Sciences* 8: 33–58.

Hillman, G. C. 2000. The plant food economy of Abu Hureyra 1 and 2: Abu Hureyra 1: The Epi-Palaeolithic. In *Village on the Euphrates: From foraging to Abu Hureyra,* ed. A. M. T. Moore, G. C. Hillman, and A. J. Legge. New York: Oxford University Press.

Hole, F., K. V. Flannery, and J. A. Neely. 1969. *Prehistory and human ecology of the Deh Luran Plain: An early village sequence from Khuzistan Iran.* Memoirs of the Museum of Anthropology Number, no. 1. Ann Arbor: University of Michigan.

Howe, B. 1983. Karim Shahir. In *Prehistoric archaeology along the Zagros flanks,* ed. L. S. Braidwood, R. J. Braidwood, B. Howe, C. A. Reed, and P. J. Watson. Chicago: The Oriental Institute of the University of Chicago.

Huss-Ashmore, R. 1982. Nutritional inference from paleopathology. *Advances in Archaeological Method and Theory* 5: 395–474.

Jaffe, Abram. n.d. [1983]. Transition from Hunter to Farmer. Unpublished manuscript, Columbia University, New York.

Jarman, M. R. 1972. European deer economies and the advent of the Neolithic. In *Papers in economic prehistory,* ed E. S. Higgs. Cambridge: Cambridge University Press.

Jones, W. F. 1910–1911. General pathology (including diseases of the teeth). In *The archeological survey of Nubia: Report on the human remains.* Report for 1907–1908, vol. 2. Cairo: National Print Dept.

Kennedy, G. E. 1986. The relationship between auditory exostoses and cold water: A latidudinal analysis. *American Journal of Physical Anthropology.* 71: 401–16.

Kirkbride, D. 1966. Beidha: An early Neolithic village in Jordan. *Archaeology* 19 (3): 199–207.

Klatsky, N. 1939. Dental attrition. *Journal of the American Dental Association* 26: 73–84.

Krogman, W. M., and M. Y. Iscan. 1986. *The human skeleton in forensic medicine.* 2d ed. Springfield, Ill.: C. C. Thomas.

Krueger, H. W. 1985. *Models for carbon and nitrogen isotopes in bone.* Cambridge, Mass.: Krueger Enterprises.

Krueger, H. W., and C. H. Sullivan. 1984. Models for isotope fractionation between *diet and bone. In *Stable isotopes in nutrition,* ed. R. Turnlund and P. E. Johnson. American Chemical Society Symposium Series, no. 258. Washington, D.C.: American Chemical Society.

Lallo, J., G. J. Armelagos, and R. P. Mensforth. 1977. The role of diet, disease, and physiology in the origins of porotic hyperostosis. *Human Biology* 49: 471–83.

Leroi-Gourhan, André. 1968. *The art of prehistoric man in Western Europe.* London: Thames and Hudson.

Leroi-Gourhan, Arlette. 1969. Pollen grains of Gramineae and Cerealia from Shanidar and Zawi Chemi. In *The domestication and exploitation of plants and animals,* ed. P. J. Ucko and G. W. Dimbleby. London: Duckworth.

———. n.d. [1976]. Les pollens de Zarzi, dans le Kurdistan Irakien. Unpublished manuscript.

———. 1981. Analyse pollinique de Zawi Chemi. In *An Early Village Site at Zawi Chemi Shanidar,* ed. R. L. Solecki. Malibu: Undena Publications.

Levi, L. 1972. *Stress and distress in response to physiological stimuli.* Oxford: Pergamon Press.

Lovejoy, C. 1985. Dental wear in the Libben population: Its functional pattern and role in the determination of adult skeletal age at death. *American Journal of Physical Anthropology* 68: 47–56.

Lovell, N. C. 1997. Trauma analysis in paleopathology. *Yearbook of Physical Anthropology* 40: 139–70.

Lowie, R. H. 1954. *Indians of the Plains.* New York: The American Museum of Natural History.

Lucas, A., and J. R. Harris. 1962. *Ancient Egyptian materials and industries.* London: Edward Arnold.

Mandel, I. D. 1979. Dental caries. *American Scientist* 67: 686–94.

Margetts, E. L. 1967. Trepanation of the skull by the medicine-men of primitive cultures, with particular reference to present-day native East African practice. In *Diseases in antiquity,* ed. D. Brothwell and A. T. Sandison. Springfield, Ill.: C. C. Thomas.

Marks, A. E., and P. A. Larson Jr. 1977. The excavations at the Natufian site of Rosh Horesha. In *Paleoenvironments in the central Negev, Israel,* vol. 2, *The Avdat/Aqev area, part 2 and the Har Harif,* ed. A. E. Marks. Dallas: Institute for the Study of Earth and Man, Southern Methodist University.

Masters, D. H., and S. W. Hoskins. 1964. Projection of cervical enamel into molar furcations. *Journal of Periodontology* 35 (1): 49-53.

Meiklejohn, C., A. Agelarakis, P. A. Akkermans, P. E. L. Smith, and R. Solecki. 1992. Artificial cranial deformation in the Proto-Neolithic Near East and its possible origin: Evidence from four sites. *Paléorient* 18: 83–97.

Mellaart, J. 1964. Excavations at Çatal Hüyük 1963: Third preliminary report. *Anatolian Studies* 14: 39–119.

————. 1970. *Excavations at Haçilar*. Edinburgh: University Press.

————. 1975. *The Neolithic of the Near East*. New York: Charles Scribner's Sons.

Merbs, F. C. 1989. Trauma. In *Reconstruction of life from the skeleton*, ed. M. Y. Iscan and K. A. R. Kennedy. New York: A. R. Liss.

Moholy-Nagy, H. 1983. Jarmo artifacts of pecked and ground stone and of shell. In *Prehistoric archeology along the Zagros flanks*, ed. L. S. Braidwood, R. J. Braidwood, B. Howe, C. A. Reed, and P. J. Watson. Chicago: The Oriental Institute of the University of Chicago.

Molist, M. 1985. Les structures de combustion de Cafer Höyük, Malatya, Turquie: Étude préliminaire après trois campagnes. *Cahiers de l'Euphrate* 4: 35–52.

Molnar, S. 1971. Human tooth wear, tooth function, and cultural variability. *American Journal of Physical Anthropology* 34: 27–42.

Müller-Karpe, H. 1966. *Handbuch der Vorgeschichte Altsteinzeit*. Munich: C. H. Beck.

Nadel, D. 1994. Levantine Upper Palaeolithic: Early Epipalaeolithic burial customs: Ohalo II as a case study. *Paleorient* 20: 113–21.

Needham, J. 1959. *Science and civilisation in China*, vol. 3. Cambridge: Cambridge University Press.

Nikiforok, G. 1981. The etiology of enamel hypoplasias: A unifying concept. *Pediatrics* 98: 888–62.

Noy, T. 1989. Some aspects of Natufian mortuary behavior at Nahal Oren. In *People culture in change*, ed. I. Hershkovits. British Archaeological Reports International Series, no. 508, part 1. Oxford, England: Archeopress.

————. 1991. Art and decoration of the Natufian at Nahal Oren. In *The Natufian culture in the Levant*, ed. O. Bar-Yosef and F. Valla. Ann Arbor: International Monographs in Prehistory.

Oakley, K. P. 1961. On man's use of fire, with comments on tool-making and hunting. In *Social life of early man*, ed. S. L. Washburn. Viking Fund Publications in Anthropology, no. 31: 176–93. New York: Wenner-Gren Foundation for Anthropological Research.

Olszewski, D. I. 1993a. Subsistence ecology in the Mediterranean forest: Implications for the origins of cultivation in the Epipaleolithic Southern Levant. *American Anthropologist* 95 (2): 420–35.

————. 1993b. The Zarzian occupation at Warwasi Rockshelter, Iran. In *The Palaeolithic prehistory of the Zagros-Taurus*, ed. D. I. Olszewski and H. L. Dibble. Philadelphia: The University Museum, University of Pennsylvania.

Ortner, D. J., and W. G. J. Putschar. 1981. *Identification of pathological conditions in human skeletal remains*. Smithsonian Contributions to Anthropology, no.28. Washington, D.C.: Smithsonian Institution Press.

Perkins, D. 1964. The prehistoric fauna from Shanidar, Iraq. *Science* 144: 1565–66.

Perrot, J. 1957. Le mésolithique de Palestine et les récentes découvertes a Eynan (Ain Mallaha). *Antiquity and Survival* 2: 91–110.

————. 1966. Le gisement Natufien de Mallaha ('Ein Mallaha), Israel. *L'Anthropologie* 70: 437–84.

Perrot, J., and D. Ladiray. 1988. *Les hommes de Mallaha (Eynan), Israel*. Memoires et Travaux du Centre de Recherche Français de Jerusalem, no. 7. Paris: Association Paleorient.

Pindborg, J. J. 1970. *Pathology of the dental hard tissues.* Philadelphia: W. B. Saunders.

———. 1982. Aetiology of developmental enamel effects not related to fluorosis. *International Dental Journal* 32 (2): 123–34.

Rathburn, T. A. 1984. Skeletal pathology from the Paleolithic through the Metal Ages in Iran and Iraq. In *Paleopathology at the origins of agriculture,* ed. M. N. Cohen and G. J. Armelagos. New York: Academic Press.

Renfrew, C., J. E. Dixon, and J. R. Cann. 1966. Obsidian and early cultural context in the Near East. *Proceedings of the Prehistoric Society* 32: 30–72.

Rose, J. C., G. J. Armelagos, and J. Lallo. 1978. Histological enamel indicators of childhood stress in prehistoric skeletal samples. *American Journal of Physical Anthropology* 49: 511–16.

Rose, J. C., K. W. Condon, and A. H. Goodman. 1985. Diet and dentition: Developmental disturbances. In *The analysis of prehistoric diets,* ed. J. Mielke and R. Gilbert. New York: Academic Press.

Rosenberg, M. 1994. Hallan Çemi Tepesi: Some further observations concerning stratigraphy and material culture. *Antolica* 20: 122–40.

Rosenberg, M., R. Nesbitt, R. W. Redding, and B. L. Peasnall. 1998. Hallan Çemi, pig husbandry, and post-Pleistocene adaptations along the Taurus/Zagros arc (Turkey). *Paleorient* 24 (1): 25–41.

Rubin, M., and H. E. Suess. 1955. U.S. Geological Survey radiocarbon dates II. *Science* 121: 481–88.

Sarnat, B., and L. Schour. 1941. Enamel Hypoplasia (chronological enamel aplasia) in relation to systemic disease: A chronologic, morphological and etiologic classification. *Journal of the American Dental Association* 28: 1989–2000.

Schmorl, G., and H. Junghanns. 1971. *The human spine in health and disease.* 2d ed. New York: Grune and Stratton.

Scott, G. R., and C. G. Turner II. 1988. Dental anthropology. *Annual Review of Anthropology* 17: 99–126.

Selye, H. 1956. *The stress of life.* New York: McGraw-Hill.

———. 1971. The evaluation of the stress concept: Stress and cardiovascular disease. In *Stress and disease,* vol. 1, ed. L. Levi. London: Oxford University Press.

———. 1976. *Stress in health and disease.* Boston: Buttersworth.

Semenov, S. A. 1964. *Prehistoric Technology.* London: Cory Adams and Mackay.

Sheely, J. L. 1958. Osteoma of the external auditory canal. *Laryngoscope* 68: 1667–73.

Smith, Phillip E. 1968. Ganj Dareh Tepe. *Iran* 6: 58–160.

———. 1974. Ganj Dareh Tepe. *Paleorient* 2: 207–209.

———. 1986. *Palaeolithic archaeology in Iran.* The American Institute of Iranian Studies Monographs, no. 1. Philadelphia: The University Museum, University of Pennsylvania.

Smoor, Bert John. The Iconographic Monuments in the Eastern Mediterranean Basin, c. 10,000 B.C. and c. 6,000 B.C. Ph.D. diss., University of California–Los Angeles.

Sognnaes, R. F., ed. 1963. Mechanisms of hard tissue destruction. American Association for the Advancement of Science, no. 75. Washington, D.C.: American Association for the Advancement of Science.

Solecki, R. L. 1972. Milling tools and the Proto-Neolithic economy of the Near East. *Proceedings of the Eighth INQUA Congress* 2: 989–94.

———. 1977. Predatory bird rituals at Zawi Chemi Shanidar. *Sumer* 33: 42–47.

———. 1981. *An early village site at Zawi Chemi Shanidar.* Bibliotheca Mesopotamica, no. 13. Malibu: Undena Publications.

Solecki, R. L., and T. H. McGovern. 1980. Predatory birds and prehistoric man. In *Theory and practice: Essays presented to Gene Weltfish,* ed. S. Diamond. The Hague: Mouton Publishers.

Solecki, R. L., and R. S. Solecki. 1963. Two hafted bone implements from Shanidar, northern Iraq. *Antiquity* 37: 58–60.

———. 1970. Grooved stones from Zawi Chemi Shanidar: A Proto-Neolithic site in northern Iraq. *American Anthropology* 72: 831–41.

Solecki, R. S. 1953. The Shanidar Cave sounding, 1953 season, with notes concerning the discovery of the first Palaeolithic skeleton in Iraq. *Sumer* 9: 229–39.

———. 1955. Shanidar Cave, a Paleolithic site in northern Iraq. In *Annual Report of the Smithsonian Institution,* l954.

———. 1957. The 1956 season at Shanidar. *Sumer* 13: 165–71.

———. 1963. Prehistory in Shanidar Valley, northern Iraq. *Science* 139: 179–93.

———. 1969. A copper mineral pendant from northern Iraq. *Antiquity* 48: 311–14.

———. 1971. *The first flower people.* New York: A. Knopf.

———. 1979. Contemporary Kurdish winter-time inhabitants of Shanidar Cave, Iraq. *World Archaeology* 10 (3): 318–30.

———. 1980. Art motifs and prehistory in the Middle East. In *Theory and practice: Essays presented to Gene Weltfish,* ed. S. Diamond. The Hague: Mouton Publishers.

———. 1994. The probable use of the elongated pebble tool as a flint chipping implement. *Bulletin of the Archaeological Society of New Jersey* 49: 88–90.

———. 1998. Archaeological Survey of Caves in Northern Iraq. *The International Journal of Kurdish Studies* 12 (1–2): 1–70.

Solecki, R. S., and M. Rubin. 1958. Dating of Zawi Chemi, an early village site at Shanidar, northern Iraq. *Science* 127: 1446.

Solecki, R. S., and R. L. Solecki. 1997. The use of acorns as food among the modern Kurds of northern Iraq. *Neolithics* 3: 2.

Steinbock, R. T. 1976. *Paleopathological diagnosis and interpretation.* Springfield, Ill.: C. C. Thomas.

Stekelis, M., and T. Yizraely. 1963. Excavations at Nahal Oren: Preliminary report. *Israel Exploration Journal* 13 (1): 11–12.

Stewart, T. D. 1958a. The rate of development of vertebral osteoarthritis in American whites and its significance in skeletal age identification. *The Leech* 28: 144–51.

———. 1958b. Stone Age skull surgery: A general review with emphasis on the New World. In *Annual Report of the Smithsonian Institution,* 1957.

———. 1977. The Neanderthal skeletal remains from Shanidar Cave: A summary of the findings to date. *Proceedings of the American Philosophical Society* 121 (2): 121–65.

———. 1979. *Essentials of forensic anthropology.* Springfield, Ill.: C. C. Thomas.

Swardstedt, T. 1966. *Odontological aspects of a medieval population in the province of Jamtland/Mid-Sweden.* Stockholm: Tiden-Barnangen AB.

Thoms, A. V. 1997. Long-term trends in the use of rock heating elements: Implications for land-use change. Paper presented at the meeting of the Society for American Archaeology, 1997, Nashville, Tennessee.

———. 2000. Cook-stone technology in North America: Evolutionary changes in domestic fire structures during the holocene. Colloque et expérimentation: Le feu domestique et ses structures au Néolithique aux Âge des Métaux, October 7–8, 2000, Bourg-en Bresse and Beaune, France.

Tomenchuck, J., and J. T. Mayhall. 1979. A correlation of tooth wear and age among modern Igloolik Eskimos. *American Journal of Physical Anthropology* 51: 67–68.

Trinkaus, E. 1983. *The Shanidar Neanderthals.* New York: Academic Press.

Trinkaus, E., and M. R. Zimmerman. 1982. Trauma among the Shanidar Neandertals. *American Journal of Physical Anthropology,* 57: 61–76.

Valla, F. R. 1991. Les Natoufiens de Mallaha et l'Espace. In *The Natufian culture in the Levant,* ed. O. Bar-Yosef and F. Valla. Ann Arbor: International Monographs in Prehistory.

Valla, F. R., F. E. Le Mort, and H. Plisson. 1991. Les fouilles en cours sur la terrasse d'Hayonim. In *The Natufian culture in the Levant,* ed. O. Bar-Yosef and F. Valla. Ann Arbor: International Monographs in Prehistory.

Van Zeist, W., and H. E. Wright. 1963. Preliminary pollen studies at Lake Zeribar, Zagros Mountains, southwestern Iran. *Science* 140: 65–67.

Watson, P. J. 1979. *Archaeological ethnography in western Iran.* Viking Fund Publications in Anthropology, no. 57. Tucson: Farming at University of Arizona Press.

Wilensky, A. O. 1932. Osteomyelitis of the jaws. *Archives of Surgery* 25: 183–237.

———. 1934. *Osteomyelitis: Its pathogenesis, symptomatology, and treatment.* New York: Macmillan.

Wright, G. A. 1978. Social stratification in the early Natufian. In *Social archaeology: Beyond subsistence and dating,* ed. C. Redman, M. J. Berman, E. V. Curtin, W. T. Langhorne Jr., N. M. Versaggi, and J. C. Warser. New York. Academic Press.

INDEX

abraders, pebble, 73, 79, 94 table 4, 156 fig. 58 [c,d]

Abu Hureyra, 116

acclimatization, 183

acorns, 47

adornments, personal, 21–22, 26, 28, 54, 62, 86, 91, 93–98, 96 table 5, 108–109, 116, 136 fig. 27, 136 fig. 28. *See under* beads; pendants

Agelarakis, Anagnostis, 4, 28–31, 28 table 1, 110–12, 117, 159

Agelarakis, Argie, xv

Anati, Emanuel, 40

Anatolia, 59, 61, 63, 116, 118

Angel, Lawrence, 90

appendicular skeletal remains, 173

archaeo-anthropological prehistoric record, 161; aspects and perspectives, 182

archaeofaunal remains, 180, 181

Baradost Mountains, xi

Baradostian (Layer C), 114

Bar-Yosef, Ofer, 40, 86, 100, 103, 116, 117, 119

bead-pendant, copper material, 13, 52, 58–59, 62–63, 93, 96, 109, 136 fig. 27 [k], 136 fig. 28 [h]

beads, xiii, 3, 12, 15, 93–94, 94 table 4, 136 fig. 27, 136 fig. 28
    animal teeth, 86, 95, 98, 114, 208
    bird bone, 95, 98
    bone, 52, 56, 95, 114, 199, 203–208, 205 table B3, 208 table B4
    crab claw, 18, 19, 52, 54, 57–58, 93, 98, 108
    dentalium shell, 86, 95–96
    gastropod shell, 16, 18, 21, 26, 52, 54, 56–58, 62–63, 93–95, 98, 108, 136 fig. 27 [i]
    stone, 15–18, 22, 33, 52–57, 62–67, 78–79, 93, 95, 98, 108–109, 114, 119, 136 fig. 27 [a,c], 136 fig. 28, 201–202
    stone spacer, 13, 15–16, 33, 53, 55, 63, 136, fig. 27 [a,c], 136 fig. 28[i], 201–202

beads and pendants, 199–218

Beidha, 41, 308

Belfer-Cohen, Anna, 82–83, 85–88, 90–92, 94–95, 98–99, 101–102, 116, 119

Bitumen (black adhesive), xiii, 22, 49–50, 62–63, 110

bone
    decorated pieces, 116
    knife with inset blade, 98
    industry, 116
    isotope analysis, 117
    ornaments, 116. *See also* adornments, personal

Bordaz, Jacques, 10, 16, 51

bow drill, 200, 203

borers, stone, 214–16, 215 table B7

Boyd, Brian, 91, 97

Braidwood, Linda, 202, 208

Braidwood, Robert, 42, 59, 115, 202, 207–208, 210

Broecker, Wallace, 117

Brophy, Gerald, 59

Burial 1 (Cat. No. 279 IV), 14, 26, 28 table 1, 130 fig. 16, 187

Burial 2 (Cat. No. 295 IV), 12, 28 table 1, 34–36, 61, 67, 89–90, 97, 99–100, 103, 112, 130 fig. 17, 131 fig. 18, 132 fig. 19, 133, fig. 20

Burial 3 (Cat. No. 296 IV), 12, 28 table 1, 77, 89, 110, 187, 191, 199, 202

Burial 4 (Cat. No. 297 IV), 12–13, 20, 26, 28 table 1, 48, 51–52, 92, 107, 133 fig. 22, 134

Burial 4 (Cat. No. 297 IV) (*cont.*)
fig. 23, 187, 194

Burial 5 (Cat. Nos. 298 IV and 371 IV), 13, 20–21, 24–26, 28 table 1, 33, 36, 48, 51, 53–54, 58, 62, 92–93, 135 fig. 25, 135 fig. 26, 187, 191, 193

Burial 6 (Cat. No. 337 IV), 13–14, 29 table 1, 34, 36, 48, 60, 72–76, 92, 112, 137 fig. 29, 138 fig. 30, 187

Burial 7 (Cat. No. 339 IV), 14, 23, 26, 29 table 1, 48, 60, 92, 138 fig. 31, 139 fig. 32, 193

Burial 8 (Cat. No. 347 IV), 14–15, 29 table 1, 187

Burial 9 (Cat. No. 350 IV), 15, 20, 24–26, 29 table 1, 48, 51, 53, 56, 60, 62, 89, 133 fig. 22, 133 fig. 23, 187–88, 191, 194

Burial 10 (Cat. No. 351 IV), 15, 17, 19, 22, 24, 26, 29 table 1, 139 fig. 33, 140 fig. 34, 141 fig. 37

Burial 11 (Cat. No. 355 IV), 16, 24, 29 table 1, 48, 51, 54, 58, 140 fig. 35, 141 fig. 36, 141 fig. 37, 188, 195, 201

Burial 12 (Cat. No. 356 IV), 16–17, 22, 29 table 1, 142 fig. 38, 188, 195

Burial 13 (Cat. No. 372 IV), 17, 24–25, 29 table 1, 48, 51, 54, 58, 141 fig. 37, 143 fig. 39

Burial 14 (Cat. No. 373 IV), 11, 15, 17–19, 24, 29 table 1, 48, 51, 54–55, 58, 60–61, 139 fig. 33, 140 fig. 34, 188, 195, 199–200

Burial 15 (Cat. No. 374 IV), 18, 20, 24, 29 table 1, 48, 51, 54, 58, 60, 110, 143 fig. 40, 144 fig. 41, 195

Burial 16 (Cat. No. 375 IV), 18–19, 29 table 1, 188, 190 196

Burial 17 (Cat. No. 376 IV), 11, 15, 17, 24, 29 table 1, 51, 58, 60, 139 fig. 33, 140 fig. 34, 189, 196

Burial 18 (Cat. No. 377 IV), 19, 29 table 1, 37, 42, 130 fig. 17, 145 fig. 42, 189, 193

Burial 19 (Cat. No. 378 IV), 19–20, 29 table 1, 145 fig. 43, 146 fig. 44, 189

Burial 20 (Cat. No. 379 IV), 20, 24, 26, 29 table 1, 133 fig. 22, 133 fig. 23, 144 fig. 41, 189, 195

Burial 21 (Cat. No. 380 IV), 20–21, 24, 26, 29 table 1, 89, 135 fig. 25, 189, 195

Burial 22 (Cat. No. 38l IV), 13, 20–22, 26, 29 table 1, 48–49, 51, 58, 62, 64, 95, 135 fig. 25, 147 fig. 45, 189, 193, 195

Burial 23 (Cat. No. 382 IV), 13, 21, 25, 29 table 1, 89, 135 fig. 25, 135 fig. 26, 189, 193

Burial 24 (Cat. No. 383 IV), 21–22, 24, 29 table 1, 49, 62, 78, 135 fig. 25, 147 fig. 45, 190, 195

Burial 25 (Cat. No. 384 IV), 22, 25, 29 table 1, 48–49, 62, 89, 94, 135 fig. 25, 142 fig. 38, 190

Burial 26 (Cat. No. 385 IV), 22, 24, 25, 29 table 1, 48, 51, 54, 140 fig. 35, 141 fig. 37, 190–91

Burial 27 (Cat. No. 186 III), 3, 9, 26–27, 37, 48, 51, 58, 60, 62, 72, 75, 78, 87, 92–93, 99, 102, 108, 149 fig. 47, 150 fig. 48

burials
    bundle, 19, 28, 107–108
    group, 23–26, 84, 88, 98, 102, 108, 191–92
    joint human/dog, 96, 100, 103
    pit, 22, 28, 92, 107
    primary, 11–14, 16, 18–20, 28, 83–84, 89–90, 99, 102, 108
    secondary, 12, 15, 28, 83–84, 89–90, 99, 102, 108, 114

Byrd, Brian F., 41, 84

Campana, Douglas, 50–51
Cafer Huyuk, 4, 202
Cayonu, 42, 59, 118–19
celts, 80, 114–15
cemetery fill, cultural materials found in, 64–81, 65–66 table 2, 136 fig. 27, 136 fig. 28, 148 fig. 46, 154 fig. 56, 155 fig. 57, 156 fig. 58, 157 fig. 59, 158 fig. 60
chipped stone industry, 65 table 2, 76–78, 115, 158 fig. 60
chisels
    pebble, 66 table 2, 74, 76, 79, 157 fig. 59 [a]
    small, 66 table 2, 74, 79, 155 fig. 57 [g,h]

chlorite, 56–57, 70, 80, 110. *See also* grooved stones

choppers, pebble, 66 table 2, 74–76, 157 fig. 59 [b,c]

Compositae, 180

cranial deformation, 112–13

De Wolf, Helen, xv

dimorphism, 167

disks, stone 75, 78

enameloblastic defects, 169

enthesophytic growth, 179

Epigenetic variation, 160

Erq el-Ahmar, 86, 95, 96 table 5

exotic materials, 56, 62, 77. *See also* trade

Ferembach, Denise, 4, 28 table 1, 29–31, 110–12, 193

Fiedel, Stuart J., 39, 83–84, 87–89, 91–92, 99–103

fire cracked rocks, 16, 34. *See also* hearths

Francis, Peter, Jr., 52, 199

French Centre National Recherche Scientifique, 160

Garrod, Dorothy A. E., 5, 39, 72, 91, 101, 114–15, 208

Gird Ali Agha, 207

Gorelick, Leonard, 56, 214

grave goods, 12–18, 21–22, 26, 28, 48–63, 78–79, 93, 98, 104, 108–109
  beads, 51–59
  bone tools, 48–51, 65 table 2
  milling tools, 48
  miscellany, 61
  personal adornments, 48 (*see also* adornments, personal)
  slabs and stones, 12–14, 17, 23, 26, 28, 48, 92, 101, 107
  small stone objects, 48
  stone tools, 60

grave markers, 23, 25, 28, 73, 93, 101, 103, 107

graves, stone lined, 26, 92, 107, 149 fig. 47, 150 fig. 48

Greater Zab River, xi, xiii, 5, 23, 59, 63, 92, 105, 117

grooved stones, 80, 115. *See also* chlorite

Guillemette, Renald N., 81

Gwinnett, A. John, 56, 214

Haçilar, 42, 202, 209

Hallan Çemi Tepesi, 103n, 118–19

Harlan, Jack R., 117

Hayonim Cave and Terrace, 40, 45, 50, 83–84, 86–87, 93, 95–96, 96 table 5, 100–101, 103

hammerstones, 65 table 2, 73, 78–9, 81, 83, 110, 116, 156 fig. 58 [e,f]

hearth lenses, 5, 104

hearths, 6–8, 28, 39–42, 45–46, 93, 99–100, 104, 106; ethnographic evidence of, 43–45; stone, 32–33, 35–36, 38, 40–44, 46

Helbaek, Hans, 47, 61

hemapoietic disorders, 179

Hillman, Gordon C., 116

Hilly Flanks, xiii

Hole, Frank, 210

Hovers, Erella, 84–87, 91–92, 94–95, 101–102

Horowitz, Mara, xv

Howe, Bruce, 37, 42, 50, 57, 115, 202, 207, 210

hypoplasias, 169, 173

idiopathic scoliosis, 176

incipient domestication, 161

Iraq Museum, Baghdad, 51–52, 54, 57, 110, 201

jadeite, 201–202

Jaffe, Abrahan, 113n

Jarmo, 207, 209

Jericho, 208

Judaideh, 202–203, 207

Karim Shahir, 37, 42, 50, 57, 201, 207, 210

Kebara, 50

Kirkbride, Diana, 208

Kurds, xii, 45, 47, 92, 105, 107, 111

Layer A (Shanidar Cave), Neolithic to Recent, 4–5, 106, 124 fig. 6, 126 fig. 8, 127 fig. 10

Layer B1 (Shanidar Cave), Proto-Neolithic, 4–10, 114, 126 fig. 8, 126 fig. 9, 127 fig. 10, 127 fig. 11, 128 fig. 12, 128 fig. 13, 129 fig. 14

Layer B1a (yellow loam layer), 7–9, 106, 124 fig. 6, 126 fig. 8, 126 fig. 9, 127 fig. 10, 127 fig. 11, 128 fig. 12, 128 fig. 13, 129 fig. 14

Layer B1b (gray sediment layer), 9–10, 106, 124 fig. 6, 126 fig. 8, 126 fig. 9, 127 fig. 10, 127 fig. 11, 128 fig. 12, 128 fig. 13, 129 fig. 14

Layer B2 (Zarzian), 5, 35, 63n

Layer C (Baradostian), 63n

Leroi-Gourhan, Arlette, 114, 117

lesions, 170

limestone slab, scratched, 19, 60

Mallaha, 39–40, 45, 50, 86, 91, 93, 96–97, 99, 103

Maranjian, George, 27, 31, 95–96

mastication, 169

matting, 12, 35, 61–62, 87, 107, 134 fig. 24

matting tools, 64, 117, 147 fig. 45

Meadow, Richard, 117, 119

Meiklejohn, Christopher, 112–13

Mellaart, James, 4, 42, 202, 210

Mesopotamia, Northern Steppe, xi, xiii, 63

milling tools, 65 table 2, 72–73, 107, 112, 117. See also mullers; pestles; querns

M'lefaat, 118

Moholy-Nagy, Hattula, 57

Molist, Miquel, 41–44

Monahan, Christopher M., 84

morphological characteristics, 160

mortars, 96

mullers, 18, 26, 33–35, 37, 60, 62, 65 table 2, 71–72, 78–80, 106, 112, 116–17, 156 fig. 58 [a]. See also milling tools

Munizaga, Juan, 4, 15, 19, 21, 28–31, 28 table 1, 51, 110–11, 185

Mureybat, 41, 44

Musslim, Buthima, 59

Nadel, Dani, 82

Nahal Oren, 39, 50, 85–87, 93, 96, 99, 100

Natufian, xiii, 38–42, 45, 51, 72, 82–86, 88, 90–93, 95–105, 104n, 108, 110, 120, 208

Nemrik, 118

Neolithic
Aceramic, 42–43, 115
Ceramic, 118
Early, 57, 119, 207
Prepottery, 87, 96n

Neolithic Revolution, xiii

nonmetric variation, 162

Oakley, Kenneth P., 38

obsidian, xiii, 36, 76, 110

Ohalo II, 82

Olszewski, Deborah, 45, 114

organic matrix, 179

osteoarthropathies, 179

osteomata, 173

ovens, earth, 43, 44, 46. See also hearths

Palegawra, 114–15

pebbles, naturally smoothed/polished, 66 table 2, 75, 77; small shaped, 22, 67–68, 155 fig. 57 [c–f]

pecking stones, 65 table 2, 73, 79, 116, 157 fig. 58 [b]

pendants, 3, 75
bone, 86, 95, 98, 114, 208, 209
shell, 114
stone, 67, 74, 78–79, 93, 96, 114–15, 209–10, 155 fig. 57 [a,b], 209, 210

Perkins, Dexter, Jr., 10

Perrot, Jean, 39–40

pestles, 14, 60, 65 table 2, 72, 96, 116

pounders, 116

population demography, 90–91, 90 table 3, 108, 186, 191, 192 table A1

population pathology, 4, 112, 118, 186

Quermez Dire, 118

querns, 12, 19, 26, 33–34, 36–37, 62, 65 table 2, 70–72, 78, 80, 93, 103, 106, 112, 114, 116–17. See also milling stones

Rakefet, 50

Reese, David S., 120n

Rehder, Harald, 120n

red pigment (hematite), 26–27, 42, 63, 66 table 2, 72, 74–76, 81, 86, 90, 108–10

Renfrew, Colin, 59

ritual paraphernalia, 120

rituals, mortuary, 32, 36–38, 40, 45–46, 73, 78, 80, 99–100, 106–107, 109, 120

Rosenberg, Michael, 103, 118–19

Rosh Horesha, 95–96

Rowanduz , xi ,xii

rubbers, 65 table 2, 69, 75, 79, 155 fig. 57 [i,j]

sacra, 173, 179

Schmörl's nodes, 176

sedentism, 162, 182

Shanidar Cave: cultural stratigraphy, xii; discovery, xi,xii; environment, xi; location, xi

Shanidar Valley, environment, xi

Shuqbah, 39, 50, 86, 93

skeletons, counts, 28–29 table 1

skull removals, 87, 97, 99, 103

slate tools and objects, 14, 60, 65 table 2, 68–69, 74, 76, 136 figs. 28 [a–g], 154 fig. 56

Smithsonian Institution, U.S. National Museum, 217

Smoor, Bert John, 68–69

spall tools, 14, 66 table 2, 79, 89, 157 fig. 59 [d]

speleologic environment, 179; domestication, 161

spondyloarthropathies, 179

Stekilis, Moishe, 39, 72, 86–87

Stewart, T. Dale, 4, 10, 110, 185, 193

stone boiling, 44

stone feature 1, 13, 32–33, 36, 58, 70, 106, 150 fig. 49, 151 fig. 50

stone feature 2, 33–34, 70, 76, 151 fig. 51, 152 fig. 52

stone feature 3, 33–34, 56–57, 70, 152 fig. 52, 152 fig. 53

stone feature 4, 12, 33, 34, 70, 137 fig. 29, 152 fig. 52

stone feature 5, 13, 34, 36, 137 fig. 29, 152 fig.52

stone feature 6, 12, 32, 34–36, 61, 67, 71, 90, 93, 99, 106, 108, 130 fig. 17, 131 fig. 18, 131 fig. 19, 132 fig. 20

stone feature 7 (the stone alignment), 12, 19, 32, 34–35, 37–38, 61, 71, 78, 100, 105–106, 130 fig.17, 132 fig.20

stone feature 8, 32, 35–36, 71, 76, 78, 93, 106, 153 fig. 54, 154 fig. 55

stone feature 9, 36, 76, 153 fig. 54, 154 fig. 55

stone features, 3–4, 9, 14, 28, 32–47, 63–64, 67–68, 71–80, 85, 91, 93, 100, 105–107, 119, 130 fig. 17, 131 fig. 18, 131 fig. 19, 132 fig. 20, 137 fig. 29, 150 fig. 49, 151 fig. 50, 151 fig. 51, 152 fig. 52, 152 fig. 53, 153 fig. 54, 154 fig. 55

stone features, functions, 58–47

subsistence (diet), 116–17; animals, 116; crabs, 16, 116; fish, 14; plants, 46–47, 116–17; snails (land), 46–47, 77, 116, 119

taconite pebbles, 75

taphonomic conditions, 163, 179

Taurus-Zagros region, 57, 116–19

Tepe Asiab, 210

Thoms, Alston, 44

Tigris River, xi, 59, 103, 118

tools, bone, 14, 21–22, 65 table 2, 69, 80, 83, 89, 94 table 4, 96, 98, 109, 114–16, 147 fig.45, 148 fig. 46; functions of, 21, 50–51 (see also matting tools); knife, with inset blade, 22, 147 fig. 45

tools and miscellany, stone (pecked, ground, or flaked), 14, 60, 62, 65–66 table 2, 67–81, 83, 89, 96, 98–99, 101, 106, 114–17, 136 fig. 28, 154 fig. 56, 155 fig. 57, 156 fig. 58, 157 fig. 59

  grooved stones, 80, 115

  hammerstones, 65 table 2, 78, 81, 83, 116, 156 fig. 58 [e,f]

  mullers, 18, 26, 33–35, 37, 60, 62, 65 table 2, 71–72, 78–80, 106, 112, 116–17, 156 fig. 58 [a] pebble abraders, 65 table 2, 73, 79, 156 fig. 58 [c,d]

pebble chisels, 66 table 2, 74, 76, 79, 157 fig. 59 [a]

pebble choppers, 66 table 2, 74–76, 79, 157 fig. 59 [b,c]

pecking stones, 65 table 2, 73, 79, 116, 156 fig. 58 [b]

pestles, 60, 65 table 2, 72, 116

pounders, 116

querns, 62, 65 table 2, 70–72, 80, 106, 114, 116–17

rubbers, 65 table 2, 69, 75, 79, 155 fig. 57 [i,j]

slate pieces, 14, 60, 65 table 2, 68–69, 74, 76, 136 fig. 28 [a–g], 154 fig. 55 [b–h]

spall tools, 14, 60, 66 table 2, 74, 76, 79, 89, 157 fig. 59 [d]

tools, chipped stone, 166 table 2, 76–78, 115, 158 fig. 60

trade, long distance, xiii, 52, 59, 62–63, 109–10. *See also* exotic materials

Trinkaus, Erik, 194

Valla, Francois R., 40–41

Wad, Mugharet, 39, 50, 72, 85–87, 91, 93, 95, 100

Wadi Hammeh, 27, 96, 99

Watson, Patty Jo, 44–45

wattle-and-daub, 12, 35, 37, 61, 100, 106, 115, 132 fig. 21

Wright, Gary A., 97, 101

Younger Dryas, 5, 117–19

Zagros, xi, xii, xiii, 5, 42, 44–46, 50–51, 56–57, 63, 82, 87–88, 97, 105, 109, 110, 114–15, 120

Zarzi, 115

Zarzian, 5, 82, 114–15, 117–19

Zawi Chemi Shanidar, xii, xiii, 4–5, 37–38, 46–47, 50, 52, 56–57, 62, 64, 67–68, 72–74, 76, 80, 90, 92, 107, 114–20, 199, 203–17

Zohary, Daniel, 117

ISBN 1-58544-272-0

90000